BAPTIST APOLOGETICS

Becoming Well-VERSED on What the Bible

Says Regarding Controversial Issues

VOLUME ONE

BY

NICHOLAS M. KROHN

FOREWORD BY

DR. JOHN WATERLOO

Dedicated to Heartland Baptist Bible College.
May the Holy Spirit ever be present in your halls,
professors, and students. May you continue to train
faithful and courageous preachers. May you continue to
teach godliness in a culture of wickedness. May you
continue to preach the Word to reach the world.

All biblical quotes are taken from the King James Bible. No variations have been made, save for the capitalization of all pronouns that refer to the Lord so as to add reverence to His holy name. All underlines to Bible verses have been added to emphasize certain portions of the verses.

Many Hebrew and Greek words are referenced throughout this book. I acknowledge that I am not an expert in either of these languages but am using Strong's Greek and Hebrew Dictionary to find the words that were originally used in the writing of the Scriptures. If there are any errors regarding the use of the Hebrew or Greek language, I sincerely apologize and would also encourage personal study of the Bible rather than fully trusting my words on these subjects.

FOREWORD

As believers, we are called to have an answer for what we believe. In a world where many are asking why we believe what we believe, it is even more necessary to articulate our positions clearly and defend our faith.

I am pleased that Bro. Nicholas has taken the time to give a Christian perspective to the cultural and doctrinal issues facing believers today. This book was not designed for scholars or experts but serves as an accessible tool for every-day Christians equipping them to articulate the Baptist position on these important topics.

We do not have a plethora of Baptist writers, so it is encouraging to have someone take the time to passionately express what they believe and why. Although this book is not designed to expound on every argument regarding each topic, it is a helpful resource that binds the author's viewpoint to a biblical worldview for answering some of the big questions facing Christians today.

– Dr. John Waterloo

TABLE OF CONTENTS

INTRODUCTION

THE CORE QUESTIONS

"What Does the Bible Say About it?"

Children get in arguments all the time. You'll see them bicker over all sorts of things. Like, who would win in a fight: Batman or Spider-Man? Or is the wind caused by birds flapping their wings or trees sneezing? Recalling my own experiences, these arguments quickly get out of hand. Each child will give the most ridiculous reasons as to why they are right and the other kid is wrong. But the quarrel usually leads to the grand-master of all argument-ending phrases: "Well, my daddy said it is!"

This book will be controversial. There is no way to avoid it. Christianity has been considered offensive since its origins and that will never change until Jesus returns. There will be some who completely agree with this book, some who partly agree with this book, and some who completely disagree with this book. But I want all three of those parties to know this: "My Father said it is." That is to say, the Word of God is going to have the final say on each of the topics we will cover. It is not my intention to expound on what I think about a certain issue. My heart is to reiterate what the Bible has already said concerning all these matters. Not what I say. Not what the culture says. Not what some institution says. Not what a certain church says. What the Bible says, because the Bible *does* have an answer for everything:

"According as His divine power <u>hath given unto us all things that *pertain* unto life and godliness</u>, through the knowledge of Him that hath called us to glory and virtue:"
(2 Peter 1:3)

My aim is to be a help. When I was younger, I found myself frequently stumped when someone would ask me why I do or don't do a certain thing:

"Why do you think homosexuality is wrong? As long as two people love each other, shouldn't that be good?"[1]

"Baptism cleanses away your sin, doesn't it?"[2]

"God is sovereign, right? He has all control. So if He does, that means He created sin. He made sin happen, right?"[3]

I didn't know the answers to those questions when I was a teenager. The Bible verses didn't just pop up into my head. Frankly, I'm terrible at impromptu speaking, so if asked on the

---

1. Answer provided in Chapter Eight: Homosexuality
2. Answer provided in Chapter Four: Baptism – Salvation and Baptism
3. Answer provided in Chapter Fourteen: The Triune God – Sovereignty

spot, I'd probably still not have the best answer. That is what this book is to be for. Sometimes, we Baptists can know a truth, but not know how to articulate it when people ask us why we believe it. Sometimes, we may even be the ones asking "Why *do* we believe that?" By God's grace, this book will be a layout of why we Baptists believe what we believe and to help other Baptists know and have an answer for why we do what we do.

"Are you really trying to please the Lord or are you simply justifying your sin?"

Another one of this book's purposes is to attack the heart of many matters. When God says in His Word that we are to abstain from something, we are to follow even if we do not completely understand why (though we often do). For those who insist that certain sins are not wrong (such as pornography, gambling, little white lies, gluttony, drinking alcohol, etc.) I feel that they must ask themselves this: Does God really feel that way about it? Does the Bible truly give evidence that these things are permitted? Or are you just trying to weasel your way out of feeling guilty for the trespasses you have committed against the Lord?

This also applies to other end of the spectrum. When God commands us to do something, we ought to do it. Giving excuses as to why you were not a witness, or why you didn't tithe, or why you didn't help a brother in need when you could have, or why you neglected prayer does not validate them. Should anyone truly think that purposely neglecting good works is permitted with the Lord, you are mistaken. Such arguments would also be feeble attempts to justify sin:

"Therefore to him that knoweth to do good, and doeth *it* not, to him it is sin."
(James 4:17)

If you are truly trying to serve and love the Lord with all of your heart, all of your soul, all of your mind, and with all of your strength, as Mark 12:30 says, would you not change your ways when you find that you are living contrary to what the Bible says? If you want to do right, and you discover that you've been doing wrong, would you not want to rectify your lifestyle? If you don't, and you dig in your heels and fight against what the Word says, that's not wanting to live righteously. That's a selfish motive. That's justifying a lust rather than endeavoring to please the Lord. That will be addressed in this book as well.

"Why '*Baptist*' Apologetics?"

Some may ask "Why just Baptist? Why not 'Christian Apologetics'?" Well, unfortunately, 'Christian' could mean a plethora of things nowadays. In the first century, it meant something simple and specific: those who follow Christ's doctrine. Today it could mean multiple different denominations and beliefs: Anglican/Episcopalian, Arminianism, Assembly of God/Pentecostal, Calvinism, Catholicism, Christian Science, Jehovah's Witnesses, Lutheran, Methodist, Mormonism, Non-Denominational, Presbyterian, etc.

Being specifically "*Baptist* Apologetics" is to help in a couple of ways. First off, it makes it more clear as to the beliefs that will be expounded on in this book. It cuts down on confusion and offended readers. Should someone who holds to the Christian Science view pick up this book, he or she will at least have an idea of what he or she is getting into.

Secondly, it is because of the dearth of Baptist writers. In my years at Heartland Baptist Bible College, one frustrating aspect was that we would often read from writers of different denominations: Catholics, Methodists, Calvinists, etc. Almost constantly, the professor would have to state something along the lines of "Now, the author does say this, but we don't hold to that belief" or "Just skip chapter seven. It delves into a false doctrine." There were a few times that we students became confused at what parts of the book were good and what parts were not. Someone might ask "Why didn't you just get books written by Baptists?" Well, there aren't many. Bible-believing, independent Baptists are known to be preachers, not necessarily authors. This book is to aid in that area. In fact, it was in one of my Heartland classes where I

11

found my calling to become a Baptist author. Ever since college, I have attempted to write books and novels that would be pleasing to the Lord.

Thirdly, it's because I believe the Baptist church is the church that most accurately follows what Christ started in the Gospels. Now, I know some people might be rolling their eyes, and I understand why. Every sect, belief, faith, religion, etc. believes that *they* are right. If people didn't think they were right, they wouldn't hold to that belief. However, we Baptists[4] follow the Bible. We do not follow what a man says. We do not follow what the culture approves of. We follow the inspired Word of God that was divinely given to mankind through the Holy Spirit. And since we are doctrinally correct, I want others to know it. I want others to realize it so that they, too, can follow the Lord in the way that He said they should. This is not arrogance, but confidence. Confidence in my God and my church.

"Aren't You Missing Some Crucial Topics?"

Tragically, yes, but not out of negligence, laziness, or ignorance. In fact, there is a verse in John that says:

---

4. Disclaimer: When I say "Baptists," I'm referring to independent, fundamental, KJV Bible-believing Baptists that follow the teachings of Jesus Christ. Unfortunately, there are many places that are Baptist in name only. They don't follow the Bible as their sole authority, nor do they exemplify what Jesus taught. One of the most obvious examples would be Westboro Baptist Church, which promotes hatred of certain people. That is *not* the message that Jesus gives.

"And there are also many other things which Jesus did, the which, if they should be written every one, I suppose that even the world itself could not contain the books that should be written. Amen."
(John 21:25)

I related much with that verse when I was writing this. I originally had over twenty chapters in this book and a page count that nearly reached 1,000 pages. One book could not contain everything I had planned. I first tried making the pages massive, which helped a great deal, but there were still over 600 pages. And that's a lot to deal with. That's a daunting book. Even with just the topics I have here, it's still over 450 pages, which is no bite-size novel. Therefore, I decided to divide the book up into different volumes, this being Volume One. So why did I have these particular topics in Volume One? Why did Tattoos make it and not The Lord's Supper? That was partly because these topics were the ones that I had already finished writing/were close to being finished and partly because I wanted more time to do some real in-depth study on the more complicated and deep topics. Rest assured, topics such as the King James Version Bible and the Lord's Supper (along with many others) are coming in future volumes. But have patience with me, it takes a long time to write a book of this magnitude. After all, I've been working on this one since 2019.

"Should I Just Take His Word For It?"

Should you just take my word for it? No. Negatory. Absolutely not. Do *not* just take my word for it. I urge those who read this book to constantly refer to the King James Bible. This book is *not* perfect, but God's Word is. This book is *not* the inspired, preserved Word of God, but it will always point back to it. This book will *not* cover every single controversial topic or every verse that speaks on a controversial topic, but we will cover a good deal. Should, the Lord forbid, this book have errors in it (it's very possible, for I am an imperfect man), I would have you realize it by the continual reading of the Holy Scriptures. For those who are reading with a heart to learn for themselves, I stress that you read the Bible along with this book. For those who are reading with a desire to better defend the faith against the world, I stress that you read the Bible along with this book. For those who are simply trying to find someone who will take their side concerning a certain argument, I stress that you put this book down and go read the Bible by itself. You are using this book in a fashion that it was not designed for. The purpose of this book is not so you can wear a smug smirk and say "I told you so." It's for the edifying of the saints and the defense of the faith. It's not a pride-booster. I hope and pray that this book may be a blessing in everyone's walk with the Lord.

"But sanctify the Lord God in your hearts: and *be* ready always to *give* an answer to every man that asketh you a reason of the hope that is in you with meekness and fear:"

(1 Peter 3:15)

CHAPTER ONE

ABORTION

Introduction

Abortion is one of the many names given to the tragically common crime known as child homicide. Many cultures don't consider it murder, however, because the baby "isn't alive." If the baby isn't alive, then it's simply a mass of cells that can be removed without any guilt on behalf of the parents or the doctors. But no matter how much our culture states that children in the womb aren't alive, they cannot change what is truth.

There are many scientific proofs and many highly educated individuals that back the truth that children within the womb are living humans. Drew Zahn writes the following:

"In McGraw-Hill's textbook, 'Patten's Foundations of Embryology, 6th ed.,' for example, biology professor Bruce M. Carlson of the University of Michigan, writes, 'The time of fertilization represents the starting point in the life history, or ontogeny, of the individual'. In other words, you and I begin our lives not when we're born, but when we're conceived. Another textbook, 'Human Embryology and Teratology, 3rd ed.,' from publisher Wiley-Liss, asserts that fertilization is the 'critical landmark' when a new, genetically distinct human organism is formed. Yet, the text explains, 'life is a continuous process' throughout the pregnancy. As Harvard University Medical School professor Micheline Matthews-Ross testified before a 1981 U.S. Senate Judiciary Committee, 'It is scientifically correct to say that an individual human life begins at conception…and that this developing human always is a member of our species in all stages of life' (New York Times, April 26, 1981). In other words, Matthews-Ross was saying, a baby is a baby – from fertilization, to heartbeat, to birth. Yes, the baby of five weeks in the womb differs from the newborn, but so does the toddler differ from the teen. Scientifically, we pass through different stages as we grow, but we don't pass from person to non-person, or vice versa. At that same 1981 government hearing, Dr. Watson A. Bowes of the University of Colorado Medical School asserted: 'The beginning of a single human life is from a biological point of view a simple and straightforward matter – the beginning is conception. This straightforward biological fact should not be distorted to serve sociological, political, or economic goals'. After examining the evidence, the Senate subcommittee reported: 'Physicians, biologists, and other scientists agree that conception marks the beginning of the life of a human being – a being that is alive and is a member of the human species. There is overwhelming agreement on this point in countless medical, biological, and scientific writings'. (Subcommittee on Separation of Powers to Senate Judiciary Committee S-158, Report, 97th Congress, 1st Session, 1981)"[5]

Unborn babies are not simply a lifeless blob that is somehow zapped alive when born. The heartbeat for an unborn baby begins as early as week three. Only *three weeks* after its conception! It is

---

5. Zahn, Drew. "The Science is Conclusive: That Fetus is a Baby." The Des Moines Register. 12, December, 2018.
desmoinesregister.com/story/opinion/columnists/iowa-view/2018/12/12/science-conclusive-fetus-baby-iowa-fetal-heartbeat-law-abortion/2286938002/

ludicrous to think that the child is *not* living when it has a heartbeat just three weeks after conception! Let us stop to think for a moment that the child is growing and developing. Stop and consider that this unborn baby, if allowed the full nine months, will become a born baby. One that is crying, squirming, and in the outside world. Eventually, that baby will become a child, the child will become a teenager, the teenager will become an adult, the adult will become an elderly person, and finally, that elderly person will pass into eternity through death. If this process is cut short by the hand of man, it is known as murder. If an elderly person is stabbed to death, it is called murder. If an adult is stabbed to death, it is called murder. If a teenager is stabbed to death, it is called murder. If a child is stabbed to death, it is called murder. If a baby is stabbed to death, it is called murder. So, why is it that when an unborn baby (who would grow to become all of those other things if given time) is stabbed to death by doctors in an abortion clinic, it is *not* called murder? It is a ploy to justify the action. To make guilty consciences feel at ease. According to Planned Parenthood, 1.2% of 1.1 million abortions that were done in the year of 2011 were done in the second trimester.[6] The rest were done in the first, which is still a horrifying, mournful tragedy. But for the moment, let us analyze the second trimester abortions. 1.2% sounds incredibly small, but of 1.1 million, it adds up to around 12,000 abortions. That is more than the

---

6. Planned Parenthood. "Abortion After the First Trimester." 2014.
plannedparenthood.org/files/5113/9611/5527/Abortion_After_first_trimester.pdf

equivalent of Poulsbo, Washington or Warr Acres, Oklahoma.[7] Those entire cities would be eradicated if compared to just the second trimester babies that were aborted in 2011. I wanted to point out the second trimester specifically because it is in the second trimester where the mother of the child feels the baby moving around within her. Yet, 12,000 mothers went to someone and paid them to stop that movement within them. As if the child they were carrying was a disease rather than a blessing from the Lord. Make no mistake, abortion is murder. Regardless of what the general public or the court systems decree, abortion is murder. If anyone takes the time to truly listen to reason, they will come to the same conclusion. However, it is maddening how much this world refuses to listen to reason. Again, it is to silence the guilt they feel.

God never intended for children to be born out of wedlock. The first step God had in mind when it came to bearing children was marriage. Marriage is when a man and a woman join together in a bond that is unlike any other. They love one another and wish to spend the rest of their lives in each other's company. It is an amazing picture of Jesus Christ and His church. Through the intimate love that this husband and wife share, children are brought forth. Once that takes place, the father and mother are designed by God to have a deep and unwavering sense of compassion for their children. It's natural. When each of my

7. Population numbers for both Washington and Oklahoma taken from 2018.

children were born, I was blown away at the overwhelming amounts of love, concern, and joy that came over me. I knew that I would die for them, even though I only knew them for a couple of hours. It didn't make sense to me, but that is how God intended parents to be when children were born to them. The child, in turn, has an affection for his or her parents as well. These relationships, whether mother to baby or father to baby, are to picture God's relationship with mankind. Like the father, the Lord is our provider and protector. Like the mother, the Lord is our nurturer and comforter.

It took me and my wife three years of marriage to have a baby. Now, in the grand scheme of things, three years is not a very long time. But when trying to have a baby, it can feel like forever. My wife began to doubt her fertility after the first year of marriage. Every time she would see a baby, hear its cry, or have someone talk to her about children, my wife would become so depressed that it was difficult to make her smile at all. And the more couples I meet, the more I find that this is a *common occurrence* among women. The desire to have children is so deeply a part of a woman's inner workings, that when they have the slightest inclination that they are barren, they can be driven to a very low emotional state. This is natural. We can even find examples in Scripture where a woman is in a desperate or miserable state when she is found to be without children (Genesis 16:2, 30:1, 1 Samuel 1:4 – 10). On the contrary, we can find great rejoicing when a woman is granted a child after years of barrenness (Genesis 21:1 – 7, Luke 1:24 – 25).

That all being said, it is the most natural thing for a married couple to bear children. It is good. It is one of the inner designs of marriage. It, like so many of God's creations, is a picture of God's relationship with man, and this is what makes abortion so devastating. It is when a man and a woman decide that they will kill something so precious. They are going to destroy the product of their love. If the parents are to represent the Lord and the baby is to represent believers in this picture, then how blasphemous it is for the picture to be skewed to show God heartlessly annihilating His own children before they ever had a chance. Abortion is not acceptable in the eyes of God. Abortion is murder. But if you think to yourself "Well, that's just *your* opinion," you'll have to think again, because Scripture has much to say about this.

What Does the Bible Say?

Onan's Sin

When it comes to passages of Scripture where a young child was slain, there are many, but let us begin with a passage that doesn't actually have a baby involved in it:

"And Judah took a wife for Er his firstborn, whose name *was* Tamar. And Er, Judah's firstborn, was wicked in the sight of

21

the LORD; and the LORD slew him. And Judah said unto Onan, Go in unto thy brother's wife, and marry her, and raise up seed to thy brother. And Onan knew that the seed should not be his; and it came to pass, when he went in unto his brother's wife, that he spilled *it* on the ground, lest that he should give seed to his brother."
(Genesis 38:6 – 9)

The context of this passage surrounds Judah, one of the twelve sons of Jacob. He had three sons, two of which are grown and ready for marriage. Er, his firstborn, is given in marriage to a woman known as Tamar. Er was a wicked man, however. In fact, he was so wicked that God took his life. Therefore, Onan was given Tamar as his wife so he might raise up children for his dead brother. This later became a part of the law:

"If brethren dwell together, and one of them die, and have no child, the wife of the dead shall not marry without unto a stranger: her husband's brother shall go in unto her, and take her to him to wife, and perform the duty of an husband's brother unto her. And it shall be, *that* the firstborn which she beareth shall succeed in the name of his brother *which is* dead, that his name be not put out of Israel."
(Deuteronomy 25:5 – 6)

Allow me to explain. If a married man (say his name was John) died before having children, the brother of John (let's call him Bill) was to take John's wife as his own so as to produce children. The first child that would be born, however, would be under the name of John, not Bill. The firstborn would be referred to as "John's kid," even though the biological father was Bill. They did this to preserve the legacy of John. Otherwise, his line would have ended. It was a way to both continue the inheritance of John and provide for John's wife after her husband had passed. In this passage, we have a similar situation. Er died before having kids. Onan was to take Tamar as his wife so Er's legacy could continue. Note where it says "when he went in unto his brother's wife, that he spilled *it* on the ground, lest that he should give seed to his brother." To avoid unnecessary mature content, I will encourage anyone who wishes to get an in-depth look at this passage to study it out for themselves. I will basically sum up the meaning of this passage with this: Onan wanted the sexual relationship with Tamar, but without the responsibility of children.[8] Does that sound familiar with today's mindset? Everyone wishes to have free and rampant immorality, but no one wants the consequence of children. This mindset is very often the spark that leads to the fire of abortion.

---

8. Full disclosure: Onan's sin here is that he took Tamar as his own but was unwilling to raise up seed for his brother, as his father commanded. That is what the Lord was displeased with. Onan was not actually guilty of anything abortion-related. He simply has a similar mindset to modern abortionists: pursuing their sexual appetites even when it is at someone else's expense.

In the Womb

One of the things that abortionists like to tell people in order to justify their actions is that life does not begin at conception. It's not a baby. It's just a mass of cells. But that is not how God views children in the womb:

"Before I formed thee in the belly I knew thee; and before thou camest forth out of the womb I sanctified thee, *and* I ordained thee a prophet unto the nations."
(Jeremiah 1:5)

In this passage, God is speaking to Jeremiah, the weeping prophet. This man would later be a faithful prophet of God even though no one would adhere to the message God gave him. He would also write two books of the Bible: Jeremiah and Lamentations. It is also believed that Jeremiah influenced both Daniel and Ezekiel to live for God, two men who would also live to be great prophets of God. Here, God says that Jeremiah had an identity before he was formed in the womb. He was not just a mass of cells, but a living soul.

"And Mary arose in those days, and went into the hill country with haste, into a city of Juda; And entered into the house of Zacharias, and saluted Elisabeth. And it came to pass, that, when Elisabeth heard the salutation of Mary, the babe leaped

in her womb; and Elisabeth was filled with the Holy Ghost:…
For, lo, as soon as the voice of thy salutation sounded in mine
ears, the babe leaped in my womb for joy."
(Luke 1:39 – 41, 44)

John was a six-month old baby inside his mother's womb at this time. Notice that the Bible calls it a "babe." Not a thing, not an it, but a person. Furthermore, a lump of cells cannot experience joy, but John did. He was a living person already even though he was only in the end of the second trimester.

Heathen Sacrifices

The most common form of ancient abortion we find in Scripture is that which dealt with sacrifices to a pagan god. There are multiple passages that refer to this heinous practice:

And thou shalt not let any of thy seed pass through *the fire* to
Molech, neither shalt thou profane the name of thy God: I *am*
the LORD.
(Leviticus 18:21)

There shall not be found among you *any one* **that maketh his son or his daughter to pass through the fire**, *or* that useth divination, *or* an observer of times, or an enchanter, or a witch,
(Deuteronomy 18:10)

Twenty years old *was* Ahaz when he began to reign, and reigned sixteen years in Jerusalem, and did not *that which was* right in the sight of the LORD his God, like David his father. But he walked in the way of the kings of Israel, yea, and **made his son to pass through the fire, according to the abominations of the heathen**, whom the LORD cast out from before the children of Israel.
(2 Kings 16:2 – 3)

Manasseh *was* twelve years old when he began to reign, and he reigned fifty and five years in Jerusalem:...**And he caused his children to pass through the fire in the valley of the son of Hinnom**: also he observed times, and used enchantments, and used witchcraft, and dealt with a familiar spirit, and with wizards: he wrought much evil in the sight of the LORD, to provoke him to anger.
(2 Chronicles 33:1, 6)

And they built the high places of Baal, which *are* in the valley of the son of Hinnom, **to cause their sons and their daughters**

26

to pass through *the fire* unto Molech; which I commanded them not, neither came it into my mind, that they should do this abomination, to cause Judah to sin.
(Jeremiah 32:35)

That they have committed adultery, and blood *is* in their hands, and with their idols have they committed adultery, and have also caused their sons, whom they bare unto me, to pass for them through *the fire*, to devour *them*.
(Ezekiel 23:37)

Now, in truth, there are some differences in the motive behind this and modern abortion. A good deal of abortions today typically deal with motives such as wanting some kind of freedom from the responsibility of children or fear of being a parent. In the days of the Bible, however, the child was already born. As far as the Bible states, the issues of modern abortion were not as much of a concern with the people in ancient times. In fact, most parents wanted to accumulate as much children as they could so as to preserve their line, increase the work capacity of the home, and show everyone how blessed they were because of their fruitfulness. But for those who served heathen gods, they believed that those gods delighted in human sacrifices. To show their devotion to such idols, people would burn their own children to these false gods. Such a difference between then and now, is it not? Some might disagree, but I perceive that they are all too

27

similar. How so? The people of the Bible sacrificed the lives of their children to the things they worshipped: the false gods. Humanity today also sacrifices their children to that which they worship: themselves. The only thing that is different is the idol. An in-depth look at one of the greatest motives behind abortion today gives a clearer picture of how two different slaughters of children are actually quite similar. For your consideration: sexual freedom.

We live in a sex-crazed culture. We are daily bombarded with advertisements, magazines, television shows, movies, novels, and fellow people that push for rampant immorality. The message is "You can be with whomever you want whenever you want. No strings attached." People find marriage unnecessary, troublesome, and imprisoning. Children are often placed in those same categories, for a child can greatly disrupt someone's entire agenda. How is our modern, immorally-driven culture likened to that of ancient heathen practices? Well, one of the things that was so appealing about worshipping false gods is that sexual freedom was not only allowed but fiercely encouraged. "Priestesses" of those religions were basically prostitutes, having sexual relations with whomever would come to "worship" at their god's temple. Unbridled licentiousness was one of the things that often ensnared the children of Israel to worship heathen gods rather than the true God of Creation, for Jehovah has many strict rules concerning the sexual relationship:

Thou shalt not commit adultery.

(Exodus 20:14)

And if a man entice a maid that is not betrothed, and lie with her, he shall surely endow her to be his wife. If her father utterly refuse to give her unto him, he shall pay money according to the dowry of virgins.

(Exodus 22:16 – 17)

Moreover thou shalt not lie carnally with thy neighbour's wife, to defile thyself with her.

(Leviticus 18:20)

And the man that committeth adultery with *another* man's wife, *even he* that committeth adultery with his neighbour's wife, the adulterer and the adulteress shall surely be put to death.

(Leviticus 20:10)

The sexual relationship was to be exclusively between a married man and his wife alone, according to the Lord, but humanity is ever so eager to have what they are not permitted to. Furthermore, the false gods had no such restrictions on the sexual relationship, but it would cost them their children, just as it does today when someone purposes to live for sex. And, in both instances, the parents seem all too ready to give up the sacred life of a baby in order to feed their own pleasure.

Other Points

Satan's Mission

Some may not agree that the desire for sexual rampancy is a key issue between heathen human sacrifices and modern abortions. So, I would like to turn your attention to another connection between the two. In fact, I would say it is the most prominent connection: Satan.

Satan is death's lover. The chief murderer. Millennia of blood stains his hands. He is ever seeking for new ways for people to kill each other. Each human life that he snuffs out is a victory for him, especially if those human lives had not turned to Jesus before death seized them.[9] Satan is the designer behind suicide, war, revenge, uncontrolled anger, the desensitizing of violence and death, and abortion. Each one has been used in Satan's arsenal to commit murder. In the past, Satan was able to convince people to slay their children because of false gods. Today, most societies have realized that such acts are heinous crimes against humanity,

---

9. Considering the subject is abortion, I will note that aborted babies do not go to hell, as some people believe. All aborted babies go to heaven. Children who are so young that they cannot understand their need for a Saviour are not held responsible for it. Though they are sinners just as the rest of us, they are incapable of being saved because they don't even know what "saved" is. It would be unjust of God to cast little children into hell, and He doesn't. Reference 2 Samuel 12:19 – 23.

but Satan is a subtle snake. When one of his more blatant lies is exposed, he conjures up less obtrusive lies that are more acceptable to the human heart. He mixes his poison of falsities with a little bit of truth:

"You can't provide for a child. You can barely take care of yourself as it is. What will happen if you let this pregnancy pan out?"

"Everyone would be miserable. It will be better for everyone if you get an abortion. Besides, it's not like it's actually a baby yet."

"You were raped. It's not your fault you got pregnant. What will everyone think? What will everyone say? You're only a teenager. You haven't even graduated high school yet. Abortion is the only way. No one can blame you. The man that raped you is to blame for all of this."

"Scientists say that the fetus inside you isn't alive. They are explaining the facts. There is no guilt in getting an abortion. You are not killing a baby, you are simply removing a mass of cells. It's just like removing a tumor."

"Humanity is populating too quickly. At this rate, over-population will cause the entire world to suffer. World hunger will sky-rocket. Animal habitats will be destroyed due to human

31

expansion. Resources will run dry and thousands will die if you don't help contribute. You already have two children. Let this one go so that the many can thrive."

People buy into those lies, and an innocent child receives the punishment. A life is lost. Destroyed at the hands of the very ones who were suppose to love that little baby. All the while, Satan is laughing. Laughing because people believed his lies to be true. Laughing because a life that God created was ended by him. Laughing at the beautiful picture that was ruined. In the dark, he cackles to himself:

"What blissful fools! Do you see them, Jehovah? Do you see the irony? They have taken their own flesh and sold it to my butchers! This is Your creation, Jehovah! Your creation that I have tainted!"

And the baby? If he or she could speak, what words would be uttered in those last moments? I'm sure we could think of many things that the baby might say. But above all, I believe the baby would simply ask "why?"

"Why are you doing this to me?"

"Why are you killing me?"

"Why don't you want me? Why don't you love me?"

"Please don't let them hurt me."

After years of conservatives pleading for the lives of thousands upon thousands of children, abortion clinics are still booming with business. And the blood on America's hands only grows greater.

"I Can't Provide for my Baby"

Now, as shown with those previous examples, there are a variety of other reasons that lead people to the terrible and ill conclusion that abortion is acceptable: financial insecurity, health issues, conception after rape, and the belief in over-population to name some. These are not necessarily selfish or sinful motives. They also deal with real, difficult scenarios that are nothing to scoff at, but to believe the killing of an innocent child is a reasonable option is a vicious crime no matter what difficulty a person may face.

Simply put, the sexual relationship produces children. That is how it was designed. That is the expected outcome of it. People who engage in sexual activity without thinking that a baby may be conceived from it are fooling themselves. If there are legitimate issues that would keep you from being able to properly provide for a child, take precautions. The most reasonable option that comes to my mind is giving a child away via adoption. There are countless couples in the world that are unable to bear their own children and would love to adopt. There are also families that would love to take in more children than they already have. Lord forbid they end up in the foster system, but that is still better than *death*. If a person is not able to care for a baby, or if they truly do not want the baby, that does not mean the child has to die. Give the baby to someone who would be able to care for and would cherish him or her with all of their hearts.

Health Issues

Concerning health issues, it would be better to abstain from sexual activity than to put anyone's life in danger, whether it is the mother, the child, or both. Now, I understand that the sexual relationship is to be enjoyed when in marriage. It is in the nature of human beings to enjoy it, but there are multiple medical options that would prevent a woman from getting pregnant rather than destroying the baby after conception.[10]

My wife and I had our second child only thirteen months after our first. Then we had our third child only nineteen months after that. After our first, we didn't expect to have another child for quite some time because it took over three years for Marissa to

10. Rather than describe such medical options, it would be better for you to consult your doctor concerning these, should your situation call for it.

get pregnant the first time, but when we found out she was pregnant again and again, we were delighted. However, there were some problems that came with that. Marissa's body was still recovering from the last pregnancies. Because of that, the pregnancy with our second and third took much heavier tolls on Marissa's body. We were told that Marissa needed to have some time before having another child. So, we proceeded with a medical solution that would keep Marissa from getting pregnant for a time. Once her body has fully recovered, we can have the procedure reversed and we'll be open to however many more children God decides to give us.[11]

I told that story to show that I am not exempt from the reality of these issues. Health problems with pregnancy are real. Just looking at history, giving birth has claimed the lives of thousands of women. It's nothing to laugh at. But at the same time, killing the baby isn't the answer.

Furthermore, an abortion is not a wise alternative when it comes to health issues. Many women have died because of an abortion alone. Countless women have been physically and

---

11. I understand this may rouse controversy. It's a tricky situation because some would claim that we're playing God. Others might argue that it's perfectly within our right to do this. But I would have everyone understand the motive. The heart of the matter is not to abstain from having children but to allow my wife to recover. If people seek out a medical operation for the sake of rampant sexual freedom with whomever they want without the consequence of children, that is sinful.

emotionally scarred due to abortions. And the cost is so much greater than people realize.

Conception by Rape

There is no easy way to discuss it. Rape is an unspeakable evil that no one should ever endure. Alas, we live in a sinful world. It does happen. For women/girls, it can be all the more terrifying when they discover that they have become pregnant with their rapist's child.

A multitude of reasons suddenly surface in the mind of the rape victim as to why she should not keep the baby. The younger she is, the more horrifying it can be. A teenage girl could reason that her life has barely begun and she's not ready to start taking care of another life. It also is not fair for her. Assuming she did nothing to incite the rape, she was completely blameless of the act. The man was the one who did this to her. She was defiled against her will and then given the responsibilities of a single parent at a very young age. It is a monumentally stressful and horrible situation to be in.

It is still a terrible situation with adult women. Being an adult woman that has conceived after being sexually assaulted does not make it easier. She may not have any parents in her life that could help her with the baby. On top of that, if she is already married, the husband will certainly be disinclined to care for the child and more ready to despise it. He may see the baby only as the spawn of the evil man that hurt his wife. That being said, the mother may even see her child as such. Especially if the baby has a physical resemblance to the man that abused her. She may be consistently reminded of her scarring incident every time she looks at the child. However, none of those reasons are valid to end the child's life.

Remember that the baby is just as blameless as the rape victim. The child is not responsible for the actions of his or her father. Therefore, getting an abortion is pinning the punishment on an innocent party. As stated before, adoption is a much better option if a woman is not able to care for her baby or is too emotionally scarred to keep the child of her rapist. A child is not defined by his or her father's actions. I believe that even a rape victim should do everything she can to keep her baby because, though the child was given to her through a terrible circumstance, that child very well may be a monumental blessing in her life. Children are, after all, gifts from God. They are not nightmares or weights to one's life. Look at what Psalms has to say about them:

"Lo, children *are* an heritage of the LORD: *and* the fruit of the womb *is His* reward. As arrows *are* in the hand of a mighty man; so *are* children of the youth. Happy *is* the man

that hath his quiver full of them: they shall not be ashamed,
but they shall speak with the enemies in the gate."
(Psalms 127:3 – 5)

Over-Population Theory

There have been those that say the world has already been over-populated and that the Earth does not have the resources to support the approximate eight billion lives that are in the world today. Talks of such issues have been prominent for a number of years and have even made their way into pop-culture, such as with the movie *Avengers: Infinity War*. In the film, the antagonist, Thanos, has a mission to destroy half of the universe's population. His reasoning? Over-population. He even states something along the lines that if the population is left unchecked, all will suffer. In real life, however, many people's conclusions to help over-population have been abortion. The entire country of China even has rules set in place that, if a couple becomes pregnant after already having two children, the woman will barbarously be subjected to a forced abortion. One without her consent.

Now, is over-population a real concern? Yes, I believe it is. There are numerous ecosystems that have been destroyed due to human growth. A number of animals are critically endangered or have even gone completely extinct because of human expansion. Certain areas of the world are extremely cramped due to the amount of people all living in one, small space. That certainly creates a lot of problems. Now, do I believe that over-population is as dire as some secular "experts" are saying? Definitely not, because we have a God of gods who is consistently watching over all of the affairs of His creation. See, if God did not exist, the over-populationists and Thanos would both be right: Life would have to be controlled and cut down from time to time so that the whole can thrive. But that's just it: God *does* exist, and is fully aware of the current population. He manages our world so that there are enough resources for the whole of humanity. There are multiple promises in the Bible to God's servants about providing for their needs:

"Trust in the LORD, and do good; *so* shalt thou dwell in the land, and verily thou shalt be fed."
(Psalms 37:3)

"I have been young, and *now* am old; yet have I not seen the righteous forsaken, nor his seed begging bread."
(Psalms 37:25)

"The LORD preserveth all them that love Him: but all the wicked will He destroy."
(Psalms 145:20)

"He shall feed His flock like a shepherd: He shall gather the lambs with His arm, and carry *them* in His bosom, *and* shall gently lead those that are with young."
(Isaiah 40:11)

"*When* the poor and needy seek water, and *there is* none, *and* their tongue faileth for thirst, I the LORD will hear them, I the God of Israel will not forsake them."
(Isaiah 41:17)

"But my God shall supply all your need according to His riches in glory by Christ Jesus."
(Philippians 4:19)

Such promises are not to the wicked. In fact, the opposite is found to be true:

"For the LORD loveth judgment, and forsaketh not His saints; they are preserved for ever: but the seed of the wicked shall be cut off."
(Psalms 37:28)

"But the wicked shall be cut off from the earth, and the transgressors shall be rooted out of it."
(Proverbs 2:22)

"The LORD will not suffer the soul of the righteous to famish: but He casteth away the substance of the wicked."

(Proverbs 10:3)

"The righteous shall never be removed: but the wicked shall not inhabit the earth."

(Proverbs 10:30)

"But it shall not be well with the wicked, neither shall he prolong *his* days, *which are* as a shadow; because he feareth not before God."

(Ecclesiastes 8:13)

Those are just a few in the grand expanse of Scripture. It basically comes down to this: we ought to be responsible with our resources and this Earth that God has gifted to us, but we need not be so extreme that we turn to abortion to solve the problem of over-population. There are enough wars, sickness, and natural disasters to see that the population stays in check. Just look at all the damage the coronavirus has done. Murdering unborn babies is not the answer to this dilemma. Remember that we have an Overseer who is all-knowing and all-wise. Do you really think He would make Earth the way He did if it was going to over-populate? He knows what He's doing.

Summary

- Abortion is the murder of an unborn child, regardless of what the media or the "experts" say. From conception, the child is alive. Once the abortion is completed, the child is dead. (Jeremiah 1:5, Luke 1:39 – 41, 44)

- It is the modern comparison to ancient heathen child sacrifices. (Leviticus 18:21, Deuteronomy 18:10)

- Abortion is one of Satan's greatest and most terrible tools/lies.

- The sexual relationship leads to children. If you're not ready for children, take precautions.

- Seek other options before choosing abortion, such as adoption. The child doesn't deserve to die.

CHAPTER TWO

ALCOHOL

Introduction

Abraham Lincoln once stated, "The legalized liquor business is the tragedy of our civilization. Alcohol is the greatest and most blighting curse of our modern civilization. The liquor seller is simply and only a privileged malefactor – a criminal."[12] And I agree completely. While many people try their best to condone the consumption of alcohol, the facts remain that it is deadly and that it brings misery. I must say that I am very passionate concerning this subject. Alcohol was a torture to my family when I was a child. I have seen its evils, which is why I have never once taken a drop of any kind of liquor, and neither should you.

Alcohol is the third leading cause of preventable death. The second would be poor diet and exercise. The first would be smoking, which could also be talked about in great lengths as to why it should be done away with. Alcohol has cost billions of dollars in property damage, is consistently involved in lawsuits, fills hospitals with dying people (both those who have poisoned their own body with alcohol and those who have been physically

---

12. "Abraham Lincoln Quotes about Alcohol," AZ Quotes, https://www.azquotes.com/author/8880-Abraham_Lincoln/tag/alcohol

harmed because of a drunk person), and is behind an unspeakable amount of lost virginity.

The World Health Organization has this to say about alcohol consumption:

> "Alcohol is a toxic, psychoactive, and dependence-producing substance and has been classified as a Group 1 carcinogen by the International Agency for Research on Cancer decades ago – this is the highest risk group, which also includes asbestos, radiation, and tobacco. Alcohol causes at least seven types of cancer, including the most common cancer types, such as bowel cancer and female breast cancer…To identify a 'safe' level of alcohol consumption, valid scientific evidence would need to demonstrate that at and below a certain level, there is no risk of illness or injury associated with alcohol consumption. The new WHO statement clarifies: currently available evidence cannot indicate the existence of a threshold at which the carcinogenic effects of alcohol 'switch on' and start to manifest in the human body."[13]

I would first like to note that the title of this article is "No Level of Alcohol Consumption is Safe for our Health." And that's precisely what this is saying. Alcohol consumption is compared to the dangers of breathing in asbestos or being subjected to dangerous radiation. Why do people think drinking alcohol is acceptable? It's like saying bashing one's head into a cement wall is fun. Now, I have been told that alcohol has some pros: It allows

13. "No Level of Alcohol Consumption is Safe for our Health." World Health Organization. 4, January, 2023. who.int/europe/news/item/04-01-2023-no-level-of-alcohol-consumption-is-safe-for-our-health.

people to have a good time and it lets people forget their problems. Compared to the cons, that is some agonizingly poor reasoning. Think of the damage alcohol brings upon the body and brain, the binding addiction it nurtures, the monetary loss it causes, etc. But don't just take my word for it or the World Health Organization's word for it. Take God's Word for it.

What Does the Bible Say?

Noah's Failure

One of the most notable things about Noah is that he was a godly man. This is nearly the first thing mentioned about him:

"…Noah was a just man *and* perfect in his generations, *and* Noah walked with God."
(Genesis 6:9)

He was a good man, but not sinless. His only recorded shortcoming dealt with his drinking after the Flood. Observe:

"And Noah began *to be* an husbandman, and he planted a vineyard: And he drank of the wine, and was drunken; and he was uncovered within his tent. And Ham, the father of Canaan, saw the nakedness of his father, and told his two brethren without. And Shem and Japheth took a garment, and laid *it* upon both their shoulders, and went backward, and

45

covered the nakedness of their father; and their faces *were* backward, and they saw not their father's nakedness. And Noah awoke from his wine, and knew what his younger son had done unto him."

(Genesis 9:20 – 24)

Some don't see this as an issue. There are those who propose that Noah accidentally drank too much and acted somewhat foolishly. But one of the things that needs to be understood is the difference between modern alcohol and biblical wine. This will be addressed in detail later in this chapter, but the short answer is this: the alcoholic content of biblical wine was so low that, if compared to modern wine, it wouldn't even be considered alcohol. So, with the alcoholic content being so low, one would have to drink a great amount of it in order to become drunk. One would have to **purposely try** to get drunk. There is the sin: Not only permitting a foreign substance to take control of his mind, but actually making an effort to do so. Noah wanted the darkness of alcohol to overwhelm his senses. And what happened? He stripped naked and passed out in his tent. Ham walked in on his father's shame, and Ham's son was later cursed for it. Did any good come from Noah's rampant consumption of alcohol? No. This is one of the mild examples of how alcohol can make life worse. Allow me to present some of the more extreme examples.

The Three Behaviors of Alcohol

It is commonly found in our day today, when someone becomes intoxicated, that they behave in one of three ways: foolishness, rage, or lust. A combination of those three also takes place rather frequently. Where is this found in the Bible? Well, in the metaphorical court room that is this book, with the case of alcohol as the subject at hand, I would like to call three witnesses to the stand: Solomon, Ahasuerus, and Lot. These three will give eye-witness accounts of how alcohol can affect someone's mind so much that it will lead them to commit foolish, wrathful, and lecherous things.

Solomon: Foolishness – The most commonly used passages of Scripture that combat alcohol are found in Proverbs, Solomon's book. And it makes sense, for Proverbs is the book on how to live wisely. There are three sections that speak against alcohol. See what the wisest man in all of history (aside from Jesus Christ) had to say about alcohol:

"Wine *is* a mocker, strong drink *is* raging: and whosoever is deceived thereby is not wise."
(Proverbs 20:1)

Many of the verses in Proverbs have little context beyond that particular verse. However, there are themes that connect certain groups of proverbs together. With Proverbs 20:1, that theme would be "foolish things." Consider the context:

"Judgments are prepared for scorners, and stripes for the back of fools. Wine *is* a mocker, strong drink *is* raging: and whosoever is deceived thereby is not wise. The fear of a king *is* as the roaring of a lion: *whoso* provoketh him to anger sinneth *against* his own soul. *It is* an honour for a man to cease from strife: but every fool will be meddling. The sluggard will not plow by reason of the cold; *therefore* shall he beg in harvest, and *have* nothing."
(Proverbs 19:29 – 20:4)

Each of these verses points out something that is done by someone who risks his or her own well being. In 19:29, fools are punished because they refuse to learn from their mistakes or abide by the law. Proverbs 20:2 demonstrates that only fools provoke a sovereign's wrath, thereby endangering their own life. Proverbs 20:3 attests that only foolish people meddle in strife because of the unpleasantness it could lead to. So what about 20:1? The punishment/end result of the deception of alcohol is not mentioned. Why? Because alcohol does not always lead to the same disaster. But two things are listed along with alcohol: mockery and rage.

We'll look at the "rage" part of alcohol later. With Solomon, I would like to first focus on the "mockery" side. It is no secret to anyone who has ever witnessed alcohol's dark ways that it brings about mockery. When enough alcohol is consumed, the drinker begins to act like a fool. He either mocks others, is mocked himself for his behavior, or both. How many people have been found ridiculing their employer after drinking? Was that a wise decision? Just ask them after they lost their job for the things they said. How many times has someone been shamed for the things they did while drunk? How many idiotic things made them regret putting that bottle to their lips? Now, mockery follows them. And if they were wise, they would come to the conclusion that they were deceived by the lie that alcohol brings nothing but good times. That is just the first of the three sections of Proverbs.

Ahasuerus: Rage – Solomon briefly told us that strong drink is raging. Ahasuerus, however, will *show* us. But before I get to that, I would like to explain a little bit of background concerning King Ahasuerus. Ahasuerus is one of the major characters in the book of Esther. When it comes to the history books, he is more commonly remembered as Xerxes, his Greek name. Why? Because he was defeated by the Greeks. The empire of the Medes and the Persians was eventually stomped down by Greece. Before that took place, Ahasuerus ruled the largest empire in the world of that time. He had everything he could ever have wanted, but he lacked wisdom. The man who sat on the Medo-Persian throne acted more like a spoiled child.

In the first chapter of Esther, Ahasuerus threw a massive banquet. This was to display his wealth and power before he and his troops march off to fight against Greece. It was to encourage morale and inspire his troops to believe that no one could be greater than their king. To further prove how great Ahasuerus was, he had the feast last six full months. And at the end of those six months, he threw another party for seven days that allowed everyone in Shushan to attend the finale to the banquet, so to speak. All this time, he was consuming alcohol, drowning himself into a drunken stupor. On the seventh day of the feast, Ahasuerus' drunken mind conceived a terrible idea:

"On the seventh day, when the heart of the king was merry with wine, he commanded Mehuman, Biztha, Harbona, Bigtha, and Abagtha, Zethar, and Carcas, the seven chamberlains that served in the presence of Ahasuerus the king, To bring Vashti the queen before the king with the crown royal, to shew the people and the princes her beauty: for she *was* fair to look on. But the queen Vashti refused to come at the king's commandment by *his* chamberlains: therefore was the king very wroth, and his anger burned in him."
(Esther 1:10 – 12)

A good deal to unpack here. First off, what was so wrong about Ahasuerus' order? He wanted to show off his wife, right? Yes, but it is believed he wanted her to appear naked to show off *all* of her beauty. Vashti, having some dignity, refused to do this, and as soon as Ahasuerus heard the reply, all of his merriment immediately transformed into hot wrath. There are many times when the phrase "very wroth" is in the Bible, but there is only one time where the Bible has the phrase "very wroth, and his anger burned in him." The Hebrew word here that is used for "anger" is "חֵמָא חֵמָה" (pronounced "khay-maw', khay-maw'") which means "heat," "hot displeasure," "furious," "rage," and "wrath." He was fuming with anger.

If he just took a moment to stop and think with a sober mind, he would realize that she was right, and he was very much wrong. As his wife, Vashti's body was for his eyes alone, not for thousands of his drunken troops. Ordering her to do this was humiliating, disrespectful, selfish, vulgar, and cruel. A command such as this could be devastating to her. Exposing one's nudity to the public eye is always shameful. Ever since Adam and Eve's sin, nakedness is unnatural to us. Not only that, but Vashti held a place of authority. She was not a concubine or a slave girl.[14] She was the

---

14. I am not saying that it would be acceptable for Ahasuerus to ask a concubine/slave girl to disrobe in front of thousands of men. It's wrong no matter who the woman is. I am simply pointing out that this was even more absurd, given Vashti's position as queen. Her title demanded respect and Ahasuerus refused to show that in this instance.

queen, but Ahasuerus took none of these things into consideration because of how his mind was overthrown by alcohol. When his intoxicated idea was denied, the alcohol transformed into an irrational fit of rage.

At this point, Ahasuerus should have taken time to think and sober up. Perhaps even talk to Vashti herself for her to plead her case, but his intoxication poisoned him with anger so that he could not think rationally. He immediately turned to his counselors for how he was to punish Vashti:

"If it please the king, let there go a royal commandment from him, and let it be written among the laws of the Persians and the Medes, that it be not altered, That Vashti come no more before king Ahasuerus; and let the king give her royal estate unto another that is better than she. And when the king's decree which he shall make shall be published throughout all his empire, (for it is great,) all the wives shall give to their husbands honour, both to great and small. And the saying pleased the king and the princes; and the king did according to the word of Memucan:"
(Esther 1:15 – 21)

In his anger and his drunkenness, Ahasuerus thought this was a great idea: to rip Vashti's title away and to never be with her again. Now, we do not know much about the relationship between

Ahasuerus and Vashti. Considering Ahasuerus' character, we know he did not value Vashti as a husband should, but we do know that he did care for her in some degree:

"After these things, when the wrath of king Ahasuerus was appeased, he remembered Vashti, and what she had done, and what was decreed against her."
(Esther 2:1)

After Vashti was banished and after Ahasurerus woke up from his wine, he remembered his former queen. Perhaps this is reading too much into it, but I feel that this verse depicts regret from Ahasuerus. Why would he recall her to mind if he didn't miss her? He had allowed his wrath to take over him while he was drunk, and it resulted in a decision that he could never revoke. His Vashti was gone forever. It was written in the laws of the Medes and Persians. It could not be undone.[15] Ahasuerus, who had always gotten whatever he desired, was not able to rewrite this law so that he could have Vashti back, and it was because he had made a hasty decision while he was consumed with drunken wrath.

Now, all things considered, that is not the worst thing that could happen when someone's anger has been kindled while

15. Let's be honest: making it so laws can *never* be reversed after they are decreed is a terrible idea. This has been shown at least twice with Ahasuerus and once with Darius (Daniel 6:7 – 15).

drunk. Was it a terrible decision with lasting consequences? Yes, but there are countless stories of lives that were changed in a far worse way by someone who exploded while drunk. There is the idea floating around that alcohol gives people courage and boldness. It does not. Rather, it frees people of their inhibitions by erasing their clear thinking. When I was growing up, I lived in a small town. Small towns out in the country are wonderful. One of the reasons why is because there is a great lack of crime. Homicide, larceny, gang violence, and such tend to happen in bigger cities. None of them really happened in my little town.

However, there is one story where a gun was brandished in a public place. From what I remember, a man's girlfriend had cheated on him. Once that man found out, she left him altogether. One night, the woman and her new boyfriend went out to the only bowling alley in town to have some fun. Then, her old boyfriend showed up with a loaded pistol. He was clearly drunk, and he was ready to murder. Whether he was going to kill his old girlfriend, her new boyfriend, or both, it wasn't clear. I was told that he shouted some things and then aimed the gun at them. Thankfully, a courageous man behind him tackled him to the ground before the gun could be fired. No one was hurt.

Now, I never knew this man. I didn't know his personality or how he behaved whilst not intoxicated, but I do know that he was never expected to try and kill his former girlfriend and her new boyfriend. He had allowed the rage of alcohol to push him to do something rash, violent, and very horrible. Because of his actions, he faced the consequences of being arrested for attempted homicide. It is wonderful that he was stopped, but not everyone is stopped before they do something of this nature while drunk. How many families have suffered at the wrath of a drunk person? How many deaths have occurred because of intoxicated rage? How many innocent people's lives have been scarred because of alcohol? How many children live in a prison of fear, wondering if their parent will come home sober or drunk? Is this drink really worth bringing out such a terrible monster to the people you care about most?

Lot: Lust – Though he was the nephew of a God-honoring man, Lot was known more for his mistakes than his godliness. That being said, we know he trusted in Jehovah, for he was labeled as a just man in 2 Peter 2:7. Furthermore, when Lot was given the chance to stay in Ur or follow his righteous uncle, Abram, he chose the latter. He made some good decisions, but he also made many poor ones. Choosing to live in Sodom began this ungodly lifestyle. The vile culture corrupted him along with his family. Although he reverenced God and was spared from the devastation of Sodom and Gomorrah, the years of being saturated in Sodom's filth did not easily fade. When Lot was left alone with his only two living daughters, they conceived a horrendous plan, and alcohol was at the core of it.

"And Lot went up out of Zoar, and dwelt in the mountain, and his two daughters with him; for he feared to dwell in Zoar: and he dwelt in a cave, he and his two daughters. And the firstborn said unto the younger, Our father *is* old, and *there is* not a man in the earth to come in unto us after the manner of all the earth: Come, let us make our father drink wine, and we will lie with him, that we may preserve seed of our father. And they made their father drink wine that night: and the firstborn went in, and lay with her father; and he perceived not when she lay down, nor when she arose. And it came to pass on the morrow, that the firstborn said unto the younger, Behold, I lay yesternight with my father: let us make him drink wine this night also; and go thou in, *and* lie with him, that we may preserve seed of our father. And they made their father drink wine that night also: and the younger arose, and lay with him; and he perceived not when she lay down, nor when she arose. Thus were both the daughters of Lot with child by their father."

(Genesis 19:30 – 36)

Alcohol lowers the wall of one's conscience and moral restrictions. In a sober state, Lot would have never agreed to have sexual relations with his own daughters. In order to convince him otherwise, his daughters made him drink wine until his basest desires started sprouting in his mind. After the drunkenness had passed, Lot had no recollection of what had taken place, for the alcohol had warped his memory also.

For those who are advocates of alcohol, please analyze this passage and learn from it. There are many sins that some consider "not that bad," but when it comes to incest, even the most reprobate minds still cringe in disgust at the thought. Alcohol caused a *saved* individual to commit incest. Lot was not a heathen man. He believed in and worshipped Jehovah, but when he had permitted alcohol to overwhelm his mind, he set aside his conscience altogether and did that which is disgusting and unnatural.

These would be the three characteristics that alcohol brings out in people: Foolishness, rage, and lust. Time and time again, it is shown to be true, whether people read it in history books or see a real life example. The world may try to deny it with deceptions of how alcohol makes people feel good and whatnot, but the facts do not lie. Alcohol is damaging to you and damaging to the people you care most about. I beg you to abstain from alcohol. It will bring out aspects of yourself that are dark, evil, and dangerous.

It Doesn't Solve Problems but Creates More

The following verses are probably the most well-known when it comes to preaching against alcohol:

"Who hath woe? who hath sorrow? who hath contentions? who hath babbling? who hath wounds without cause? who hath redness of eyes? They that tarry long at the wine; they that go to seek mixed wine. Look not thou upon the wine when it is red, when it giveth his colour in the cup, *when* it moveth itself aright. At the last it biteth like a serpent, and stingeth like an adder. Thine eyes shall behold strange women, and thine heart shall utter perverse things. Yea, thou shalt be as he that lieth down in the midst of the sea, or as he that lieth upon the top of a mast. They have stricken me, *shalt thou say, and* I was not sick; they have beaten me, *and* I felt *it* not: when shall I awake? I will seek it yet again."
(Proverbs 23:29 – 35)

Proverbs 20:1 showed how alcohol brings about mockery and rage. Proverbs 23:29 – 35 shows another aspect here: sorrow. People have been known to turn to alcohol when depressed. Alcohol does not solve the depression. In fact, it may well only increase their sorrow when they awake from it. It is true the alcohol may give people a high, but there is an inevitable low after the high wears off. Look at the other adjectives that Solomon uses for those who drink wine: woe, contentions (brawling), babbling, wounds without cause, redness of eyes. These are not characteristics that the average man or woman seeks. But alcohol is associated with all of them. Furthermore, it is yet again made clear here that alcohol leads to other sins. In these verses,

Solomon specifically mentions sexual sin ("Thine eyes shall behold strange women") and a break down of mental filters by way of speech ("Thine heart shall utter perverse things"). They stagger back and forth because of how the drink has affected their brain and their balance ("Yea, thou shalt be as he that lieth down in the midst of the sea, or as he that lieth upon the top of a mast"). Finally, it ends where it began. The drinker returns to sobriety and says to himself, "I will seek it yet again." A terrible cycle that produced no good. What evil came of it? A lowering of the moral senses, an allurement to fornication, a dependence upon alcohol, and ultimately nowhere closer to solving the original problems that persuaded him to drink in the first place.

Paul's Stand against Alcohol

As with so many controversial issues, people might say "But that was the Old Testament! That means it doesn't apply to Christians today! We go by the New Testament!" Now, I must interject that such thinking is flawed, for the Old Testament was not written simply to be thrown away once the New Testament was penned. They are to be a complete set together: the Old Testament picturing the coming of the Messiah and the New Testament being the coming of the Messiah that brings salvation to all. Secondly, many things that are forbidden in the Old Testament are still forbidden in the New Testament. This includes alcohol. Paul, the author of half of the New Testament, has something to say about alcohol:

"And be not drunk with wine, wherein is excess; but be filled with the Spirit;"
(Ephesians 5:18)

Many people read this wrong. They tend to be advocates of moderate drinking but are against getting drunk. They typically read it as something along the lines of this: "Drinking alcohol is fine, as long as you don't drink it excessively. Also, be filled with the Spirit." See how it feels like the two subjects don't fit? Why jump from talking about alcohol to the Spirit? In reality, they are connected because the two are opposites. Drinking alcohol encourages sin while being filled with the Spirit encourages righteousness. So, the verse should really be read more with this message: "Be filled with the Spirit rather than being filled with alcohol."

Furthermore, a mindset of "just don't drink too much" is ignorant, for the human nature is to gravitate beyond set boundaries. Every sinner naturally wants to go further than what is advised. A similar situation would be to purposely be alone with someone to whom you are sexually attracted to. Nothing may happen, but with desire and opportunity both present, the risk is too great to be considered anything but foolish. Another comparison would be over-eating. We can all be tempted to eat more than our hunger requires. Appetites are often larger than one's stomach, and when someone habitually over-eats, an unhealthy lifestyle begins. The same goes with moderate drinking. Eventually, people who drink moderately will want to see where they go if they drink excessively. They want to see what will happen, what they will feel, if it truly is as fun as some say, etc. It's our nature to never be satisfied, but to always desire "just a little more."

Moreover, we have already established that alcohol brings out a darkness in people. It incites moronic behavior, nurtures wrath, and sets fire to even the most unnatural passions. This darkness that fills them would be the opposite of what the Holy Spirit is, for the Holy Spirit extinguishes all evil behavior in a person. When one is filled with the Spirit, their life brings out the fruit of love, joy, peace, longsuffering, gentleness, goodness, faith, meekness, and temperance (Galatians 5:22 – 23). But someone cannot be filled with the Spirit and filled with the dark essence of alcohol at the same time. Like a cup, we can only be filled with one thing at a time. Like oil and water, the Holy Spirit does not mix with the devices of Satan. Be not filled with wine, but be filled with the Holy Spirit.

Lastly, before we move on, I know that many are wondering what the word "excess" refers to. As mentioned with Noah, biblical wine did in fact have some alcoholic content. Very, very little, but it was there. So, it was possible to get drunk off of grape juice, but in order to do it, you had to drink a huge amount. One could say you would have to drink *excessively*. This is what is likely being referred to with the fact that Paul says "wherein is excess." I would encourage personal study, however.

"Know ye not that the unrighteous shall not inherit the kingdom of God? Be not deceived: neither fornicators, nor idolaters, nor adulterers, nor effeminate, nor abusers of themselves with mankind, Nor thieves, nor covetous, nor <u>drunkards</u>, nor revilers, nor extortioners, shall inherit the kingdom of God. And such were some of you: but ye are washed, but ye are sanctified, but ye are justified in the name of the Lord Jesus, and by the Spirit of our God. All things are lawful unto me, but all things are not expedient: all things are lawful for me, but I will not be brought under the power of any."
(1 Corinthians 6:9 – 12)

This passage is not typically the first one people go to when speaking against alcohol, but it is a very good one. Among other things, drunkenness is mentioned. It is said that drunkards will not inherit the kingdom of God. Now, just to clarify, this is not saying that anyone who has ever done any of the things listed cannot be saved. For instance, David was an adulterer, but was called God's servant. What Paul is saying here is those whose life is characterized by these things will not inherit the kingdom of God. Why? Because they are not saved. They have rather given themselves over to these sinful lifestyles and are happy to wallow in their condemnation.

Moving on, the important part of the passage is at the end. Paul says that all things are lawful for him to do, but all things are not edifying. What is he saying here? Well, after Christ came, the law of God was overruled by grace. They go together, but if one breaks the law, he or she is able to be washed by God's grace. So Paul is saying that he could do any number of the things he mentioned and then ask for forgiveness of it, but that is not expedient. It is not profitable. If we, as Christians, think that we can rampantly sin consequence-free just because we ask for forgiveness right after, we're fooling ourselves. What you sow, you will reap (Galatians 6:7).

Lastly, Paul made it a point that those who are going to pursue the office of pastor or deacon must not associate with alcohol:

"A bishop then must be blameless, the husband of one wife, vigilant, sober, of good behaviour, given to hospitality, apt to teach; Not given to wine, no striker, not greedy of filthy lucre;

but patient, not a brawler, not covetous;…Likewise *must* **the deacons** *be* **grave, not doubletongued, <u>not given to much wine</u>, not greedy of filthy lucre;"**
(1 Timothy 3:2 – 3, 8)

"For a bishop must be blameless, as the steward of God; not selfwilled, not soon angry, <u>not given to wine</u>, no striker, not given to filthy lucre;"
(Titus 1:7)

They are to be officers of God's church. After all we've looked through, I don't think it's hard to understand why a pastor or deacon should not drink alcohol. In fact, all Christians should stay away from the toxicity of alcohol, but it is far more crucial for spiritual leaders to abstain. They are charged with leading God's people. A very serious responsibility is placed upon their shoulders. As often as possible, they must seek to be filled with the Spirit so as to rightly live. I can only imagine how much Satan endeavors to push pastors and deacons to be caught up in drinking, so he might destroy their reputation and image as men of God. Think of how many men have had to step down from the pulpit after succumbing to alcohol and committing senseless actions. Acting like a fool, being filled with wrath, overwhelmed with lust.

Now, some might think, "Well, I'm not going to be a pastor or a deacon." That's still not a license for you to drink. If you name the name of Christ, you are to disassociate yourself from alcohol. Satan still wishes to destroy you as well, and he will use whatever avenue he can to do so. Why open the door for him? Be done with that vile drink!

Various Other Bible Passages

Now, I could go on forever with every single Bible verse that condemns consumption of alcohol, but I feel that I've already made my point crystal clear. So, instead of beating the same horse over and over, I will simply put a few other Bible verses that I have found against alcohol here in case readers would like to study it out for themselves:

"Woe unto them that rise up early in the morning, *that* they may follow strong drink; that continue until night, *till* wine inflame them!…Woe unto *them that are* mighty to drink wine, and men of strength to mingle strong drink: Which justify the wicked for reward, and take away the righteousness of the righteous from him!"
(Isaiah 5:11, 22 – 23)

"But they also have erred through wine, and through strong drink are out of the way; the priest and the prophet have

erred through strong drink, they are swallowed up of wine, they are out of the way through strong drink; they err in vision, they stumble *in* judgment. For all tables are full of vomit *and* filthiness, *so that there is* no place *clean.*"
(Isaiah 28:7 – 8)

"And the king appointed them a daily provision of the king's meat, and of the wine which he drank: so nourishing them three years, that at the end thereof they might stand before the king…But Daniel purposed in his heart that he would not defile himself with the portion of the king's meat, <u>nor with the wine which he drank</u>: therefore he requested of the prince of the eunuchs that he might not defile himself."
(Daniel 1:5, 8)

"Whoredom and wine and new wine take away the heart."
(Hosea 4:11)

"And they have cast lots for my people; and have given a boy for an harlot, and sold a girl for wine, that they might drink."
(Joel 3:3)

"Behold, his soul *which* is lifted up is not upright in him: but the just shall live by his faith. Yea also, because <u>he transgresseth by wine</u>, *he is* a proud man, neither keepeth at home, who enlargeth his desire as hell, and *is* as death, and

cannot be satisfied, but gathereth unto him all nations, and
heapeth unto him all people:"
(Habakkuk 2:4 – 5)

"The aged women likewise, that *they be* in behaviour as
becometh holiness, not false accusers, <u>not given to much wine,</u>
teachers of good things;"
(Titus 2:3)

"For the time past of *our* life may suffice us to have wrought
the will of the Gentiles, when we walked in lasciviousness,
lusts, <u>excess of wine</u>, revellings, banquetings, and abominable
idolatries:"
(1 Peter 4:3)

Other Points

Unfermented vs. Fermented Wine

The most common retort to all of these verses is this: "What
about all of the positive verses in the Bible where people drank
wine? Countless people condoned wine in the Bible. Even *Jesus*
turned water into wine!" Though that seems like a good argument,
it is an uneducated one, for people need to take the culture and
method of how wine was produced in ancient Israel. According to
www.bibleinfo.com:

67

"Ancient civilizations had several ways of preventing fruit and fruit juices from fermentation, and thus were able to have non-alcoholic wine (grape juice) throughout the year.

1) One method involved boiling the juice and reducing it to a syrup that could later be diluted with water.

2) Another was to boil the juice with minimum evaporation and then immediately seal it with beeswax in air-tight jars.

3) Drying the fruit in the sun and then reconstituting it with water, adding sulfur to the fruit juice, or filtering the juice to extract the gluten were also methods that would prevent the juice from fermenting.

These means of preservation were known to the ancients, who also practiced boiling fermented juice to eliminate the alcohol.

'The Mishna [a collection of oral Jewish traditions] states that the Jews were in the habit of drinking boiled wine' (Kitto's Cyclopedia of Biblical Literature, vol. 2, p. 447). Naturally, this wine would be entirely free of alcohol as a result of the boiling, if not also from the manner of preservation.

In his commentary on the Gospel of John, Albert Barnes wrote, 'The wine of Judea was the pure juice of the grape, without any mixture of alcohol. It was the common drink of the people and did not produce intoxication.' And Adam Clarke, commenting on Genesis 40:11, wrote, 'From this we find that wine anciently was the mere expressed juice of the grape without fermentation. The saky, or cupbearer, took the bunch [of grapes], pressed the juice into the cup, and instantly delivered it into the hands of his master'."[16]

---

16. "What are the Facts about Fermented Drinks in the Bible?" Bibleinfo, https://www.bibleinfo.com/en/questions/what-are-historical-and-scriptural-facts-about-fermented-drinks-bible

As you can see, the Hebrew people's wine in biblical times was essentially grape juice. If there was any alcohol level in it, it would be so extraordinarily insignificant that it would not even be considered alcoholic today. Therefore, it would also take a great amount of consumption before ever influencing the mind or getting anyone drunk. So, for all of those who say, "Drinking alcohol is fine! Plenty of godly people did it in the Bible!" it shows how little they understand what biblical wine was. Jesus did not promote alcohol at the wedding of Cana. He created non-alcoholic grape juice, which is what the word "wine" usually refers to throughout the Bible.[17]

Common Sense

Now, for those who are still not convinced, let's look at alcohol in the light of science and common sense. Even leaving the Bible out, alcohol is still shown to be a poison. And I don't mean a figurative poison. I mean a literal, killing poison. Here are some things that are affected by alcohol:

- Brain – Interferes with the communication pathways and how the brain works. This can affect mood, behavior, and make concentration and physical coordination difficult.

---

17. There are passages that do speak strictly of intoxicating beverage while using the word "wine," however. The word "strong drink" is sometimes used to distinguish it, but each verse needs to be taken in its context so as to know exactly what is being referenced.

- Heart – Can lead to stretching of heart muscle, irregular heart beat, stroke, and high blood pressure.

- Liver – Can lead to steatosis, alcoholic hepatitis, fibrosis, and cirrhosis.

- Pancreas – Can lead to inflammation and swelling of certain blood vessels that will impede proper digestion.

- Immune system – Can weaken the immune system and make you more susceptible to disease and infection.

This information was taken from the National Institute on Alcohol Abuse and Alcoholism (NIAAA).[18] Alcohol poisons you. In the medical field, alcohol is used to disinfect. It is a substance that is magnificent at killing viruses, bacteria, and other harmful germs. It cleans everything from counter-tops in a kitchen at home to equipment at hospitals that will be used for tests. When alcohol is used properly, it can promote health by way of sanitation. However, when used as a beverage, alcohol is a substance that brings destruction to the body. The liver is commonly one of the primary organs that suffers greatly from drinking alcohol. Why is that? Because the liver is the organ that filters out toxicities in the body. When alcohol is placed within the body, the liver does

18. "Alcohol's Effects on the Body." National Institute Alcohol Abuse and Alcoholism. N.D. niaaa.nih.gov/alcohols-health/alcohols-effects-body.

everything it can to rid the body of it. But all too often, the liver is overwhelmed by the amount of poison that is placed in the body when it comes to drinking.

Honestly, if people would unbiasedly weigh the rewards against the consequences of recreational consumption of alcohol, they would find that there are very few, shallow rewards. And what grave, life-changing consequences there are. We've looked through many of them and I don't think they need to be rehashed, but this author pleads with you: don't drink alcohol. In the end, it will harm you and others around you. The small benefits it brings will not comfort you when the massive tragedies come.

<u>Summary</u>

- Alcohol is a literal poison. It's original purpose was not for consumption, but for sanitation by way of killing harmful germs.
- Alcohol unlocks dark parts of the sin nature in a person (foolishness, wrath, and lust), and will cause people to do even the most vile of things. (Proverbs 20:1, Esther 1, Genesis 19:30 – 36)
- The Bible never condones the drinking of alcohol. The acceptable "wine" in the Bible is referring to unfermented grape juice.

- Alcohol and the Holy Spirit cannot coincide. When people give themselves over to alcohol, they nurture darkness within them. The opposite is true when people surrender to the Holy Spirit. (Ephesians 5:18)
- Alcohol will not solve your problems, but will likely contribute to them. (Proverbs 23:29 – 35)
- The benefits of drinking alcohol are greatly outweighed by the multiple negative aspects that alcohol brings to someone's life.

CHAPTER THREE

AUTHORITY

Introduction

No matter where you are in life, you have someone that you answer to. People don't tend to like that fact. Everyone would rather be their own boss doing what they want, how they want, and when they want. Many cultures, including America's, push people to excel in the business area, to climb the corporate ladder so that they can one day reach the glamorous position of "manager," "supervisor," or even "C.E.O." Though there is nothing wrong with wanting to be a leader, do we not struggle with wanting to overthrow authority so that we can be our own authority?

We are, by our very nature, rebellious. If someone tells us to do something undesirable, there is an automatic response of "No" that flashes in our mind. Whether or not we comply, the resistance still emerges in our spirit. Children really show this in a more unfiltered way. For those of you who are parents, how many times have you told your kids to pick up their toys, clean their room, stop running through the store, not touch something fragile, etc. and they just buck against you? They say "No!" They whine and cry. They throw a fit. We, as parents, have a choice to either let it slide or put the fear of God in that child.

Now, take that image in your mind. Whether or not you are a parent, you've seen it. Take that picture of a five year old, screaming in the checkout line because he didn't get the piece of candy he wanted, and realize this: that's us. Little rebels that grow up into adult rebels. It is not natural for us to submit to authority. We want to be our own authority, as foolish as that idea is. Look at it this way: A child has the authority of parents over him. Once that child becomes an adult and starts work, that adult has the authority of a boss over him. That adult may become the boss of that specific building, but that boss has the authority of the C.E.O. over him. That boss may eventually become the C.E.O. of the company, but he still has the law as an authority over him. That C.E.O. may run and be elected as President of the United States of America where he can move to change the laws, but he still has the authority of the nation over him. That President may overthrow the nation's authority and change America's government into a dictatorship, but that dictator is still under the authority of Almighty God. As shown here, the idea of becoming higher than every authority is not only foolish but impossible.

Now, I genuinely don't feel like I need to hammer this idea down too much. If anyone thinks about it for too long, they realize that they cannot be free from authority. At the same time, however, knowing that we have authorities over us is not what's important here. **Submitting** to those authorities is what's important. As Christians, we are called to willingly put ourselves under all ordained authorities. This includes parents, government, police officers, teachers, and, if you're a married woman, your husband. Now, God will not make us submit, but it is best if we just cast away our rebellious spirit and become submissive.

What Does the Bible Say?

Submission to God

God has complete sovereignty. Sovereignty is a fancy word for being in control over or being a ruler over. It's why a king can also be known as a sovereign, and God is sovereign over all. He has authority over everything because He made everything. There is no one equal or higher than Him.

Of course, this attribute also brings about a question: "How can we have free will if God is in control of everything?" That question can be taken further to ask: "Is God responsible behind everything that happens?" For the answers to those questions, please refer to Chapter Fifteen: Wrath, Love, and Other Enigmas – "Why do Bad Things happen in Life if God is Good and in Control over Everything?" and "How can we have Free Will if God is Sovereign over Everything?" I don't want to get too off topic here and those sections go more in depth.

There have been a few times in the Bible when someone rejected God's sovereignty. Now, rebellion against any authority is ultimately rebelling against God,[19] but we'll look at just a few times when someone wasn't necessarily fighting against a man, but God Himself:

Satan

"How art thou fallen from heaven, O Lucifer, son of the morning! *how* **art thou cut down to the ground, which didst weaken the nations! For thou hast said in thine heart, I will ascend into heaven, I will exalt my throne above the stars of God: I will sit also upon the mount of the congregation, in the sides of the north: I will ascend above the heights of the clouds; I will be like the most High."**
(Isaiah 14:12 – 14)

The greatest and most consequential rebellion of all time. Lucifer, who may have been an arch-angel like Michael, being consumed by pride and blasphemously wanting to be equal with God, and he has been trying ever since. I've heard it more than a few times from some people that they think God and Satan are equally powerful entities that are battling for the fate of humanity, but God and Satan are nowhere near equal. The Lord is above all.

---

19. Unless that authority commands us to do something that contradicts God's commandments. See The Exception on page 112.

"I *am* the LORD, and *there is* none else, *there is* no God beside Me: I girded thee, though thou hast not known Me: That they may know from the rising of the sun, and from the west, that *there is* none beside Me. I *am* the LORD, and *there is* none else."

(Isaiah 45:5 – 6)

"To whom will ye liken Me, and make *Me* equal, and compare Me, that we may be like?"

(Isaiah 46:5)

"Remember the former things of old: for I *am* God, and *there is* none else; *I am* God, and *there is* none like Me"

(Isaiah 46:9)

Lucifer, who very well knew all of this, wanted to attain to the same level as God anyway. Thus he went from Lucifer, meaning "brightness" and "morning star," to Satan which means "accuser" and "adversary." Now, the rest of the story hasn't happened yet, but Satan's rebellion is only going to lead him to an eternal seat in the Lake of Fire. It was, after all, designed for him and his demons.

"And the devil that deceived them was cast into the lake of fire and brimstone, where the beast and the false prophet _are,_ and shall be tormented day and night for ever and ever."
(Revelation 20:10)

The greatest rebellion will be met with the greatest triumph. Though Satan has and will continue to war against the things of God until that fateful day, he will ultimately be defeated. His pride cost him his heavenly position,[20] his pure nature, and total separation from the God who made him. He will likely burn in the hottest places of the Lake of Fire, for he saw God for who He is and rejected Him anyway.

Pharaoh:

"And afterward Moses and Aaron went in, and told Pharaoh, Thus saith the LORD God of Israel, Let my people go, that they may hold a feast unto me in the wilderness. And Pharaoh said, Who _is_ the LORD, that I should obey his voice to let Israel go? I know not the LORD, neither will I let Israel go."
(Exodus 5:1 – 2)

---

20. Some believe that Lucifer was an arch-angel along with Michael and possibly Gabriel (there is some debate whether Gabriel is an arch-angel also. Michael is the only one who is actually called one in Jude 1:9). Even if Lucifer wasn't an arch-angel, he appears to have had some sort of significant status among the angels before his fall.

This is a rather brazen statement, but it's only natural since Pharaoh thought himself a god. He was raised as such. Like the pharaohs before him, Pharaoh would have been told all his life that, once he ascended to the throne, he was the sun god Ra in human flesh. He was told that he was a deity and all of Egypt was to obey his every whim as if it were a divine decree. God eventually obliterated that concept with Pharaoh by showing him he was powerless against the Lord's plagues. However, when Moses first confronted Pharaoh to let the Hebrews out of bondage, Pharaoh immediately pushed back against this authority. Why? Because *he* was the supreme authority. He told others what to do. No one told him what to do. He stiffened his neck, hardened his heart, and said "No."

Being one of the most popular stories in the Bible, most people know how that went. Egypt was dealt ten catastrophic plagues: the Nile turning to blood, frogs, lice, flies, sickness on the livestock, boils, hail mingled with fire, locusts, darkness that could be felt, and the death of the firstborns. Eventually, Pharaoh was broken and he released Israel. Shortly after doing this, however, his stubbornness revived. He chased Israel down with six hundred chariots and very likely lost his life in the Red Sea. He rebelled against God time and time again. Eventually, it cost him everything.

<u>Achan:</u>

"And ye, in any wise keep *yourselves* from the accursed thing, lest ye make *yourselves* accursed, when ye take of the accursed thing, and make the camp of Israel a curse, and trouble it.... But the children of Israel committed a trespass in the accursed thing: for Achan, the son of Carmi, the son of Zabdi, the son of Zerah, of the tribe of Judah, took of the accursed thing: and the anger of the LORD was kindled against the children of Israel."

(Joshua 6:18, 7:1)

The book of Joshua is known for the victories that take place for the children of Israel. It is the book where the Hebrew people conquered the land that God promised them. Unfortunately, because of a man named Achan, there is a black mark where God's people were shamefully defeated.

When Israel was going to fight against Jericho, God ordered them not to take anything. The city, and everything in it, was cursed.[21] This was very clearly explained before they attacked the city, but Achan took items that he coveted: a Babylonish garment, two hundred shekels of silver, and a wedge of gold. Because of that, he was in direct violation of what God had ordered. In fact, the silver and the gold were supposed to be given to God by being

---

21. Except for Rahab and her family due to her faith.

placed within the tabernacle treasury. So, he was not only disobeying God, but stealing from Him as well.

Achan hid the items in his tent, his family being privy to it. From Jericho, the Israelites moved on to Ai. There, they were defeated because of the curse. Thirty-six men died because of Achan's sin. Once Joshua knew that someone had taken of the cursed items of Jericho, God providentially led him to Achan. Achan and his family were stoned because of Achan's rebellion. He, like Pharaoh, lost everything.

Saul:

"And Samuel said, When thou *wast* little in thine own sight, *wast* thou not *made* the head of the tribes of Israel, and the LORD anointed thee king over Israel? And the LORD sent thee on a journey, and said, Go and utterly destroy the sinners the Amalekites, and fight against them until they be consumed. Wherefore then didst thou not obey the voice of the LORD, but didst fly upon the spoil, and didst evil in the sight of the LORD? And Saul said unto Samuel, Yea, I have obeyed the voice of the LORD, and have gone the way which the LORD sent me, and have brought Agag the king of Amalek, and have utterly destroyed the Amalekites. But the people took of the spoil, sheep and oxen, the chief of the things which should have been utterly destroyed, to sacrifice unto the LORD thy God in Gilgal. And Samuel said, Hath the LORD

as great delight in burnt offerings and sacrifices, as in obeying the voice of the LORD? Behold, to obey *is* better than sacrifice, *and* to hearken than the fat of rams. For rebellion *is as* the sin of witchcraft, and stubbornness *is as* iniquity and idolatry. Because thou hast rejected the word of the LORD, he hath also rejected thee from *being* king."

(1 Samuel 15:17 – 23)

Saul started out so well as being the first king of Israel, but along the way, he began to think that his ideas were better than what God had told him. First, when he was in trouble in chapter 13 with the Philistines, he offered up a burnt sacrifice to the Lord, which was not lawful for him to do; he was not a priest. Then, when God ordered him to utterly destroy all of the Amalekites and their animals, Saul decided that he would only destroy most of them and keep the best of the animals.

Twice, he had rebelled. So, his position as king was removed from him. It was passed on to David. And Saul, so eager to hold onto his kingdom, became so mad with jealousy that he endeavored to murder David. Straying further and further from the Lord, Saul digressed to the point where he ended his own life after being wounded on the battlefield.

Jonah:

"Now the word of the LORD came unto Jonah the son of Amittai, saying, Arise, go to Nineveh, that great city, and cry against it; for their wickedness is come up before me. But Jonah rose up to flee unto Tarshish from the presence of the LORD, and went down to Joppa; and he found a ship going to Tarshish: so he paid the fare thereof, and went down into it, to go with them unto Tarshish from the presence of the LORD."
(Jonah 1:1 – 3)

Here is a rebellion that didn't go as far as it could have, thankfully. At first, Jonah was so set on *not* preaching at Nineveh. He first tried going to Tarshish, which was the furthest place from Nineveh in the known world at that time.[22] God, as we know, brought a great storm. At that point, Jonah was ready to die before he would go and preach at Nineveh. He had the men of the ship throw him overboard. Then, after being swallowed by a great fish for three days, Jonah broke. He prayed in repentance, was vomited up, and went and did what God originally told him to do.

Now, Jonah ends with a bittersweet tone. Unlike Pharaoh, Achan, or Saul, Jonah didn't hold to his rebellion so tightly that it ended his life. He asked for forgiveness and was given a second chance. Now, did he carry it out with the spirit that God would

---

22. Tarshish was believed to be located in Spain. Estimated to be around 2,500 miles away from Nineveh.

have been proud of? Absolutely not, but he forsook his rebellion, and God saved him from dying in the fish.

These are just a few examples of what happens when people fight against God, but there are also multitudes of stories where people were obedient to the Lord instead of kicking against Him. So many, in fact, that I wouldn't be able to fit them all in a concise manner. Rather, it would be good for you, reader, to study them out in the Bible for yourself:[23]

- Noah
- Abraham
- Joseph
- Moses
- Joshua
- Rahab
- Gideon
- Samuel
- David
- Isaiah
- Ezekiel
- Jeremiah
- Daniel
- Mary and Joseph

23. Now, take into account that being obedient to God does not mean these people had an easy life. Most of these people, rather, had a life that was full of difficulties and hardships, but God was with them in life. And now, they are experiencing great rewards in heaven.

- The Twelve Apostles
- Paul

These and so many others. Don't fight against God. It'll only be worse for you in the end. Obey Him. After all, the best life you could ever live would be the life that God has planned for you.

The Authority of God's Man

Now, I would like to first clarify that, when I say "God's man," I am meaning a man that is given direction by the Lord to lead God's people in the way of holiness and truth that is clearly defined through the Bible. In simpler terms, a pastor, missionary, or evangelist who is wholly devoted to the Lord and follows the Bible.

Of course, God's man is a slightly different authority for us because he will not be telling us what to do in every aspect of our lives. Rather, he is a spiritual authority for the church. Outside of the church, he has no authority to command people. He can't order someone to mow his yard, so to speak. He will be putting forth God's word, commanding what God already commanded. Now, let's look at some biblical examples of what happened when people stood against and attacked God's man:

<u>Moses</u>:

"And they gathered themselves together against Moses and against Aaron, and said unto them, *Ye take* too much upon you, seeing all the congregation *are* holy, every one of them, and the LORD *is* among them: wherefore then lift ye up yourselves above the congregation of the LORD?...And it came to pass, as he had made an end of speaking all these words, that the ground clave asunder that *was* under them: And the earth opened her mouth, and swallowed them up, and their houses, and all the men that *appertained* unto Korah, and all *their* goods. They, and all that *appertained* to them, went down alive into the pit, and the earth closed upon them: and they perished from among the congregation."

(Numbers 16:3, 31 – 33)

Korah, Dathan, and Abiram, in the days of the forty-year wilderness wandering, came and stood against Moses with this idea that Moses had exalted himself when he ought not have. More than likely, these men were wanting positions of authority as well, and were trying to make Moses look bad in order to get what they wanted. Now, God didn't appreciate that.

God commanded Moses with all those who submitted to him and Korah with all those who were following him, to separate into two companies. On the next day, God showed who was the one who had been in the right. Korah and all that were with him were consumed in a massive pit that opened underneath them. Once they fell in, it closed back up above them.

Korah, Dathan, and Abiram treated Moses with dishonor, falsely accused him, and outright rebelled against him. God made sure everyone else knew that was not acceptable.

The Prophet that Spoke against Jeroboam:
"And it came to pass, when king Jeroboam heard the saying of the man of God, which had cried against the altar in Bethel, that he put forth his hand from the altar, saying, Lay hold on him. And his hand, which he put forth against him, dried up, so that he could not pull it in again to him."

(1 Kings 13:4)

Now, this man's name is not given in the Bible. He is simply known as a man of God from the tribe of Judah. He was led by God to give a message against Jeroboam's altar of false gods. Jeroboam tried to have him taken, but God sent a swift punishment and withered his hand. Jeroboam actually had to ask the man of God to pray for him in order to have his hand restored.

Elijah:
"Then the king sent unto him a captain of fifty with his fifty. And he went up to him: and, behold, he sat on the top of an hill. And he spake unto him, Thou man of God, the king hath

said, Come down. And Elijah answered and said to the captain of fifty, If I *be* a man of God, then let fire come down from heaven, and consume thee and thy fifty. And there came down fire from heaven, and consumed him and his fifty."
(2 Kings 1:9 – 10)

J.R.R. Tolkien once wrote "Never laugh at live dragons."[24] I'm sure if anyone saw a massive, carnivorous, fire-breathing reptile, they would have to be pretty foolish to laugh at such a dangerous creature. Men of God do not have such a frightening appearance, but it is always good to remember that they serve a dangerous God. Now, God is good, but He has also brought harm to more than a few lives when someone mocked, insulted, or treated His man badly.[25] People ought to have humility and graciousness when addressing a man of God. Is he anything more than just an ordinary man? No, but he has been called out by God to do His ministry. And if you mock or insult the man of God, the Lord may not be pleased with that.

Now, this captain was following the orders of his king, but he had the audacity to command God's man in such a way. Judging from the passage, I don't believe he was being overly respectful.

24. Tolkien, J.R.R. 2001. "*The Hobbit.*" 215 Park Avenue South, New York, NY 10003. Houghton Mifflin Company.

25. See Numbers 12, Judges 16:25 – 30, and 2 Samuel 6:20 – 23 for a few examples.

He and his fifty, along with another band that came after him, paid the price.

On the contrary, see what happened when someone honored and listened to God's man:

Nathan:
"And David said unto Nathan, I have sinned against the LORD. And Nathan said unto David, The LORD also hath put away thy sin; thou shalt not die."
(2 Samuel 12:13)

David and Nathan had a wonderful relationship. Most kings and prophets in the Bible were often found at war with each other, but these two had a strong friendship. Even when David stooped to his lowest point (morally speaking), he made the right decision when he was confronted by God's man.

David had been, for some time, hiding the fact that he had committed adultery with Bath-sheba and murdered her husband. When Nathan brought God's message of judgment to him, David could have fought against that. He could have had Nathan imprisoned or even put to death, but he didn't. He listened and he repented, and for that, his life was spared. According to the law, adulterers and murderers were both crimes that were worthy of the death penalty, but God showed mercy to David because he made the right decision once he was confronted.

Elisha:

"Now Naaman, captain of the host of the king of Syria, was a great man with his master, and honourable, because by him the LORD had given deliverance unto Syria: he was also a mighty man in valour, *but he was* a leper…Then went he down, and dipped himself seven times in Jordan, according to the saying of the man of God: and his flesh came again like unto the flesh of a little child, and he was clean. And he returned to the man of God, he and all his company, and came, and stood before him: and he said, Behold, now I know that *there is* no God in all the earth, but in Israel: now therefore, I pray thee, take a blessing of thy servant."

(2 Kings 5:1, 14)

Naaman, at first, wasn't satisfied with the message that he would have to wash in the Jordan seven times to be cleansed of his leprosy. However, when he did what God's man told him to do, he reaped the reward of it. He was free of his disease and he became a follower of Jehovah.

Jonah:

"And Jonah began to enter into the city a day's journey, and he cried, and said, Yet forty days, and Nineveh shall be

90

overthrown. So the people of Nineveh believed God, and proclaimed a fast, and put on sackcloth, from the greatest of them even to the least of them."
(Jonah 3:4 – 5)

Now, Jonah does not get much praise here. As far as we can tell from the Bible, he was doing just the bare minimum when it came to preaching for Nineveh to repent. Later on, he still believed the city was worthy of destruction. However, he's not the focus. The people of Nineveh are the focus here. They hearkened to Jonah's message and repented. They submitted to this prophet of God that barely put any effort into his preaching. Because of this, God spared them.

Another point to add to this section is the fact that we are to follow spiritual authorities even when they are not right with God. This can be backed up by what Jesus says about the Pharisees:

"Then spake Jesus to the multitude, and to His disciples, Saying, The scribes and the Pharisees sit in Moses' seat: All therefore whatsoever they bid you observe, *that* observe and do; but do not ye after their works: for they say, and do not."
(Matthew 23:1 – 3)

Jesus was saying to follow the Pharisees' orders (to a degree. See The Exception on page 112.) due to their spiritual authority,

91

but not to follow their example because of their hypocrisy (Matthew 23:13 – 29). We, likewise, ought to follow our spiritual authority. Even if God's man is not living right, he still has authority.

Parental Authority

Kids are going to love this section (blatant sarcasm), but if we stop and think about it, we're all someone's kid, aren't we? The Lord made it very clear how He feels when it comes to how children ought to treat their parents:

"Honour thy father and thy mother: that thy days may be long upon the land which the LORD thy God giveth thee."
(Exodus 20:12)

"Honour thy father and thy mother, as the LORD thy God hath commanded thee; that thy days may be prolonged, and that it may go well with thee, in the land which the LORD thy God giveth thee."
(Deuteronomy 5:16)

"Honour thy father and *thy* mother: and, Thou shalt love thy neighbour as thyself."
(Matthew 19:19)

"Children, obey your parents in the Lord: for this is right. Honour thy father and mother; (which is the first commandment with promise;)"
(Ephesians 6:1 – 2)

"Children, obey *your* parents in all things: for this is well pleasing unto the Lord."
(Colossians 3:20)

Rather self-explanatory, but there are a couple of things I do want to go over. Through the years, I've heard some questions concerning the relationship between children and parents:

Question #1: "So, does that mean that I have to still obey my parents when I'm thirty years old, out of the house, and married?"

It is important to look at the specific words that the Bible says concerning this. Most of the verses do not say "obey," but "honor." "Honor" in the Hebrew comes from the word "כָּבֵד   כָּבַד" (pronounced "kaw-bad, kaw-bade"), which means "to make heavy or weighty." Now, what does making something heavy have to do with honoring? Well, it means "to make heavy" in the sense that it is not a light thing. If something weighs on you, that means that it is important. Serious. Significant. So, what God is saying is for us to keep our parents important to us. Don't think lightly of what they say.

In the Greek, "honor" comes from the word "τιμάω" (pronounced "tim-ah'-o"), which means "to prize or revere." Sounds much like the Hebrew version, huh? The Lord cares more about how we respect and appreciate our parents than actually obeying them. Why? Because if we honor our parents, obedience comes naturally.

But to answer the question, no. Someone who no longer lives with his or her parents does not have to obey everything they say. Until a child is grown and as long as a child lives under their parents' roof, they should obey them. It's the parents' house. Being a parent myself, I am a big advocate of the verses that tell kids to obey, but once children come of age and go out on their own, they are free from their parents' authority. This is what the Lord establishes in Genesis:

"Therefore shall a man leave his father and his mother, and shall cleave unto his wife: and they shall be one flesh."
(Genesis 2:24)

Now, don't get me wrong. This does not mean you are free from honoring your parents. You should *always* honor. But obedience is not a requirement once you go out on your own. Does that mean you can go up to your parents and rub it in their face, saying, "Ha! I'm out on my own! I don't have to obey you anymore"? Absolutely not, because that is not honoring your parents. Even if you're living on your own, you should always listen and consider what your parents have to say. They have experience that you don't. They may see things in a way that you do not, and, if you take their words to heart, you might save yourself a lot of trouble. At the end of the day, you can disobey them if you're not under their authority anymore, but that also doesn't mean that you should disrespect them. Honor, listen, respect, and love your parents.

Question #2: "What about the verses that *do* say to obey your parents? We can't just throw those verses away."

Very good point. Paul clearly says twice that children are to obey their parents, but again, we need to look closely at the words that were used. In Ephesians 6:1 and Colossians 3:20, the word that is used for "children" is "τέκνον" (pronounced "tek'-non") which means "child" or "young person from birth to adolescence," not the grown children. As stated previously, those who are still growing up in their parents household are to obey their parents commands.

Now, in Paul's day, people in their twenties were still considered children. This is why children are to submit to their parents' authority as long as they are living under their parent's roof. If you don't want that, you have to move out.

95

Question #3: "What if my parents order me to do something that's against what God wants?"

See The Exception on page 112

Question #4: "What about when my parents get older and can no longer take care of themselves? Is is all right for me to put them in an assisted living place/nursing home?"

This can get complicated, so bear with me. Part of this can be answered with what was talked about previously: honor your parents. If your parents don't want to be put in an assisted living place or a nursing home, it may be wrong of you to put them there. They took care of you when you couldn't take care of yourself. It is right for you to repay the favor. This is not to say that it is *always* wrong to put your elderly parents in an assisted living place or nursing home, but I'll get to that in just a moment.

In biblical times, children would care for their parents when parents grew too old to provide for themselves. Now, in Jesus' day, certain people would try to get out of taking care of their parents by way of being "religious":

"Why do ye also transgress the commandment of God by your tradition? For God commanded, saying, Honour thy father and mother: and, He that curseth father or mother, let him die

the death. But ye say, Whosoever shall say to *his* father or *his* mother, *It is* a gift, by whatsoever thou mightest be profited by me; And honour not his father or his mother, *he shall be free.* Thus have ye made the commandment of God of none effect by your tradition."

(Matthew 15:3 – 6)

The Pharisees basically told their parents they couldn't take care of them because they had offered money to God. Jesus harshly and rightly condemned them for this. They didn't do this to give more to God. They did this to get out of providing for their aged parents. If you're just trying to weasel your way out of helping your parents, that is sinful. No assisted living establishment or nursing home is going to provide the emotional care and well-being that a parent's own child can give. Assisted living places do that work because it is their *job*. Grown children should take care of their parents because they *love* them.

However, there is much more to consider. What if someone's parents have become a danger to themselves and others? There have been instances where elderly people were driving who should not have been, and it ended in catastrophe and multiple deaths. What if someone's parents have growing mental instability? What if the care they require is more than you can provide? The parents may not want to be put into such an institution, but it may be what is best for everyone involved,

97

including the parents. There are a multitude of situations that would make a nursing home a very reasonable and right solution. So, here is my full answer: the grown children should do their best to take care of their aging parents. If it is best for an elderly parent or parents to be put in an assisted living or nursing home, it is not wrong to do so.[26] However, if the grown children are simply trying to weasel out of responsibilities for their parents, that is wrong. Basically, you just need to do what is best for everyone with a heart of love and a right standing with God.

Governmental Authority

Now, most of the time when Christians hear the term "the government," it usually doesn't bring good, warm feelings to mind. Why not? Because our country is not what it once was, spiritually speaking. Many people in government have skewed ideas towards life. Many promote evil things, such as homosexuality and abortion. Make no mistake, there are some very wicked people in our government.[27] However, let us never forget that government was instituted by God. This began in Genesis:

---

26. I would also like to add that visits should be regular, or as much as the children are able. Having parents left at a nursing home without ever seeing their relatives can be incredibly disheartening and miserable.

27. There are also decent and godly people in government as well. Not everyone with a governmental position is out to destroy Christianity.

"Whoso sheddeth man's blood, by man shall his blood be shed: for in the image of God made He man."
(Genesis 9:6)

A very simple start in government's origin, but a beginning nonetheless. If someone murdered another person, it was society's responsibility to see that justice was carried out. For the longest time, Israel operated under the government of a theocracy: man was ruled directly by God. This changed in 1 Samuel when the people demanded a king to rule over them. It transitioned from a theocracy to a monarchy. This monarchy continued until the kingdoms of Israel and Judah were taken away into captivity. From then on, throughout the rest of the Bible, the children of Israel were ruled by foreign powers. Babylon, Persia, and then Rome. They were under the thumbs of some vicious and cruel dictators, but how were they instructed to treat the government they were under?

"Let every soul be subject unto the higher powers. For there is no power but of God: the powers that be are ordained of God. Whosoever therefore resisteth the power, resisteth the ordinance of God: and they that resist shall receive to themselves damnation. For rulers are not a terror to good works, but to the evil. Wilt thou then not be afraid of the power? do that which is good, and thou shalt have praise of the same: For he is the minister of God to thee for good. But if

thou do that which is evil, be afraid; for he beareth not the sword in vain: for he is the minister of God, a revenger to *execute* wrath upon him that doeth evil. Wherefore *ye* must needs be subject, not only for wrath, but also for conscience sake. For for this cause pay ye tribute also: for they are God's ministers, attending continually upon this very thing. Render therefore to all their dues: tribute to whom tribute *is due;* custom to whom custom; fear to whom fear; honour to whom honour."

(Romans 13:1 – 7)

Paul was commanding this to believers who were under the government of Rome. This was possibly during the reign of Nero, an insane individual who fiercely persecuted the Christians. For, as stated previously, God created government. He made it to establish order in the realm of law and justice. Therefore, we are to obey the authorities that are set over us. This is a recurring theme throughout the Bible:

"Thou shalt not revile the gods, nor curse the ruler of thy people."
(Exodus 22:28)

"My son, fear thou the LORD and the king: *and* meddle not with them that are given to change:"
(Proverbs 24:21)

100

"Then said Paul unto him, God shall smite thee, *thou* whited wall: for sittest thou to judge me after the law, and commandest me to be smitten contrary to the law? And they that stood by said, Revilest thou God's high priest? Then said Paul, I wist not, brethren, that he was the high priest: for it is written, Thou shalt not speak evil of the ruler of thy people."
(Acts 23:3 – 5)

"Put them in mind to be subject to principalities and powers, to obey magistrates, to be ready to every good work,"
(Titus 3:1)

"Submit yourselves to every ordinance of man for the Lord's sake: whether it be to the king, as supreme; Or unto governors, as unto them that are sent by him for the punishment of evildoers, and for the praise of them that do well. For so is the will of God, that with well doing ye may put to silence the ignorance of foolish men: As free, and not using *your* liberty for a cloke of maliciousness, but as the servants of God. Honour all *men.* Love the brotherhood. Fear God. Honour the king. Servants, *be* subject to *your* masters with all fear; not only to the good and gentle, but also to the froward. For this *is* thankworthy, if a man for conscience toward God endure grief, suffering wrongfully. For what glory *is it,* if, when ye be buffeted for your faults, ye shall take it patiently? but if, when ye do well, and suffer *for it,* ye take it patiently,

this *is* acceptable with God. For even hereunto were ye called: because Christ also suffered for us, leaving us an example, that ye should follow His steps:"

(1 Peter 2:13 – 21)

Even though governments can be harsh and corrupt, God wants His people to be subject under them. Now, that doesn't mean that Christians ought to blindly follow whatever their government says. Many countries today do not live underneath totalitarian governments nowadays. There are many places where the people have a voice. It is the responsibility for Christians to use what sway they have to put righteous people in authority, so as to push for a more God-honoring nation.

There is also a time when it is right for Christians to reject the orders of their government, but we will discuss that further in The Exception on page 112.

The Authority of the Husband

Of all the sections on authority, I imagine this one will draw the most contempt. The feminist movement is constantly shoving their ideals in everyone's face, saying women can and should do everything men do. See, but men and women are not only built differently, they are wired differently. God did this on purpose. When a man and a woman get married, one is to be the authority.

It's just like with a church. There is one man who is the highest human authority in a church: the pastor. Even though he is the authority, that doesn't mean he reigns in a dictatorial sense. He is to be as a loving, guiding lead-sheep, while he himself answers to God for his actions and his teachings. The same is true for the home:

"Wives, submit yourselves unto your own husbands, as unto the Lord. For the husband is the head of the wife, even as Christ is the head of the church: and He is the Saviour of the body. Therefore as the church is subject unto Christ, so *let* the wives *be* to their own husbands in every thing."
(Ephesians 5:22 – 24)

"Wives, submit yourselves unto your own husbands, as it is fit in the Lord."
(Colossians 3:18)

Scripture makes it clear that the authority in the home falls under the responsibility of the man. If a woman wants to honor the Lord, she will honor her husband and submit to him. Now, there is some confusion as to when and why this all started. Some believe it was the natural order at the very beginning of Creation, while others perceive it to be a part of woman's curse at the fall:

103

"Unto the woman he said, I will greatly multiply thy sorrow and thy conception; in sorrow thou shalt bring forth children; and thy desire *shall be* to thy husband, and he shall rule over thee."
(Genesis 3:16)

I can see why some people think the wife's submission is a part of the curse. The verse here does sound like it might be a proclamation of judgment. However, Paul states differently:

"But I suffer not a woman to teach, nor to usurp authority over the man, but to be in silence. For Adam was first formed, then Eve. And Adam was not deceived, but the woman being deceived was in the transgression."
(1 Timothy 2:12 – 14)

So, what is this verse saying? Many have taken it to be quite offensive, thinking that the Bible is saying women ought not have a voice at church. That's not what it's saying. The Greek word here for "silence" is "ἡσυχία" (pronounced "hay-soo-khee'-ah"), which means "quietness or stillness." When service has begun at church, we should all be quiet and still. Not just the women, but all members. The only one who should be speaking is the pastor. The women are emphasized because Paul was instructing that women ought not teach or preach to men in churches because that would place them as an authority over the man, and, going from

God's original design, the order of authority in the church is the same as the authority in the home. Adam was formed first, then Eve.

Now, why is that significant? Well, Paul is stating that the headship of man was not a part of the curse, but originated in the perfect Creation. Furthermore, in the Creation account, we constantly find God speaking to Adam directly, not with Eve. This was to show Adam's headship. God would speak to Adam and Adam would pass it down to Eve. The only passage where God spoke directly to Eve was when He was pronouncing judgment upon her for eating the forbidden fruit, and this was done because Adam was not fit to proclaim the judgment, seeing he was caught up in the same sin.

Moreover, I would like to take another look at 1 Timothy 2:14: "And Adam was not deceived, but the woman being deceived was in the transgression." Adam and Eve both had different reactions to Satan's tempting. Eve bought into it. She was deceived by Satan. He lied to her, and she thought that God was holding back something good from her. With Adam, this was not the case. Now, we don't know for certain where Adam was when Eve was speaking with the serpent. Some think he was off doing work. Others think he was right there with Eve. I don't think it matters all that much where he was at the time. If he wasn't with Eve, Eve should have consulted with him before taking the fruit. If he was with Eve, he remained silent throughout all of Satan and Eve's conversation when he should have been speaking.

Regardless, Eve was deceived whereas Adam knew it was wrong, but did it anyway. Look at the difference of Adam and Eve's confessions to God:

"And the man said, The woman whom Thou gavest *to be* with me, she gave me of the tree, and I did eat. And the LORD God said unto the woman, What *is* this *that* thou hast done? And the woman said, The serpent beguiled me, and I did eat."
(Genesis 3:12 – 13)

Eve blames the serpent, saying that he beguiled her while Adam never confesses that he was deceived. Adam knew that it was 100% wrong, but he decided to sin with his wife anyway. This has carried over all the way to men and women today. I've heard countless stories of young women giving up their virginity to a terrible man because he was able to deceive and manipulate her into doing it. I've also heard countless stories of men going into sinful situations, knowing full well what was going to happen and that they were wrong.

Now that we have gone through all of that, what *is* Genesis 3:16 meaning when it says, "thy desire *shall be* to thy husband, and he shall rule over thee"? Pastor John Yates put it this way:

> "The word 'desire' is the same as the word used in Genesis 4:7. The meaning there is clearly that sin desired to control Cain and that a **battle** for control was now underway. The parallel is clear. The perfect loving harmony and order God intended for marriage has been replaced with a selfish battle for control. The curse produced a rebellious nature in the woman, which resents her husband's headship and desires control for herself."[28]

Put simply, part of the curse is that women don't want to have men as authorities over them. Taking that into consideration, it makes sense why the feminist movement is fighting so desperately to overthrow the natural authority of man, but if you're a married woman who wants to please the Lord, you have to realize that submission to your husband is a part of His perfect will.

Now, I get it. "Submission" is a taboo word in our society today. Angry outcries can sometimes voice this question: "Why do I have to submit and my husband doesn't?! It's not fair!" but let's first look at what else Paul says:

---

28. Yates, John. "*Faith Bible Institute Commentary Series, Volume I.*" (Genesis and Job). Monroe, Louisiana. Faith Bible Institute Press. Page 149.

"But I would have you know, that the head of every man is Christ; and the head of the woman *is* the man; and the head of Christ *is* God."
(1 Corinthians 11:3)

It does say that the head of the woman is the man, but does it say that the man is his own head? No, Christ is the head of every man. So, a husband with a rebellious spirit who feels that he doesn't have to answer to anyone is just as wrong as a wife thinking she doesn't have to listen to her husband. Let me use a contemporary example for this: a husband who abstains from church, thinking that church is just for his wife and children, is as in as much rebellion as a wife who treats her husband like garbage. We all need to submit. Ladies, also remember that Jesus was submissive to God the Father. Jesus demonstrated both roles perfectly while on Earth: loving the church more than Himself and being submitted to godly authority. So, wives, before any rejection of this subject comes to your mind, remember that Jesus, our Saviour, was willing to submit. God in the flesh submitted, and He didn't just submit to God the Father. He submitted to Mary and Joseph. Imperfect, sinful parents. Jesus could have said "I don't need to listen to either of you." He honestly didn't need to submit, but He did. You should as well.

I understand that not all husbands seem to be qualified to be the head of the home. Not all husbands are worthy to be submitted to, but that's not the point. Like with governmental authority, God calls wives to submit to their husbands regardless if he is a good one or not. Now, a woman ought to make sure she marries a good man in the first place. Don't marry a man for his looks, his possessions, his wealth, his social status, or anything of the like. You should only marry the man that God directs you to. Any other reason outside of that is a poor reason. If you diligently search for God's will when it comes to the man He wants you to marry, He will lead you to the right guy.[29] The Lord often does this through godly parents and godly counsel, who have insight (and aren't as biased towards the guy you fancy) that can help you find the one God wills for you. This should be a man that loves the Lord, demonstrates fruit of the Spirit in his life, shows kindness and respect to his parents, and adores you and treats you with dignity.[30]

Now, what if a woman has married an abusive man? Is it still right to submit to him? The answer is not so cut and dry to be simplified down to a "yes" or "no." Instead, see The Exception of page 112.

---

29. This, of course, depends on whether or not God has the gift of singleness in mind for you.

30. Now, take into account that he's going to mess up and have flaws. We're all sinners, after all. No man is going to be a perfect Disney movie prince.

Another thing to consider is the cycle of love and respect. Now, to most men, respect is the monumental thing in a relationship. To most women, they want to be loved above all else.[31] That is why God commands for wives to submit and for husbands to love. It's what the other person needs. If a man doesn't have respect, he will either turn bitter and angry, or deflated and depressed. He needs that respect from the person he cares about most. If a woman doesn't have love, she'll have a similar reaction: bitter and angry, or deflated and depressed. She needs that love just as much as the man needs respect, but, if both are followed, something amazing happens.

If a man is given the respect he needs from his wife, he will be inclined to show love to her; if a woman is shown the adoration she needs from her husband, she will more readily submit to his authority; and they'll feed off one another. The more respect the wife gives, the more love the husband gives. The more love the husband gives, the more respect the wife gives. The opposite is also true. If a woman withholds respect from her husband, he will be more likely to withhold love; if a man is not very loving to his wife, her respect for him will diminish; and they'll feed off each other in that way. The less respect the wife gives, the less love the

---

31. This doesn't mean that love is not important to the husband and that respect is not important to the wife. It also doesn't mean that the husband doesn't need love and that the wife doesn't need respect. A husband ought to love and respect his wife and a wife ought to respect and love her husband, but what tends to be the most crucial is respect to the husband and love to the wife.

husband gives. The less love the husband gives, the less respect the wife gives. So, just follow what God commands. Wives, respect and submit to your husbands. Husbands, love and appreciate your wives. If you both do that, the relationship will naturally begin to thrive.

There's another snag that can happen in the marriage relationship, however. The "I'll start when they do" situation. Basically, it is when a wife and a husband both have the idea that the other person needs to pick up their part first. A husband will say, "I'll start loving her when she starts respecting me." The wife, likewise says, "I'll submit to him when he starts treating me like he should." And the relationship just spirals downward. Now, in my humble *opinion*, I do believe the husband ought to take the initiative. He's the head, after all. He's the authority. The responsibility of leadership falls upon his shoulders. If he, as a Christian husband, wants to honor God and keep his marriage from crumbling, he ought to be the man of his relationship and start loving his wife even if she doesn't show him respect.[32] Before you start shouting "But she-!" you need to ask yourself "Did Jesus love us only when we submitted to Him?" No, Jesus loved us when we hated Him, if we'll be honest with ourselves. Does Romans 5:8 come to mind? Speaking to the wives now, this is not saying that you get off easy. Just because I think husbands ought to take the initiative doesn't mean you can disrespect him if

---

32. The movie *Fireproof* shows this fairly well.

he doesn't. No, you need to step up and be submissive even if he doesn't show you love. If both the husband and the wife have Jesus as their example, what ought they to do? Wait for the other person to change? No! We need to be willing to give before receiving. Wives, respect your husband even if he doesn't deserve it. Respect him even if he's not loving you the way he should. Likewise, husbands, love your wife even if she doesn't submit to you. Love her like Christ loves you. That is what will be the best way to get back what you need in return.

The Exception

What if our earthly authority commands us to do something that is contrary to Scripture? What if God's man tells us we need to perform legalistic works in order to keep our salvation? What if our parents say we have to forsake our faith? What if a woman's husband orders her to stop reading her Bible? What if any of the above individuals are physically, mentally, or emotionally abusive? What if the government tells us to stop going to church? Peter gave us that answer in Acts:

"And they called them, and commanded them not to speak at all nor teach in the name of Jesus. But Peter and John answered and said unto them, Whether it be right in the sight of God to hearken unto you more than unto God, judge ye.

For we cannot but speak the things which we have seen and heard."

(Acts 4:18 – 20)

"And when they had brought them, they set *them* before the council: and the high priest asked them, Saying, Did not we straitly command you that ye should not teach in this name? and, behold, ye have filled Jerusalem with your doctrine, and intend to bring this man's blood upon us. Then Peter and the *other* apostles answered and said, We ought to obey God rather than men."

(Acts 5:27 – 29)

Now, what all do these verses imply? Simply this: God is the highest authority. He outranks every human that we have in our lives. Therefore, if He has commanded us to do something in Scripture, we are to follow Him even when our earthly authority tells us not to.

Now, for clarity's sake, what are these verses ***not*** saying?

1. This is an **exception**, not a rule

Know that these two verses do not give any Christian the license to rebel willy-nilly. The Apostles were doing exactly what Jesus had told them to do: spreading the Gospel. The chief priests, who were the spiritual authorities of that day, commanded them to stop. And that is when the Apostles rebelled and stood their ground. The spirit behind it was "I will follow God."

Remember that Peter, the very person who stated "We ought to obey God rather than men," was the same person who said "Submit yourselves to every ordinance of man for the Lord's sake." One of God's commands is to follow authority. If we just seek to rebel because we want to, we are actually rebelling against God Himself. Don't look for loopholes that give you an out when you don't want to do something that your authority is asking you to do. That is serving self, which is the opposite of serving the Lord.

2. We don't have the right to dishonor

Another point that needs to be addressed is the attitude. Should our earthly authority command us to do something that is against what God has instructed, we are still to show our authority honor. Whether that authority is God's man, parents, the government, or husband. Do not insult them, belittle them, or mock them. If you do, what are you showing them? That God condones you treating them poorly? That would paint a bad picture of God to them. If we want to win over our authority to see why we are doing what we are doing, we will show them respect, but calmly stand fast to our decision. Rather, if you act nasty to them and shout "You can't make me do this!" that will only spur them on to escalate the situation to a worse state. Solomon put it like this:

"A soft answer turneth away wrath: but grievous words stir up anger."
(Proverbs 15:1)

Lastly, I feel that the situation of abuse of any kind ought to be addressed with a little more specific attention. Now, to be clear, I am talking about true abuse. I am talking about where someone's godly authority brought significant, deliberate, and/or continual harm by way of the physical, the mental, or the emotional realm. Being yelled at one time by your parents is not abusive. That being said, abuse does happen. Sadly, it can happen from the people we hold close and love dearly. It can also happen from those we are told by God to submit to. We all need to understand that it is not God's will for someone to submit to abuse.

So, what ought someone to do if they are subject to abuse? Whether it be God's man, parents, or a husband, they ought to be reported to the right authorities.[33] Seek help if you are being hurt.

_____

33. I left out government in this sentence because we very well may have to endure evil that is brought to us by the government. Christians of the New Testament certainly dealt with that. Many were tortured and slain by the hands of their governmental authority and we should not write that off, thinking that would never happen in our day. It very well could.

To reiterate a point I said earlier, make sure to seek a godly individual for a pastor and for a husband before committing to a church or to a marriage. Of course, we cannot choose our parents, but we have a great amount of control when it comes to the other two. When it comes to choosing a husband, I think I must urge the greatest caution, ladies. God designed the husband/wife relationship to be the closest relationship possible amongst humans. If you choose a man that God is not pointing you towards, you may be signing up for some of the most miserable years of your life.

Regardless, if someone is doing vile, harmful things to you, please tell someone so that it can be stopped. Don't think of it as selfish, because if they're being abusive to you, odds are they will be or even currently are being abusive to someone else.

Summary

- You can't escape authority. Even if you become the highest authority in the world (very unlikely. The only one who will probably accomplish that before Christ's return is the Anti-Christ), you still answer to God.
- Submit to the Lord's leading. Those who don't usually regret it tremendously.
- Listen to God's man. He is appointed by the Lord to be a proclaimer of God's Word. But don't just take his word for it.

Study the Bible so that you are aware of what is truth and what is error.

- Treat God's man well, even if you disagree with him.
- Honor your parents. If you live under their roof, you should obey them. If you're grown and out of the house, you should still show them the admiration and honor they deserve.
- Wives, submit to your husband. His role is to be the leader of the home, regardless if you think he is qualified. Respect him and his decisions.
- Husbands, honor your wife. Both the husband and the wife ought to honor each other, even though the husband is the authority. It is about mutual love and respect. Remember that the husband and wife relationship is a bond that is between two equals that simply have different roles.
- Obey the government, within godly reason. Government was appointed by God to carry out justice and uphold law.
- The only time you shouldn't obey your authority is if they tell you to do something contrary to what God has told us to do. We are then to obey our highest authority and follow God rather than man.
- If your godly authority is being physically, mentally, or emotionally abusive to you, report them to the proper authorities. It is not God's will for you to be subjected to torture in this fashion.

CHAPTER FOUR

BAPTISM

Introduction

Baptism: the thing that we are named after. Interestingly enough, before we were called "Baptists," we were called "Ana-Baptists." This word means "To baptize again," since we would baptize those who joined from the Catholic church who had "already been baptized."[34]

Now what is baptism? There are many definitions out there and many are incorrect. Just looking at a Merriam Webster Dictionary, it provides these three definitions:

"A Christian sacrament marked by ritual use of water and admitting the recipient to the Christian community."

"A non-Christian rite using water for ritual purification."

"An act, experience, or ordeal by which one is purified, sanctified, initiated, or name."

---

34. The Catholic church's method of baptism is completely incorrect, not even adhering to the actual meaning of the word "baptize." See more in Method.

All three of those definitions bear errors. Baptism is not a sacrament, it is an ordinance.[35] Baptism does not purify or sanctify in any way. So, how is baptism biblically defined? To put simply, baptism is a picture of Jesus' death, burial, and bodily resurrection. It is showing outwardly of the washing away of sin that has taken place inwardly once the believer called on Jesus Christ to be saved.

A form of baptism began thousands of years ago when Gentile proselytes wanted to become a part of the Jewish nation and faith. It was required because it would demonstrate that they were identifying with Jehovah God and His doctrines while denouncing their previous false gods. This is why people, in some cultures (especially those of Islam), are cast out from their families when they become baptized into Bible-believing church. Their baptism states that they hold to the church's beliefs while recanting of their previous religion.

Baptism is very important to Christianity. It, like many other aspects of Christianity, shows a beautiful picture. Though, it has sadly been misunderstood and misused throughout the ages and still is today in many circles.

---

35. A sacrament is something someone must do in order to be saved. An ordinance is something a believer ought to do because it was brought up in the Gospels, practiced in Acts, and instructed upon in the Epistles. Baptism and the Lord's Supper both fulfill these requirements and therefore are the only two ordinances.

What Does the Bible Say?

Salvation and Baptism

First things first, we need to discuss what baptism is not. It is *not* the means of salvation. Baptism does not save anyone. Baptism is a picture of spiritual regeneration, not the actual process.

"The like figure whereunto *even* baptism doth also now save us (<u>not the putting away of the filth of the flesh, but the answer of a good conscience toward God,</u>) by the resurrection of Jesus Christ:"
(1 Peter 3:21)

Baptism does not regenerate a sinner's soul; it does not wash away sins; it does not redeem man in the eyes of God. Do you know what baptism does if a person is not saved? You get dunked into a body of water. Without salvation being the predecessor, baptism means nothing. The only requirement to receiving salvation from Jesus is crying out to Him in faith for it:

"For God so loved the world, that He gave His only begotten Son, that whosoever believeth in Him should not perish, but have everlasting life."
(John 3:16)

"And it shall come to pass, *that* whosoever shall call on the
name of the Lord shall be saved."
(Acts 2:21)

"That if thou shalt confess with thy mouth the Lord Jesus,
and shalt believe in thine heart that God hath raised Him
from the dead, thou shalt be saved."
(Romans 10:9)

"For whosoever shall call upon the name of the Lord shall be
saved."
(Romans 10:13)

After someone calls upon the Lord to be saved, being
baptized into a Bible-believing church is the very next step they
ought to do. Baptism is not only a public demonstration that a
believer has been converted to the teachings of biblical
Christianity, but it also establishes him or her as a member of the
church they were baptized into. If anyone is still unconvinced that
baptism does not save, let us take a look at some other verses that
deal with baptism:

"Then Peter said unto them, Repent, and be baptized every one of you in the name of Jesus Christ for the remission of sins, and ye shall receive the gift of the Holy Ghost."

(Acts 2:38)[36]

"But when they believed Philip preaching the things concerning the kingdom of God, and the name of Jesus Christ, they were baptized, both men and women."

(Acts 8:12)

"And as they went on *their* **way, they came unto a certain water: and the eunuch said, See,** *here is* **water; what doth hinder me to be baptized? And Philip said, If thou believest with all thine heart, thou mayest. And he answered and said, I believe that Jesus Christ is the Son of God. And he**

---

36. Now, some have taken this verse to mean that people need to repent *and* be baptized to be saved. Not only does that not match up with the rest of Scripture, but this confusion is due to how the Greek syntax compares to the English. Linguistic elements in the Greek and Hebrew don't always match that of the English language. Take Spanish, for instance. In Spanish, adjectives come after the subject, not before. "*Chocolate calientes*" literally translates to "chocolate hot" instead of "hot chocolate." Similarly, this verse is worded in a way that doesn't always make sense to English speakers. Another verse that does this is Philippians 4:13 – "I can do all things through Christ which strengtheneth me." Many people take that to mean "I can do all things through Christ, who gives me strength," but that's not what it's saying, because it says "which." Christ is not a "which," but a "who." Rather, the verse is saying "I can do all things which strengtheneth me through Christ" meaning "I can do all things that make me stronger through Christ." Similarly, this verse is not saying that baptism is a requirement for salvation, but this: "Repent every one of you in the name of Jesus Christ for the remission of sins, and be baptized, and ye shall receive the gift of the Holy Ghost." I know it's perplexing, but Greek is not English. And the study of the Greek and Hebrew will help us better understand what was originally intended to be said in the Bible.

commanded the chariot to stand still: and they went down

both into the water, both Philip and the eunuch; and he

baptized him."

(Acts 8:36 – 38)

"While Peter yet spake these words, the Holy Ghost fell on all

them which heard the word. And they of the circumcision

which believed were astonished, as many as came with Peter,

because that on the Gentiles also was poured out the gift of the

Holy Ghost. For they heard them speak with tongues, and

magnify God. Then answered Peter, Can any man forbid

water, that these should not be baptized, which have received

the Holy Ghost as well as we? And he commanded them to be

baptized in the name of the Lord. Then prayed they him to

tarry certain days."

(Acts 10:44 – 48)[37]

"And a certain woman named Lydia, a seller of purple, of the

city of Thyatira, which worshipped God, heard *us:* whose

heart the Lord opened, that she attended unto the things

which were spoken of Paul. And when she was baptized, and

her household, she besought *us,* saying, If ye have judged me

---

37. After Pentecost in Acts 2, the Holy Spirit's ministry changed (more on that
in Chapter Fourteen: The Triune God – The Holy Spirit). He now only
descends upon believers and does so permanently. The Holy Spirit coming
upon Cornelius and his family demonstrated that they have believed the word
of God and were saved.

to be faithful to the Lord, come into my house, and abide *there.* And she constrained us."
(Acts 16:14 – 15)

"Then he called for a light, and sprang in, and came trembling, and fell down before Paul and Silas, And brought them out, and said, Sirs, what must I do to be saved? And they said, Believe on the Lord Jesus Christ, and thou shalt be saved, and thy house. And they spake unto him the word of the Lord, and to all that were in his house. And he took them the same hour of the night, and washed *their* stripes; and was baptized, he and all his, straightway."
(Acts 16:29 – 33)

"And Crispus, the chief ruler of the synagogue, believed on the Lord with all his house; and many of the Corinthians hearing believed, and were baptized."
(Acts 18:8)

Each one of these verses show that salvation came *prior* to baptism. It tells that the individual or group of people believed first. Only after believing are they baptized. With the eunuch, Philip even clearly stated that he must believe first before getting baptized. Furthermore, Jesus Himself was baptized:

124

"Then cometh Jesus from Galilee to Jordan unto John, to be baptized of him. But John forbad Him, saying, I have need to be baptized of thee, and comest thou to me? And Jesus answering said unto him, Suffer *it to be so* now: for thus it becometh us to fulfil all righteousness. Then he suffered Him. And Jesus, when He was baptized, went up straightway out of the water: and, lo, the heavens were opened unto Him, and He saw the Spirit of God descending like a dove, and lighting upon Him: And lo a voice from heaven, saying, This is my beloved Son, in whom I am well pleased."

(Matthew 3:13 – 17)

So, let's analyze this passage here real quick. Jesus Christ, the sinless, perfect, Saviour of all humanity, was baptized. God in human form was baptized. If people hold to the belief that baptism saves, this would mean that Jesus was not saved before He was baptized. That doesn't make sense. Jesus didn't have to get saved because He was and is perfect. Without sin. If He had sin, He would not be God nor able to save us from our sins.[38] Jesus was baptized to show the correct process for us. Thinking that Jesus was needing salvation just like the rest of us is not only erroneous but opens up all other sort of incorrect doctrinal theories.

---

38. More on this in Chapter Fourteen: The Triune God.

While I'm at it, it must also be made clear that someone can be saved *without* Baptism:

"And one of the malefactors which were hanged railed on Him, saying, If Thou be Christ, save Thyself and us. But the other answering rebuked him, saying, Dost not thou fear God, seeing thou art in the same condemnation? And we indeed justly; for we receive the due reward of our deeds: but this man hath done nothing amiss. And he said unto Jesus, Lord, remember me when Thou comest into Thy kingdom. And Jesus said unto him, Verily I say unto thee, To day shalt thou be with Me in paradise."
(Luke 23:39 – 43)

I love that these verses are in the Bible. It obliterates all works-based salvation theories in Christianity. This man was a criminal. He had not done good works to earn his way to heaven, but had done so much evil that the Romans condemned him to the cross. Remember that crucifixion was arguably the worst way to die. I wager that his crimes were not minor. Regardless, as he was dying on the cross next to Jesus, he simply asked for Jesus to remember him. In this statement, it shows us that he believed who Jesus was and called out to Him for salvation. And Jesus answered him, telling him that he would be with Him in paradise, otherwise known as Abraham's bosom.[39] This criminal had no chance to be baptized. He died without baptism. Yet, he was saved. This, along with all of the other arguments made in this section, should make it very evident that baptism is not synonymous with salvation.

Baptism's Origins

Baptism is not talked about in the Old Testament. The first time we see it in Scripture is with John the Baptist:

"John did baptize in the wilderness, and preach the baptism of repentance for the remission of sins. And there went out unto him all the land of Judaea, and they of Jerusalem, and were all baptized of him in the river of Jordan, confessing their sins. And John was clothed with camel's hair, and with a girdle of a skin about his loins; and he did eat locusts and wild honey; And preached, saying, There cometh one mightier than I after me, the latchet of whose shoes I am not worthy to stoop down and unloose. I indeed have baptized you with water: but He shall baptize you with the Holy Ghost."

(Mark 1:4 – 8)

---

39. The place all believers who had died went to before Christ paid the sin debt. They could not yet be in heaven because justice had not yet been satisfied with the atonement of Christ. It was a temporary place located across from Hades (temporary hell as opposed to the Lake of Fire) in the center of the Earth. Jesus spoke about this place in Luke 16:19 – 31.

So, was this a brand new thing that John invented? No, this was actually an adaptation of what was called the mikvah, or ritual immersion bath. This had been a part of the Jewish culture for generations at this point. It symbolized spiritual cleansing and was part of the preparation for undertaking a new beginning. Jewish men took a mikvah each Sabbath day in preparation for a new week. Jewish women took a mikvah after each monthly period as a spiritual cleansing. On Yom Kippur, the day of atonement, the high priest would take seven mikvot (plural of mikvah) in preparation for entering the Holy of Holies.

The reason John the Baptist implemented the mikvah as a part of his ministry was for people to show that they had repented and acknowledged their need for a Saviour. They were looking for the coming Redeemer that John was frequently announcing. John was bridging the dispensation between law of the Old Testament and grace of the New Testament. In both, salvation was the same: putting faith in God that His Messiah would save us from our sins. Those in the Old Testament, such as Abraham, Moses, and David were looking forward to the Messiah. We in the New Testament look back to the Messiah.

Nowadays, the baptism still shows spiritual cleansing, but instead of it being the means to be cleaned, it shows that it has already happened. That's why, when someone gets saved, they only need to be baptized once. The mikvah, on the other hand, was done consistently throughout one's life. However, that is no longer needed, since the Lamb of God has come and paid the price in full.

The Purpose

So, what is the purpose for baptism? As stated prior, it is two-fold: to publicly show that you are a believer and follower of Jesus Christ and to become a member of a church body of other believers. And though baptism does not save, it is still important. Jesus did command for it to be done:

**"Go ye therefore, and teach all nations, baptizing them in the name of the Father, and of the Son, and of the Holy Ghost:"
(Matthew 28:19)**

The Candidate

The candidate is one who must have the prerequisite of salvation. The candidate should also make sure the church in which he or she is being baptized in is following the Bible as the sole authority and not the ideals or philosophies of mankind.

The Mode

This one will probably stir the waters some (pun intended), but baptism is to be done by immersing the candidate fully in water. Baptism does not mean sprinkling water on someone. It does not mean pouring water on someone's head. It comes from the Greek word "βαπτίζω" (pronounced "bap-tid'-zo") which is a derivative of the Greek word "βά πτω" (pronounced "bap'-to") which means "to whelm, that is, cover wholly with a fluid."

Also, it's a picture of Jesus' death, burial, and resurrection. When someone dies, people don't just sprinkle a little bit of dirt on them. They are completely buried into the ground. The picture is lost when someone just pours water on the candidate's head and likens that to Jesus' burial.

The Administrator

The administrator is a Bible-believing church. This is backed by when Jesus gave the Great Commission to the Apostles:

"Then the eleven disciples went away into Galilee, into a mountain where Jesus had appointed them. And when they saw Him, they worshipped Him: but some doubted. And Jesus came and spake unto them, saying, All power is given unto Me in heaven and in earth. Go ye therefore, and teach all nations, baptizing them in the name of the Father, and of the Son, and of the Holy Ghost: Teaching them to observe all things whatsoever I have commanded you: and, lo, I am with you alway, *even* unto the end of the world. Amen."
(Matthew 28:16 – 20)

It is important to note that He was speaking to the eleven when Jesus was giving this.[40] The Apostles were the first church that Jesus began. Just like it is the duty of churches to witness to unbelievers, it is also the duty of churches to administrate baptism once someone does get saved. Getting baptized by someone who is not a part of a church doesn't really do anything, especially since part of the reason for baptism in the first place is to join into the membership of a body of believers.

Summary

- Baptism does not save. It is an ordinance, not a sacrament. It pictures spiritual regeneration, but isn't the actual process. Salvation strictly comes from calling out to the Lord in repentance and asking for His saving grace (Luke 23:39 – 43, John 3:16, Acts 2:21, Romans 10:9, 10:13).
- To be done correctly, baptism must be administered to the right candidate (a saved individual) by the right administrator (a pastor or appointed leader in a Bible-believing church) in the right mode (full immersion in water) to accomplish the right purpose (publicly displaying of what has taken place within and establishing one's self as a member in a church).

---

40. Another aspect to keep in mind is that Jesus was talking to the appointed leaders of the first church. This goes to show that, when it comes to baptizing, it should be done by either the pastor or an appointed leader within the church.

CHAPTER FIVE

DANCE

Introduction

Dance has been on the Baptist no-no list for quite some time. It's been a hot debate for decades and will likely continue to be so. Conservatives and liberals alike will argue their point until they are blue in the face. In order to better understand what the right answer is concerning dance, we should first ask ourselves what dance is.

First, I must establish that dancing is not inherently sinful. Claiming that dance is sinful is like saying a rock is sinful. A rock is a part of this Earth's ecosystem. It's supposed to be there, but that same rock can be used to commit murder when bashed against the skull of another human being. *That* is sinful. The same is true with dancing. It can be used for sin, and often is (Let me say that again just to make sure you all read that: *dancing is often used in sinful ways*. Remember that). Therefore, it ultimately depends on how it is used. Because dancing, whether people acknowledge it or not, is a part of the human makeup. Like singing, it is something we do when we celebrate or when we are simply joyous. It can often be done involuntarily or without even being recognized. No matter what culture or time-frame you look at, dancing can be found. This goes to show that God placed dancing within the design of humanity. It's supposed to be there, and the Lord never put anything within mankind that wasn't supposed to be there.[41] This is also shown by how people from every era have an inclination to watch dancing as well. It's why people go to see dance performances such as ballets and musicals. So, what is the answer here? Is dancing sinful or is dancing a good thing? It can be either; it depends on how it is used.

At its core, dancing is an outward expression of inner delight, but over time, it has evolved into something else in various cultures. Since dancing involves one's body, it is very easily sexualized. That is the greatest danger with dancing. Our world often displays dancing as a thing of immodesty and seduction. It is more used as a tool of lust than anything else in our modern world. Even when dancing is not sexualized, there is still the danger of allowing pride or vanity to be the focus – a sort of "look at me" mindset.

Like with so many things in this world, there is a balance to it. It is best when we stay in the center and not move too far to the right hand or the left. Now, dancing does not have to be done at all. If George wishes to abstain from it completely, that's fine, but

---

41. I am not including the sin nature or any consequence of the fall into sin. That was a result of humanity's decision and not a part of God's perfect plan.

when George is watching his favorite football team score a winning touchdown with only thirty seconds left on the clock, you can bet that he will jump up off of his couch and start dancing. That is to say, dance is a part of us. It is a physical display of celebration. It is what we do and it is meant to be enjoyed, but when young people start gyrating their hips all over the place to impress the opposite gender, we've got a problem. In that scenario, dance is being misused. If dancing is to be done, it should be done with the right heart and the right method. There are multiple Bible verses that show when dancing was done right and when dancing was done wrong.

What Does the Bible Say? – NEGATIVE

I will take the time to split up what the Bible says about dancing into two categories: negative and positive. And since I like to get the bad news out of the way first, we shall dive into the negative of dancing.

Choosing Wives

What better book of the Bible to look at for examples of moral decay than the book of Judges? In this book, we find Israel constantly caught in a spiritual downward spiral. They go from being victorious and God-fearing under the leadership Joshua, to being physically enslaved by foreign powers and spiritually enslaved to their own wickedness. In the final chapters of Judges, the tribe of Benjamin was at war with the other tribes of Israel. In the end, Benjamin was slaughtered almost to the point of extinction. The other tribes recognized it would not be right to completely eliminate a fellow tribe, but in their rashness, they previously swore to not give any of their daughters to a Benjamite. Now, the tribe of Benjamin had quite a dilemma. In order for the tribe to repopulate once more, the Benjamite men that were left needed wives. The tribes thought of a way they should obtain them without breaking their vows:

"Then they said, Behold, *there is* a feast of the LORD in Shiloh yearly *in a place* which *is* on the north side of Bethel, on the east side of the highway that goeth up from Bethel to Shechem, and on the south of Lebonah. Therefore they commanded the children of Benjamin, saying, Go and lie in wait in the vineyards; And see, and, behold, if the daughters of Shiloh come out to dance in dances, then come ye out of the vineyards, and catch you every man his wife of the daughters of Shiloh, and go to the land of Benjamin. And it shall be, when their fathers or their brethren come unto us to complain, that we will say unto them, Be favourable unto them for our sakes: because we reserved not to each man his wife in the war: for ye did not give unto them at this time, *that* ye should be guilty. And the children of Benjamin did so, and took *them* wives, according to their number, of them that

danced, whom they caught: and they went and returned unto their inheritance, and repaired the cities, and dwelt in them."

(Judges 21:19 – 23)

Now, among other very wrong things that are found in this passage, I would like to focus on how each Benjamite chose his wife: by her dancing. It wasn't based on her personality or her character, or God's will. It was based on how she moved her body. Now, was this *sinful*? That is harder to pin down. It could have been if the men were lusting after the women whose dancing pleased them the most, but the Bible doesn't necessarily say that's what happened. For all we know, the Benjamites may have simply just picked the first lady that got close enough to the vineyards. Regardless of the motives, it was not right what they did.

Did anyone ask the Lord what should be done? No. Were the women asked if they wanted to marry these men? That wasn't even a thought. Were the women's families involved in this decision? Not in the slightest. Instead, this passage feels like the script for *Seven Brides for Seven Brothers*.[42] These women were kidnapped and forced against their will to marry these men. Now, was this because of their dancing? It's a possibility. At the very least, it was a factor. Given the spiritual destitution of the time frame, I feel that these women were not dancing in an appropriate

---

42. Good movie, but using the abduction of the Sabine women as dating advice is a terrible way to get a wife.

fashion. It is likely that they were showing off their bodies in a wrongful way. How many times has that kind of dancing been used to have someone look at a man or a woman in an impure light? How many times has inappropriate dancing been the beginning of something that turned very sinful and caused many regrets?

Herod's Birthday

Before we get into the Bible passage, allow me to take a moment to describe who Herod Antipas was. Herod Antipas was one of the sons of Herod the Great (the man that sought to kill Jesus when he was born in Bethlehem). He, along with his brother, Herod Archelaus, and his half-brother, Philip (also known as Herod II) were set to govern Israel by Rome.[43] Herod Archelaus ruled over Judea, Idumea, and Samaria. Herod Antipas ruled over Galilee and Perea. Philip ruled over Gaulanitis and Batanaea.

Now, Herod Antipas had married Phasaelis, the daughter of King Aretas IV of Nabatea. However, when he had stayed with his half-brother, Philip, and his wife, Herodias, for a time, Antipas decided that he wanted Herodias for himself. Evidently, Herodias preferred Antipas over Philip as well, for the two schemed together to be married. Antipas divorced Phasaelis (which actually

---

43. It can get pretty confusing when everyone's name is still Herod. Friendly advice: don't name your kids names that sound the same or all start with the same letter. I knew a family that had a Kayla, Kailey, and Katie. Don't do that. People will never get their names right.

started a war between him and Aretas IV), and Herodias divorced Philip shortly before Philip died. This sounds like a soap-opera, doesn't it? Herod Antipas, when it comes to most of his historical accounts, does not seem to follow in his father's footsteps of being a tyrannical, power-hungry monster. So, at least he had that going for him. However, he was more loyal to Rome than he was to his own people. He also had a sexual appetite for what was forbidden. As John the Baptist stated in Mark 6:18, it was not lawful for Herod Antipas to have Herodias. She was Philip's wife. This violated God's commandment in Leviticus 18:16, and it showed a flippancy for God's institution for marriage.

Not only that, but Herodias probably should not have been married to either Philip or Herod due to their family ties. Many do not realize that Herodias was actually the granddaughter of Herod the Great. Philip and Herod Antipas were both Herodias' uncles. Though disgusting, this is not surprising, for incest was common with rulers. They did this because they believed it "preserved the royal bloodline." Pharaohs in Egypt did this. Roman Caesars did this. Later on, European kings and queens would do this as well. It is why many of those royals had notable health defects, such as Charles II of Spain, George III of England, and Tutankhamen of Egypt (popularly known as "King Tut").

So, now that we have established who Herod Antipas was, let us get into the passages concerning his birthday:

138

"But when Herod's birthday was kept, the daughter of
Herodias danced before them, and pleased Herod."
(Matthew 14:6)

"And when a convenient day was come, that Herod on his
birthday made a supper to his lords, high captains, and chief
estates of Galilee; And when the daughter of the said Herodias
came in, and danced, and pleased Herod and them that sat
with him, the king said unto the damsel, Ask of me whatsoever
thou wilt, and I will give *it* thee. And he sware unto her,
Whatsoever thou shalt ask of me, I will give *it* thee, unto the
half of my kingdom."
(Mark 6:21 – 23)

Now, Herodias was believed to be about five to ten years
younger than Herod Antipas.[44] At the time of John the Baptist's
death, she would have been around forty-three to fifty years of
age. Now, Herodias was married to Philip when she was around
ten years old (gross). Combining that with her alleged age at this
period could have made her daughter, Salome, anywhere between
the ages of ten to thirty-five years old.[45] Salome came before her

44. Herod Antipas was believed to be born around 25 to 20 BC, while Herodias
was born around 15 BC. This is all supposed, however, so I would study it out
for yourselves.

45. According to Hebrew culture of that time, she still would have been
considered a child. Especially if she was still unmarried and living with her
mother.

great uncle/uncle/step-father and danced for him. Now, can we be dogmatic as to what kind of dancing Salome was doing? No. The Bible simply says that she danced, but consider two things:

Firstly, Salome was, obviously, raised by Herodias. Herodias was a woman who was perfectly fine with throwing away her first husband in order to have his brother. Then, when that was challenged by John the Baptist, she desired to have his head on a charger. Really take that in for a second. She didn't just want him killed. She wanted him to be beheaded and have his head brought to her on a literal silver platter. That's pretty messed up. And she was the one who raised Salome. Now, every soul has the choice to be who they want to be, but I reckon that some of Herodias transferred over into her daughter.

Secondly, Salome pleased Herod Antipas. We've established that Herod was twisted in his romantic views. He, like Herodias, callously threw away his first spouse. He did this to then wrongfully take his own brother's wife, which was also his niece. Considering all that, positive thoughts do not arise when it says that the dancing of Salome pleased Herod Antipas. In fact, Herod Antipas enjoyed it so much that he vowed he would give his great niece/niece/step-daughter anything she wanted. It is because of this vow that John the Baptist was murdered.

Disgusting as it may be, I feel the need to point out again that Herod Antipas and Salome were blood-related. Herod Antipas was her uncle, yet it is likely that Herod Antipas was having impure thoughts toward this young woman. Yes, Herod Antipas was a sick individual, but that is also the danger of dancing. If it is done the world's way, it incites ungodly passions. God did not intend this to be.

Demons in Babylon

One of the passages that is not as well-known in the realm of dancing would be the passage about Babylon's destruction in the book of Isaiah. In Isaiah's time, Babylon didn't yet exist as the world power it would become, but God was already telling of Babylon's fall through His prophet. In one of the verses, dancing is mentioned.

"It shall never be inhabited, neither shall it be dwelt in from generation to generation: neither shall the Arabian pitch tent there; neither shall the shepherds make their fold there. But wild beasts of the desert shall lie there; and their houses shall be full of doleful creatures; and owls shall dwell there, and <u>satyrs shall dance there</u>."
(Isaiah 13:20 – 21)

So, what is a satyr? In mythology, it was known as a half-goat, half-man creature. In the Bible, this word "satyr" comes from the Hebrew word "שָׂעִיר שָׂעִר" (pronounced "saw-eer', saw-eer'") and can be translated to mean just a regular goat. However, this word can also mean "devil," which is what I believe the passage is referring to.

The location where Babylon once stood can be found in modern day Iraq. There are even tours of the ruins of Babylon, but there is an interesting rumor about those tours: the tour guide will refuse to stay after dark. The reasoning behind it? Because the locals believe that demons come there at nightfall. If that's true, I would like to point out that this is a prophetic fulfillment of Isaiah 13:20. Look up at it again. It states that the Arabians will never pitch their tents there. Secondly, it shows why in the very next verse: The satyrs dance there. Wherever devils dance, wise people avoid.

Demons are degenerate creatures. They chose that path near the beginning of time when Satan sinned. Ever since their fall, demons cannot do good.[46] They must obey God's decrees, yes,

---

46. There have been books and TV shows that display demons as creatures that are bent towards evil, but can still be good if you're nice to them, do something for them, etc. I must emphasize how that is not true when talking about demons in reality. They are not entities to mess around with. They, like Satan, want you to burn in hell. They do not want to befriend you, they are not adorably mischievous creatures, they are not dumb monsters that you can tame. They are intelligent, powerful, evil beings that are consistently seeking for your *destruction*. Do not seek out demons. That is only asking for misery.

because God still has authority over them, but they never obey with a willing and submitted heart. Every chance they get, they cause chaos, destruction, misery, and evil. Their main goal is to bring every soul they can to hell with them. That all being said, I do not think anyone in their right mind would want to be a part of a demon's dance. As stated earlier, dancing is an outward expression of inner delight; but what would a demon have delight in? Only wicked and abominable things. This points back to the motive behind the dancing. Dancing should not be centered around one's self, or trying to entice someone to lust. Christians ought only dance with right motives. The ultimate one being giving praise to the Lord. You can know that the demons who dance at the ruins of Babylon are *not* doing so to praise the Lord.

What Does the Bible Say? – POSITIVE

Contrary to some people's beliefs, there are actually more positive verses about dancing in the Bible than there are negative. Which, honestly, I find odd. With the way that I was raised, many godly people I knew told me that dancing was a sinful thing. Now, again, it can be a slippery slope, so don't think that everything is sunshine and roses concerning dance. However, at the same time, it's not purely sinful. If dancing is done right, it is actually a praise unto the Lord, and God actually encourages it in various passages:

When God's Man Danced

David was called the man after God's own heart (1 Samuel 13:14). That is a very important detail about the shepherd boy who became king. Does that mean he was perfect? Absolutely not. But he was godly. He walked with God to a very close and intimate degree. Now, we have seen before that godly men and women can make very wrong decisions. David is, of course, one of them, and his sins are very well known. However, David was also known to promote dancing before God. Consider the following:

"And it was *so*, that when they that bare the ark of the LORD had gone six paces, he sacrificed oxen and fatlings. And David danced before the LORD with all *his* might; and David *was* girded with a linen ephod. So David and all the house of Israel brought up the ark of the LORD with shouting, and with the sound of the trumpet."
(2 Samuel 6:13 – 15)

This is how dancing is supposed to be. David's motive for his dancing was to honor the Lord as the ark of God was finally brought into Jerusalem, and all of Jerusalem was celebrating with him. Well, except for one person. Just a few verses after this, David's first wife, Michal, condemns David for how he danced:

144

"Then David returned to bless his household. And Michal the daughter of Saul came out to meet David, and said, How glorious was the king of Israel to day, who uncovered himself to day in the eyes of the handmaids of his servants, as one of the vain fellows shamelessly uncovereth himself!"
(2 Samuel 6:20)

Now, did David really do this? Did he dance to be seen by women? Did he start removing clothing so as to seduce the women around him? No, Michal simply thought that David's display was beneath him. He was the king of Israel, yet he danced among the people like he was one of them. To her, a woman who had been raised in royalty, this was shameful. To her, the royal family should not be seen in such a light. To her, they were to be the embodiment of honor, dignity, respect, and nobility. And showing such raw adoration for the Lord was not included in her mind, which is why she thought little of her husband in that moment. You might wonder, "How do you know David wasn't doing it to show off to the women around him?"

First, because the Bible states twice that David danced "before the Lord" (2 Samuel 6:14, 16)[47] Not "before the people." Not "before the handmaidens." His attention was firmly on God. Remember that the Bible doesn't flatter its heroes. If David had done wrong in this, the Bible would have said so, but it doesn't. In

_____
47. Three times if you include David's explanation to Michal (2 Samuel 6:21).

fact, when I read it, it seems more like this was a very *good* thing that David was doing. He danced because he was overjoyed in what God had done, and he was praising the Lord with it.

Secondly, because who is punished at the end of this chapter? Is David smitten by God because he was shaming himself or dishonoring his wife by vying for the attention of other women? Not at all. Rather, Michal is stricken with barrenness. She would never have children because she beheld David doing something that was honoring the Lord, and she condemned it. With her sarcastic, vicious words, she spat down on David for doing something that she thought was belittling to his title as king. After David defended himself, God showed who was truly in the right, and it was not Michal.[48]

Other Positive Bible Passages

Thou hast turned for me my mourning into dancing: thou hast put off my sackcloth, and girded me with gladness;
(Psalms 30:11)

"Let them praise His name in the dance: let them sing praises unto Him with the timbrel and harp."
(Psalms 149:3)

---

48. Another example of why it is dangerous to attack God's man.

"A time to weep, and a time to laugh; a time to mourn, and a time to dance;"
(Ecclesiastes 3:4)

"Then shall the virgin rejoice in the dance, both young men and old together: for I will turn their mourning into joy, and will comfort them, and make them rejoice from their sorrow."
(Jeremiah 31:13)

"The joy of our heart is ceased; our dance is turned into mourning."
(Lamentations 5:15)

Now, I really don't feel the need to go through and explain each of these verses. I think the message they convey is rather easy to understand. However, I will say that these verses do not defend situations that include inappropriate or immodest dancing, such as high school proms and cheerleading. However, we shall get more to that in just a little bit.

Other Points

The Nature of Satan

Another aspect I would like to touch on is how Satan works when it comes to dancing. Many people believe that dancing is just intrinsically sinful. It's not. Dancing was not invented by

Satan because, as stated before, it's a part of us. You don't have to teach people what dancing is. My toddler knows how to dance. When I play music that she likes, she starts doing this adorable hopping thing. She's dancing. No one taught her that. She's physically expressing her pleasure for the music. It is my firm belief that God created that sense of dancing within us. However, Satan twisted it, as he does with so many things. He's twisted marriage into homosexuality. He's twisted righteous anger into sinful rage. He's twisted the desire for provision into greed. He's twisted godly sorrow into worldly depression and suicide. He's twisted the desire for physical intimacy into promiscuity. All these things that God created and instilled in us, Satan ever attempts to warp them into something wrong.

The same goes with dancing, and I would say that Satan has been *very* successful with this. Though I am defending dancing as a God-ordained entity, I'm not saying that there is not a great danger with it nowadays. When people think of going out to dance in this age, they don't think of using it to praise God or to be morally correct. Rather they think of nightclubs, strip-clubs, and wild parties. Each of these are usually accompanied by alcohol, drugs, sex, and bad music. So, yes, dancing can be dangerous. Dancing, if not done right, is very wrong and leads to other sins. So, great caution is advised. At the same time, don't loop dancing in with things that are 100% sinful.

Dancing Events

Now, I need to add some things to all that I have said concerning dancing. First off, there is a big difference between doing a little happy dance because you got the job you were praying for and participating in an actual dancing event. The happy dances? There is nothing wrong with them and can be done until the cows come home. Most of the time, they just make everyone laugh awkwardly because Jim is looking like a goofball. However, there need to be guidelines when one wishes to be a part of a dancing group. Whether it is a high school prom, a play, cheerleading, or something else, it needs to first go through what Scripture indicates.

I realize that there is no "thou shalt not dance" passage in the Bible. Probably because it'd be hard to put a rigid, black-and-white verse on something that is rather grey. We have established earlier that dancing is good, but can be (and often is) used in wrong ways, but that is why God shows us through principle in the Bible when it comes to dance. When it comes to the good passages, what was seen there? Firstly, a good and right motive. The dancer was using his/her dance to praise the Lord. Not to promote themselves. Secondly, there were no indications of physical contact with the opposite gender (we'll get to that point later). Thirdly, there is no seduction or sexual passions ignited.

Using these three things can help us determine what is okay and what is not okay when it comes to dancing events.

I understand that this greatly narrows down what Christians can partake in when it comes to dancing, but if we are trying to honor God, we ought to abstain from things that could lead to evil. This means high school proms. Proms, known for having the wrong kind of dancing, also have other things roped in with them. Of course, ungodly music is a big one. It's usually what gets the ungodly dancing started. However, fornication is also something that takes place at proms. Couples have been known to catch a ride with someone and go who-knows-where so that they can be alone. All in all, it's just better to stay away from them.

Moving on, cheerleading is another area that is not okay. Men gawk at cheerleaders. Why? Because of what they are wearing. And when a girl is dancing while wearing an immodest outfit, it only makes it worse. The dancing becomes more of a form of pornography rather than actual dancing. On and on we could go, but instead of just listing what is okay and what is not, I feel that whoever reads this should be able to discern from the following list:

1. What is the motive?
2. Does it involve physical contact with the opposite gender?
3. Is it immodest or sexualized?

If someone can go through those three things and come out saying, "The motive is pure, there isn't physical contact with the opposite gender, and it is perfectly modest;" then I believe it should be fine.

Touching

This section, I feel, is where I will get the most hate-rage from dance-loving readers. It is my heartfelt belief that couples should not dance together until they are married.

(insert gasps, shouts of anger, and cries of despair)

The reasoning I have behind this is that touching between two people of different genders ignites passion. The Bible speaks on this:

"Now concerning the things whereof ye wrote unto me: *It is good for a man not to touch a woman*"
(1 Corinthians 7:1)

In Middle-Eastern culture, especially in ancient times, couples did not necessarily dance together. I feel that couple-dancing was really made prominent from European culture. America, having European roots, brought that over into the American culture when it was founded. That does not mean that touching while dancing is wrong **when** the couple is already husband and wife, not boyfriend and girlfriend. Touching while dancing should not be shared by those who are not already bound together by the marital covenant. Why? Because touching ignites passion. In fact, the Greek word used in this verse for touch, "ἅπτομαι" (pronounced "hap'-tom-ahee"), is reflexive of the word "ἅπτω" (pronounced "hap'-to") which means "to set on fire, to kindle." Touching ignites passion. Dancing is also done out of passion. So Passion + Passion = A **Lot** of Passion. Putting touch and dancing together is to light a significant flame of desire, and it is not something that ought to be trifled with when the couple is not married. Now, is it morally wrong for a boyfriend and a girlfriend to dance together? No. It's not a sin. However, I do not feel it is wise because it may easily **lead** to sin, and anything that could lead to sin is foolishness.

<u>Summary</u>

- Dancing is good or bad depending on how it is used. It was instilled in us by God to be an outward display of inward delight, but twisted by sin and Satan to incite lust and lead to other sins.
- Most dancing events should be avoided by the Christian simply because the world uses dancing in a way that does not please God.
- Couples should **not** dance together unless they are married.

CHAPTER SIX

EVOLUTION

Introduction

"Billions of years ago, the universe was born by the Big Bang." Words that are found in many books on science and the origin of the universe. Every book that promotes evolution in this way can be trusted to be filled with utter falsities. Now, that's a bold statement, but one I intend on expounding upon to show the truth. This belief is considered science when it doesn't even follow the definition of science. Science is the study of structure and behavior of the natural world through observation, experimentation, and testing of theories against the evidence obtained. Evolution is said to be done over millions of years. So, it can't be observed. Though people have tried, all evolutionary experiments have started and ended with the same animal as a result, hence, not evolution.[49] Really, there's no real evidence that evolution ever took place on our planet. For something that is said to be science, it's missing the science part. That's because evolution's true purpose is really to deny the existence of God.

---

49. In order for evolution to truly take place, an animal has to change to a completely different animal.

Really quick, I want to say that this will ***not*** be exhaustive. Disproving evolution deserves to be an entire book in and of itself, especially when it comes to how much one would have to write just to show how ludicrous the theory of evolution is. This will only be a brief summary. If you wish to see a more exhaustive study, please look up Dr. Kent Hovind or Dr. Jason Lisle.[50]

There are more ways that evolution does not follow scientific fact. Take the Big Bang for instance. Boiled down, it basically says the universe exploded into existence from nothing. First off, that just doesn't make sense. What caused the explosion? How does nothing explode and somehow make physical matter? I'll elaborate further. We've all seen explosions, right? Whether it's fireworks on the 4th of July or epic pyrotechnics on movies, explosions are cool to look at, but they're also very dangerous. Why? Because explosions ***destroy*** things. It's a mixture of heat and pressure the spreads out from a single point. Explosions can destroy cars, houses, landscapes, and even entire cities. Here's what explosions don't do: create. If you put dynamite in a rabbit warren, you will not find that rabbit warren with firmer structure and foundation once that dynamite goes off. If you use a grenade to blow up a Scrabble board, the letters won't fall together and line up to write out the Declaration of Independence.

---

50. I do not endorse everything that these men are behind, most particularly the Bible version that they use. However, they are very intelligent and have excellent arguments against the theory of evolution and arguments for Creation.

Explosions cause chaos, not order. You will find this every time. There is no logical way that a big explosion formed our tiny blue planet at the exact place it needed to be in the solar system to sustain life, along with all of the complexities that make up just one single-celled organism. The chance of the Big Bang causing everything that we see now is the same as throwing a banana at a wall and it suddenly turning into a talking piano that can juggle.

What Does the Bible Say?

The True Origin of Creation

"In the beginning God created the heaven and the earth."
(Genesis 1:1)

The very first words of the Bible establish that everything we see, hear, taste, smell, and feel around us was brought into existence by a Creator. For anyone who believes that evolution and Christianity can go together, this verse shows the direct contrast of what evolution describes, but that's not where it ends. Evolution also states that life started with an explosion that led to cells, which evolved into fish, which evolved into lizards, which evolved into apes, which evolved into us – constantly changing. Here is what the Bible says:

"And God created great whales, and every living creature that moveth, which the waters brought forth abundantly, after

their kind, and every winged fowl after his kind: and God saw that *it was* good…And God said, Let the earth bring forth the living creature after his kind, cattle, and creeping thing, and beast of the earth after his kind: and it was so. And God made the beast of the earth after his kind, and cattle after their kind, and every thing that creepeth upon the earth after his kind: and God saw that *it was* good."
(Genesis 1:21, 24 – 25)

Evolution says that animals evolved from simple cells into what they are now. The Bible says that God created everything as it is already. The phrases "after his kind" and "after their kind" show that everything reproduces offspring of the same species. Kangaroos reproduce kangaroos. Owls reproduce owls. Eels reproduce eels. Nowhere in the Bible does it give weight to the idea that any animal warped into another animal over time.

We Are Different from Animals

"And God said, Let Us make man in Our image, after Our likeness: and let them have dominion over the fish of the sea, and over the fowl of the air, and over the cattle, and over all the earth, and over every creeping thing that creepeth upon the earth. So God created man in His *own* image, in the image of God created He him; male and female created He them."
(Genesis 1:26 – 27)

156

One of the main points of the evolution theory is that mankind is no more than an advanced animal. That we are nothing else except a really smart ape. This is not what the Bible declares. We are made in the image of God, and we were created to have dominion over the animal kingdom. That, of course, does not give us the right to be cruel to or reckless with the animal kingdom, but have rule over them as responsible stewards. Care-taking over what God has given us. The animals are here for our benefit. Whether it be for companionship, food, beauty, or simply maintaining the balance of nature. We are not a part of them, nor are they akin to us. And let me give you some simple examples as to how they are not:

Animals Kill Each Other: And I'm not talking about the predator-prey aspect.[51] I'm talking about animals of the same species. There is a *huge* list of animals that kill each other over things like breeding rights and territory. We're talking deer, swordfish, tigers, meerkats, Komodo dragons, bears, horses, bald eagles, lions, and the list goes on and on and on and on.

---

51. Though something could be brought up about that. If all life generated and evolved from the same cells, that means that all life on Earth is related. That means geese, starfish, cows, trees, tomatoes, watermelon, and everything else living is all related to humanity. If that's true, the argument could be made that when we chop down a tree, we are committing murder. When we eat an orange, we are committing cannibalism. See how the theory of evolution can lead to such looney conclusions?

These animals have no problem ending the life of one of their fellow species for reasons we would consider less than substantial. If a man killed another man because they were both flirting with the same girl, no one would think, "Oh, that's understandable." No, we'd think the guy is nuts for doing something like that. Clearly, there is a drastic moral distinction between us and the animal kingdom when it comes to murder.

Mating: With animals, mating is little more than an instinct. It usually goes like this: a male mates with as many females as possible so as to reproduce as many offspring as possible. Why? Because many animals die before they reach adulthood. If the species is to continue, they need a lot of offspring. This is not how it is with humanity. With humanity, God desires one man and one woman to be together for a lifetime. The purpose of people coming together in a relationship is far more than just reproducing children. Marriage is a resemblance of Jesus Christ and the church. Sadly, many people have adopted the animals' way rather than God's way. When people act like animals when it comes to the sexual nature, what follows? Heartbreak, guilt, life-changing consequences, and it could even go so far as to end in suicide. Do you see that happening with buffalo when one male mates with fifty females? No, because we are made differently. Now, are there some animal couples that truly share a type of love that we could relate to? Yes, I would say so. There are animals that mate for life, such as swans, wolves, barn owls, and various others, but the majority are not that way. There is simply an instinct that is to be fulfilled and then they are done with each other. Concerning those out there that like to have relationships with "no strings attached," this is not how it should be. God put it this way:

"Therefore shall a man leave his father and his mother, and shall cleave unto his wife: and they shall be one flesh" (Genesis 2:24).

This word "cleave" comes from the Hebrew word "דָּבַק" (pronounced "daw-bak") which means "to cling, to abide, to be joined together." It was never in God's mind that marriage should be something that was flippant or temporary.

The Gap of Intelligence: Animals rely mainly on instinct while humans regularly use intellect in every-day life. Many animals are more physically adept than humans, but humans have more than made up for it with superior intelligence. The gap of intellect between the animal kingdom and humanity is staggeringly obvious. Even the smartest animals like dolphins, elephants, and chimpanzees are not on the same level as humanity. For if they were, would not elephants invent a better way to keep poachers from slaughtering them and taking their ivory? Would not chimpanzees come up with a solution to keep humans from destroying more of their habitat? Would not dolphins think of a way to cause their population to increase rather than decrease by way of fisheries? If human intelligence were in the same situations, you can bet brains would be racked until a valid solution came along. Rather, humans have built modes of transportation that allow us to travel from one side of the planet to the other in less than a day. We have established institutions to assist the poor, the homeless, the disabled, the elderly. We have invented weapons to defend ourselves from even the most powerful animal out there. We have even built machines that allow us to visit the furthest depths of the sea, as well as the vast expanse of space. If we are all just animals, why is there such a monumental gap of intellect? It's because we're not animals. We are higher than they, as God designed us. Dr. Jean Lightner adds more on this subject as well:

"Humans are clearly distinct from other animals in cognitive and language ability. Occasionally, the ability of chimps to use tools or simple sign language is touted as evidence for their close relationship with us. In reality, chimps are not significantly different in these areas from many other mammals and birds (except that they can use their hands more like us). Chimps lack the anatomy for human speech. Ironically, a few birds have been known to use human language quite well, at least for an animal. Simple tool making ability is also seen in a variety of animals. While intelligence in animals is quite fascinating, it is still significantly different from that of humans and gives no hint of common ancestry. The similarities are much more easily explained by the fact that these animals all had a common designer who reused certain excellent design elements much like engineers do in their creations today."[52]

The Spiritual Nature: Humanity is the only creature on Earth that possesses a spiritual nature. For everyone has a faith or belief system. Even evolution and atheism is a type of belief. No matter who you talk to or what culture a person is from, everyone holds to a higher belief of some kind. Even if we were to exclude atheists, which is said to be around 500 to 750 million people worldwide,[53] that still leaves *billions* of people who do have some sort of deity, faith, religion, or doctrine. Billions of people that pray, follow some weekly ritual, practice a creed so as to be accepted by their deity, evangelize others to join their faith, etc. Animals, on the other hand, do not do any of the sort. If we are all animals, why does humanity very consistently cling to the thought of a higher power while animals do not? You can preach the Bible all you want to your dog, and your dog will not be bothered by it at all. Preach the Bible to a person though, and that person will either get uncomfortable or get convicted. Why? Because there's a spiritual nature to us that God readily communicates to. It's why we reflect on our purpose in life while animals don't. It's why people go to great lengths to "discover themselves" while animals

---

52. Lightner, Jean. "A Tale of Two Chromosomes." "Answers in Genesis." November 14, 2007. answersingenesis.org/genetics/dna-similarities/a-tale-of-two-chromosomes/

53. This is a very generic estimate and is not to be taken as incredibly accurate, since the demographics of atheism vary depending on how someone is viewed to be "atheist," as well as how some atheists do not make their belief public information.

don't. It's why we always put someone or something as our god in life even when we don't have a religion.

I have more I could go through, but I said this wasn't going to be exhaustive. Time would fail me to try and bring up every flaw in evolution's theory when it comes to the thought that we are advanced animals. Rather, I'd just like to get you thinking. For anyone with common sense who is willing to face reality, it is quickly realized that we are simply not animals. We never were.

Theistic Evolution

Theistic evolution can be fairly popular in some Christian circles. After all, since so many scientific professionals hold to evolution, it can be rather daunting to think they are just so completely off. So, in a riding-the-fence kind of way, some Christians hold to the belief that God made the world, but He did so through evolution. However, it just doesn't work. Let's take a look at the Creation account:

"In the beginning God created the heaven and the earth. And the earth was without form, and void; and darkness *was* upon the face of the deep. And the Spirit of God moved upon the face of the waters. And God said, Let there be light: and there was light. And God saw the light, that *it was* good: and God divided the light from the darkness. And God called the light

Day, and the darkness He called Night. And the evening and the morning were the first day. And God said, Let there be a firmament in the midst of the waters, and let it divide the waters from the waters. And God made the firmament, and divided the waters which *were* under the firmament from the waters which *were* above the firmament: and it was so. And God called the firmament Heaven. And the evening and the morning were the second day. And God said, Let the waters under the heaven be gathered together unto one place, and let the dry *land* appear: and it was so. And God called the dry *land* Earth; and the gathering together of the waters called He Seas: and God saw that *it was* good. And God said, Let the earth bring forth grass, the herb yielding seed, *and* the fruit tree yielding fruit after his kind, whose seed *is* in itself, upon the earth: and it was so. And the earth brought forth grass, *and* herb yielding seed after his kind, and the tree yielding fruit, whose seed *was* in itself, after his kind: and God saw that *it was* good. And the evening and the morning were the third day. And God said, Let there be lights in the firmament of the heaven to divide the day from the night; and let them be for signs, and for seasons, and for days, and years: And let them be for lights in the firmament of the heaven to give light upon the earth: and it was so. And God made two great lights; the greater light to rule the day, and the lesser light to rule the night: *He made* the stars also. And God set them in the firmament of the heaven to give light upon the earth, And to rule over the day and over the night, and to divide the light from the darkness: and God saw that *it was* good. And the evening and the morning were the fourth day. And God said, Let the waters bring forth abundantly the moving creature that hath life, and fowl *that* may fly above the earth in the open firmament of heaven. And God created great whales, and every living creature that moveth, which the waters brought forth abundantly, after their kind, and every winged fowl after his kind: and God saw that *it was* good. And God blessed them, saying, Be fruitful, and multiply, and fill the waters in the seas, and let fowl multiply in the earth. And the evening and the morning were the fifth day. And God said, Let the earth bring forth the living creature after his kind, cattle, and creeping thing, and beast of the earth after his kind: and it was so. And God made the beast of the earth after his kind, and cattle after their kind, and every thing that creepeth upon the earth after his kind: and God saw that *it was* good. And God said, Let Us make man in our image, after our likeness: and let them have dominion over the fish of the sea, and over the fowl of the air, and over the cattle, and over all the earth, and over every creeping thing that creepeth upon the earth. So God created man in His *own* image, in the image of God created He him; male and female created He them. And God blessed them, and God said unto them, Be fruitful, and multiply, and replenish the earth, and subdue it: and have dominion over the fish of the sea, and over the fowl of the air, and over every living thing that moveth upon the earth. And God said, Behold, I have given you every herb bearing seed, which *is* upon the face of all the earth, and every tree, in the which *is* the fruit of a tree yielding seed; to you it shall be for meat. And to every beast of the earth, and to every fowl of the air, and to every thing that creepeth upon the earth, wherein *there is* life, *I have given* every green herb for meat: and it was so. And God saw every thing that He had made, and, behold, *it was* very good. And the evening and the morning were the sixth day."

(Genesis 1:1 – 31)

Okay, now let's compare this with what evolution says and see how much they can't coincide:

<u>Differences in Time</u>: Evolution says it took billions of years to form everything. Creation says it took six days. The Hebrew word here for "day" is "יוֹם" (pronounced "yôm"), which means "from sunrise to sunset." This is the same word that is used in passages like Exodus 16:4, Joshua 6:3 – 4, 1 Samuel 2:34, 1 Kings 4:22, etc. So, these were literal, twenty-four hour days in which God created everything, not billions of years.

For those who hold to day-age creationism who might say "Well, 'יוֹם' can also mean a time period of unspecified length. It could mean billions of years," I ask you this: how long can plant

165

life last without the sun? Because plants were created on the third day. The sun was created on the fourth day. If there were billions of years in between, that plant life would not survive without the sun, but one, twenty-four hour period? Yeah, they could last through that. Furthermore, it's true that there are passages where the word "יוֹם" is used to talk about long periods of time, but the Creation account is very specific in how it is *not* that:

"And God saw the light, that *it was* good: and God divided the light from the darkness. And God called the light Day, and the darkness He called Night. And the evening and the morning were the first day."
(Genesis 1:4 – 5)

The specific parameters of day and night are set here. It's not referring to anything beyond that. If the plain sense makes common sense, seek no other sense lest you come up with nonsense;[54] and here, the plain sense is that God has created and is referring to day and night as we know them. Remember, God knows how to talk to mankind. He's not trying to make some difficult code to crack, or some mystic message of mystery that only the spiritually elite can decipher. No, He makes things very understandable to us. Do we need to work hard and study? Yes, but we do not need try to find a secret message behind every verse

---

54. This is a summarized version of Dr. David L. Cooper's quote on "The common sense Golden Rule of Interpretation."

because God doesn't work that way. He's not trying to hide things from us in His Word.

Adam and Eve: Evolution states that man came from monkeys, that came from lizards, that came from fish, that came from slime. Creation states that God created man from the dust of the ground and breathed life into him. This is an irredeemably stark contradiction. God very plainly states how Adam and Eve were created, but evolution demands slow transforming process from ape to mankind. The only way theistic evolution can still try to mesh the Bible with evolution is if Adam and Eve are just allegorical and not real people. Now, if Adam and Eve weren't real people, why is Adam listed in the genealogy of Christ in Luke 3? If Adam and Eve weren't real people, who were the first people to sin? If Adam and Eve weren't real people, at which point in the genealogies of Genesis do we get to actual real people? If Adam and Eve weren't real people, who was the serpent talking to? Or is the serpent another allegory? See what I mean? If the plain sense makes common sense, seek no other sense lest you come up with nonsense.

Jesus Believes in Creation

Jesus quoted many Old Testament passages. One in particular shows how the theories of evolution and theistic evolution weren't even a consideration in His mind:

"The Pharisees also came unto Him, tempting Him, and saying unto Him, Is it lawful for a man to put away his wife for every cause? <u>And He answered and said unto them, Have ye not read, that He which made *them* at the beginning made them male and female</u>,"
(Matthew 19:3 – 4)

This is a reference to the book of Genesis:

"So God created man in His *own* image, in the image of God created He him; male and female created He them."
(Genesis 1:27)

This means that Jesus believes the Genesis account in a literal sense, not figurative, allegorical, or metaphorical as theistic evolution states. Since we know Jesus is God, this is ultimately God saying that Genesis is true in the literal sense. Furthermore, it was stated previously that evolution is not science because science has to be observed. Evolutionists would state that Creation is not science because that was not observed, either. Well, Jesus observed it because He was there, and Jesus, as a man, can claim that Creation is indeed scientific.

Other Points

Morals

Thought-provoking question: Where do morals come from if we were all a result of a random arrangement of atoms and chemicals? Molecules don't have consciences. So, where do we get our sense of right and wrong? Even every little child has a sense of what is right and what is wrong. Everyone feels guilty when they do something wrong. Even people who live in sin still seek to hide their sinful ways, but, if evolution is true, then there is no sense of right and wrong. It's very strange to know what is right and what is wrong when there is no right and wrong. So where did morals, conscience, and character come from? I'll give you the answer. They came from Jehovah God.

I'll put it another way. What is one of the most popular arguments against the existence of God? You've probably heard it at least once in your life when trying to witness to an evolutionist or atheist: "If God is real and if God is good, why is there so much evil in the world?" This is a good question, and a question that we're not going to answer right now. If you want the answer to this question, please refer to Chapter Fifteen: Wrath, Love, and Other Enigmas – "Why do Bad Things happen in Life if God is Good and in Control over Everything?" Now, imagine there is a debate going on between a Bible believer and an evolutionist:

Evolutionist: "If God is real, why is there so much evil in the world?"

Bible believer: "What evil?"

Evolutionist (slightly confused at the response): "What do you mean 'what evil'? Murder, racial prejudice, rape, and such."

Bible believer: "But, according to atheism, there is no such thing as evil. Evolution states that we just wound up here by accident due to an explosion and millions of years of evolving. There's no purpose or ultimate design to anything. Therefore, the concept of evil cannot exist unless there is a designer and lawmaker behind all of existence. If atheism is valid and there is no God, nothing is wrong. Nothing is evil. If it feels good for someone to do, no one really has the right to say it's evil. This includes rape, murder, thievery, torture, incest, terrorism, cannibalism, infanticide, kidnapping, bestiality, child pornography, slavery, and everything else abominable that mankind could commit. If there is no God, these are just preferences people have that are free of condemnation, but the thing is you *know* these are wrong. You *know* that rape is unacceptable. You *know* that the Holocaust was wrong. You *know* that the concept of evil does exist. Everyone does. It is a universal concept. We just choose to ignore some of them. Therefore, there *must* be a God that established what is good and what is evil."

Irreducible Complexity

Irreducible complexity can be defined simply as this: every part needs to be in its place for the whole to work. Evolution puts forth the idea that humanity came from some sludge, and we very, very slowly morphed into humans over a period of billions of years. Here's where the logic of that really breaks down. So, what evolved first? The bones or the muscles to move the bones? The heart or the blood vessels that the heart sends blood to? The retina of the eye or the cornea of the eye? See, it doesn't make sense. All of those parts had to be there simultaneously for the whole body to function properly. It shows more evidence of an intelligent Creator rather than slowly evolving those parts over billions of years.

Let's take it a step further and go with the idea that we were once fish, but we decided to grow arms and legs. If it took billions of years, how would the in-between fish function? The half-fins, half-arms and half-tail, half-legs wouldn't assist in either swimming nor walking. The fish-person would not be able to move and would therefore die. Other examples of how this doesn't work would be with woodpeckers and bombardier beetles.

First of all, the woodpecker. It uses its beak like a jackhammer to drill holes into trees in order to get bugs. So, stop for a moment and think about how that would come about in an evolutionary process. Because not all birds can do this. If they tried, they would destroy their beak and concuss themselves to death if they kept trying, but woodpeckers have a spongy bone in the front of their skull called cancellous bone. This dissipates and absorbs the shock of the constant hammering of their beak against solid wood. So, the question is this: how did the woodpecker slowly develop that cancellous bone with evolution? That type of pecking would have killed any bird that didn't have it. Woodpeckers, without that spongy bone, would have died off.

Next, we have the bombardier beetle. A very fascinating insect. When they are disturbed or in danger, they eject a hot, noxious chemical spray. It's a chemical reaction between hydroquinone and hydrogen peroxide. Heat from the reaction makes the mixture around boiling point. It can be fatal to attacking insects and very painful to larger predators. Now, how would the beetle slowly evolve to be able to do this? To mix two chemicals at just the right amount so as to use it as a defense mechanism instead of blowing themselves up? It doesn't make any sense. This isn't just with a few creatures, it's with *all* of them. Every part is needed simultaneously for the whole to function. If things had formed parts separately over billions of years, everything would have died off.

Evolution Can't Be Proven

Evolutionary author and fossil expert, Colin Patterson, the Senior Principal Scientific Officer of the Paleontology Department of the British Museum of Natural History, had this to say when asked why there were no transitional fossils forms in his book:

"I fully agree with your comments on the lack of direct illustrations of evolutionary transitions in my book. If I knew of any, fossil or living, I certainly would have included them...There are no transitional forms...There is not one such fossil for which one could make a watertight argument."[55]

Evolution cannot be proven. No one can truly bring forth evidence that the Big Bang ever happened, that we evolved from apes. It cannot be observed today. That means that evolution is *not* scientific fact. So the world ought stop saying that it's science and call evolution what it really is: the belief in a higher power, god, or supernatural force that made up our existence without proven, substantial fact. In other words, a religion.

---

55. Sunderland, Luther. 1988. "*Darwin's Enigma: Fossils and Other Problems.*" Master Books. Page 89

Where Evolution Leads

One of evolution's most destructive ideals is that it tells people that they were made on accident. Humanity was just formed out of random chance. You have no purpose. You are to just follow your instincts. Have fun, reproduce, and die. There is not much more to it than that. So, let's stop and think for a moment where that might take someone in their thinking:

No respect for authority: If evolution was truly the way everything came into being, that would mean there is only one ultimate rule – the strongest man decides everything. From this mindset, totalitarianism and dictatorship come from, and not just in governmental aspects but how the home is led. How many abusive husband/fathers have led their home with this creed: "I'm the strongest so I say what goes. If you don't agree, I'll use my strength to force you to agree"? That is not how God designed the family to be led.

Furthermore, in evolution's ideology, authority should not be respected or reverenced. Authority is simply someone who's stronger than you in the evolutionist's mind, and, if you can't run from authority or overthrow it (or don't want to), you have to obey it, usually out of fear for what would happen if you don't. Authority is only something to be feared in evolution's manual, until one has the ability or opportunity to revolt against it. What does this cause in a society? Distrust, discontentment, disrespect, hate. Nothing good, I'll tell you that, but what does God say concerning authority? Honor it. Because if citizens honor their government, if children honor their parents, if wives honor their husbands, what happens then? Mutual respect, trust, exaltation, and even love. Now, of course, that's not a guarantee. It depends on the authority, but there's a much higher chance to be honored in return if you honor first than simply obeying out of fear while resenting your authority.

The difference is clear. Evolution is the religion of "me." Christianity puts others before yourself, including authority. If everyone is only looking out for "me," that eats away at a society.

No self-worth: It hardly builds any self-esteem in anyone when people believe that they are no more than a random arrangement of atoms. If I'm an accident, who is to say that I actually should have existed in the first place? It's the first step on a tragic path of suicide. Because people want to know that they matter. Evolution says that they don't. God says the antithesis of that:

"Are not five sparrows sold for two farthings, and not one of them is forgotten before God? But even the very hairs of your head are all numbered. Fear not therefore: ye are of more value than many sparrows."
(Luke 12:6 – 7)

"For when we were yet without strength, in due time Christ died for the ungodly. For scarcely for a righteous man will one die: yet peradventure for a good man some would even dare to die. But God commendeth His love toward us, in that, while we were yet sinners, Christ died for us."
(Romans 5:6 – 8)

"In this was manifested the love of God toward us, because that God sent His only begotten Son into the world, that we might live through him. Herein is love, not that we loved God, but that He loved us, and sent His Son *to be* the propitiation for our sins."
(1 John 4:9 – 10)

Those are just a few of the multitude of verses that demonstrate our value to God. God says you matter. God says that you are of great worth to Him. So much so that He was willing to die for you. Yes, He died for the entire expanse of humanity, but He also died for you specifically. He was thinking of you when He was on that cross. Knowing that will give a person self-worth.

Much more so than thinking "I'm only here because of random chance."

Racism: Charles Darwin, the founder of the theory of evolution, was actually a racist. And evolution shows itself to be held up by racist ideology. Observe:

"At some future period, not very distant as measured by centuries, the civilised races of man will almost certainly exterminate and replace throughout the world the savage races…The break will then be rendered wider, for it will intervene man in a more civilised state, as we may hope, than the Caucasian, and some ape as low as a baboon, instead of as at present between the negro or Australian and the gorilla."[56]

Let's break down what Darwin is saying here. He's saying that, one day, the "civilized races" (ergo, white people) will *exterminate* and replace the "savage races." So here, Darwin is in approval of genocide. Furthermore, he expounds that doing so will make the evolutionary gap between man and ape wider. Then he puts a comparison. He's wishing for the gap to be even wider than it is between white men and apes, instead of how small the gap is between black men and apes or Australians and apes.

---

56. Darwin, Charles. 1871. "*The Descent of Man, and Selection in Relation to Sex.*" London: John Murray. Volume 1. 1st Edition. Page 201

Darwin is saying, in no uncertain terms, that black men and Australians (which is oddly specific, but whatever) are basically animals and deserve to be wiped out. Does everyone see that? This man cared nothing for certain ethnicities and approved of murdering them off. If that sounds familiar, it's because there was another famous man in history who tried doing that very thing: Adolf Hitler. He saw the Jewish people as an inferior race and the German people as the superior race. So, he tried to wipe out all of the Jews. Ask yourself: was that wrong? If you say "yes," that means that you don't genuinely hold to evolution's creed of "survival of the fittest." If evolution is true, there would be superior and inferior races, and if humanity is to improve, wiping out the inferior races is actually commendable. So, if you hold to evolution, Hitler should have actually been a good guy, right? Now, I wonder how many evolutionists would agree to that statement. See, because we know that what Hitler did was abominable. We know it's right to respect everyone as equals, no matter their ethnicity. Why? Because we were all created as one race, the human race. God instilled it in us to have pity for the weak, the helpless, the deformed, the handicapped, the elderly, the sick, but if evolution is true, it calls for the eradication of all of those categories. See how messed up that is?

On and on we could go about how evolution causes people to have no respect of life (abortion, euthanasia of the elderly and mentally handicapped, etc.), is a gateway to reckless and evil living, etc. Make no mistake that evolution leads to some very dark places and has produced nothing good since its origin.

Summary

- God fashioned all of Creation in six, literal days by speaking it into existence and formed mankind out of the dust of the ground. All creatures he made were designed to reproduce after their own kinds and not morph into something else.
- You cannot try to mix evolution with the Bible because one of them will have to be greatly skewed in order for the two to fit.
- Evolution is a religion, not science. There is no substantial proof that it ever occurred; it has multiple contradictions to scientific fact.
- Creation itself points to the fact that everything was made by an intelligent, powerful Designer, not a random chance with simple examples of the woodpecker and the bombardier beetle.
- Evolution cannot explain morals and conscience whereas the Bible can.
- Evolution leads to further problems such as no respect for authority, hopelessness, and racism.

CHAPTER SEVEN

GAMBLING

Introduction

Everyone wants to be rich. Everyone has fantasies of what it would be like to have millions upon millions of dollars. To be able to be a real life Bruce Wayne and just buy whatever you want without worrying about financial insecurity. There are certain ways of getting to that kind of wealth and most of them include rigorous work. However, there is one way that someone could get potentially very wealthy without hardly any work at all: gambling. Many people, even some Christians, don't see any problems with gambling, but there are many.

What Does the Bible Say?

Now, there is no cut-and-dry "Thou shalt not gamble" in the Bible, but there are principals which still condemn it.

Money Isn't Everything

"And He said unto them, Take heed, and beware of covetousness: for a man's life consisteth not in the abundance of the things which he possesseth."

(Luke 12:15)

"For the love of money is the root of all evil: which while some coveted after, they have erred from the faith, and pierced themselves through with many sorrows."
(1 Timothy 6:10)

As Christians, we need to remember that money has its place. Yes, we need it in order to survive. Money provides food, transportation, housing, and all sorts of other necessities to life, but money is not the answer to all of life's problems. Being rich won't satisfy everything. In fact, wealth can also bring about problems. As Ecclesiastes 5:11 states, "When goods increase, they are increased that eat them."

The Cost of Gambling

"Wealth *gotten* by vanity shall be diminished: but he that gathereth by labour shall increase."
(Proverbs 13:11)

"For even when we were with you, this we commanded you, that if any would not work, neither should he eat."
(2 Thessalonians 3:10)

Work is good. It is one of the things that was established in Creation before the fall. Adam was to dress and to keep the Garden of Eden. With work, comes fulfillment. It's the feeling of satisfaction and pleasure that we all get after we accomplish a job well done. God's approval is on work. He does not approve of laziness, which is one of the many ill aspects of gambling. Now, someone might say, "But there's no way I'd ever get millions of dollars otherwise!" There are many problems with that statement:

1. Would gaining millions of dollars really be beneficial for you?

2. You will likely *never* win the lottery.

3. You actually can get millions of dollars otherwise.

<u>1. Would gaining millions of dollars really be beneficial for you?</u> Most of the time, the answer is an emphatic no. God is the answer to all of our problems, not money. Now, can money help some things? Yes, God does use money to bring about blessings and to help those who are in need, but if you gained millions of dollars today, consider all that comes with it:

• Friends, family members, and even complete strangers would be asking for financial favors from you.
• Your spending habits can easily get out of control and lead to unhealthy lifestyles.

- Your security needs have greatly increased since you've become a potential target for robbery, and much of your winnings may need to be spent on that alone.

- You're a societal anomaly; you can't exactly associate with the poor or middle class anymore, but the upper class doesn't see you as one of their own since you stumbled into riches rather than worked for them or inherited them.

- The most crucial danger: your dependence falls more on your money than on God.

There are other problems that come with winning big at the lottery, but the main thing I want to address is our dependence on God. Whether we are rich or poor, we need to rely on God every day. Money doesn't bring salvation, the peace that passes understanding, lasting joy, or true fulfillment. We can get in our mind that it does, but so often we find rich people who are just as depressed and unsatisfied as the poorest people. Sometimes, the poorest people are even happier.

Getting back on track, trying to win the lottery shows our state of contentment. People buy lottery tickets, go to casinos, put money down while playing card games because they are not content with the financial status they have right now. Now, if we have a financial need, go to the Lord about it. Not the casinos. God will be much more gracious, I promise you. However, if you're just wanting to make more money because you want more money, I would first ask you where your heart is at. Are you making money your god? Are you wanting the fruit of labor without the labor? Are you being consumed by lust (thinking of all the things you could buy with tons of money) or pride (thinking of how people will look up to you if you had tons of money)? Are you upset at God for the financial status that you're in? All of these things can be the start of a terrible turn in your life. Because this moves us to #2: You're probably not going to win the lottery.

2. You will likely never win the lottery. "I could get lucky" many people think. Let's analyze the odds, shall we? The chances of being struck by lightning is around 1 to 1 million. Those are terrible odds. It's why most people aren't struck by lightning, but the chances of winning the lottery are 1 to 292 million. You are more likely to get struck by lightning multiple times then getting one jackpot win at the lottery. Casinos and gambling organizations have *designed* it that way. How else would they run a business if not to ensure they receive enough funds to pay for vast expenses and still make a profit? Casinos have shows, buffets, large amounts of alcohol, big lots of land, employees, building maintenance, and so much more to worry about when it comes to finances. It is said that the Wynn casino in Las Vegas spends around $154,000 for every hour that the casino is open.[57] Not

---

57. Take this with a grain of salt because I just googled this. It wasn't any in depth research.

month, not week, not even day. Every *hour*. That's not even considering the profit side to casinos. Do you think casinos and gambling organizations are really just trying to give away money? No, they want to *appear* like they're giving away money so you will come to spend your money and add to their financial gain. They are not charities; they are businesses. They are there to make a profit off of services you pay for. In this case, the service is the very, very low chance that you might win some money.

Even on the off chance that you do win, what exactly are you winning? It's not like Monopoly where $100 magically appears in your hand when you land on Free Parking. No, what you're winning is other gamblers' money. Those who gambled and lost. Feels a little more sour when you think of it that way, doesn't it? In order for someone to be a winner, there have to be multiple losers. That's not the Christian way of earning riches. God wanted you to work for the money you receive, not take from someone else's losses.

3. You actually can get millions of dollars otherwise. However, it's not fun or glamorous. Most of it really just comes down to the discipline of investing and saving your money. Putting money into an account that will make interest and then keep adding to that account every payday. One day, you'll have a decent amount of funds there. It requires sacrifice, determination, diligence, intelligence, and consistency. Dave Ramsey is a good financial advisor to consult in one of his many books to see how regular Joes and Janes can make great deals of money if they're willing to put in the work. However, few of us are likely to become the next Elon Musk or Jeff Bezos or Bill Gates. Honestly, I'm okay with that. I'm fine with living within my means and being content with what I have. I feel like that's the heart that the Lord wants when it comes to finances. When in a tight spot, God usually shows Himself strong by putting forth the money we really need. An example of this in my own life is that in 2019, I was facing my last year of college. I didn't have the means to pay for it, but I knew God wanted me to finish, so I started registering. Before I finished, my father called me. My father is not a wealthy man, and therefore surprised me when he said, "I'm going to pay for your last year of college." The whole thing. I thought that my wife and I were going to have to scrape by financially, but God changed that with that phone call. Part of the praise goes to my father for being willing to help me out with a bill that was not small, but I know it was the Lord that provided him that money so he could send it my way.

Circling back towards gambling, wealth is not fit to be given to those who cannot be the master of it. For if you are not the master of your money, money will be the master of you. A rather poetic way to say this: if you didn't earn it, you don't deserve it. Those who work hard to make millions of dollars know the true value of it. They have poured time, effort, stress, planning, and many other things into accumulating the wealth that they have. They have managed both themselves and their money in order to be where they are. Furthermore, those who become wealthy are not heavy spenders, nor are they people who spend their money on foolish things. If they were, they wouldn't have their millions. On the flip side, those who try to win the lottery usually are foolish spenders, hence the fact that they are wasting money on gambling. Instead of paying for a lottery ticket, try putting that amount into a savings account and keep it up on a monthly basis. If you put just $20 in a savings account and continue to do that every month, you will have over $1,000 in five years, plus interest. If you still hold on to the hope that you could win big, I assure you that you will be out over $1,000 in far less time.

Other Points

Casting lots

Many people believe that the lot in the Bible was a form of gambling. This is not the case. Gambling is putting your money on the line to get other gamblers' lost money. The lot was used to make impartial decisions. The lot can be more appropriately compared to drawing straws. It was sometimes used by God as a way of singling someone out as well. It was never a form of gambling. Observe:

"Ye shall therefore describe the land *into* seven parts, and bring *the description* hither to me, that I may cast lots for you here before the LORD our God."

(Joshua 18:6)

"And Saul said, Cast *lots* between me and Jonathan my son. And Jonathan was taken."

(1 Samuel 14:42)

"And the rulers of the people dwelt at Jerusalem: the rest of the people also cast lots, to bring one of ten to dwell in Jerusalem the holy city, and nine parts *to dwell* in *other* cities."

(Nehemiah 11:1)

"They said therefore among themselves, Let us not rend it, but cast lots for it, whose it shall be: that the scripture might be fulfilled, which saith, They parted my raiment among them, and for my vesture they did cast lots. These things therefore the soldiers did."

(John 19:24)

"And they prayed, and said, Thou, Lord, which knowest the hearts of all *men,* shew whether of these two thou hast chosen, That he may take part of this ministry and apostleship, from which Judas by transgression fell, that he might go to his own

place. And they gave forth their lots; and the lot fell upon Matthias; and he was numbered with the eleven apostles."

(Acts 1:24 – 26)

Insurance and Stocks

Some people compare gambling to being the same thing as insurance and investing in stocks. They all involve risk, right? Yes, they do, but the purpose behind them is different. Gambling is putting your money on the line to get other gamblers' lost money. Insurance is paying a company so that if anything happens to your car/house/etc. it can be repaired or replaced. Insurance *safeguards* your assets while gambling essentially throws them away.

As for stocks, investment and gambling are not the same thing. Investing in stocks is saying, "I want to put my money in this company to help it grow and benefit from its growth." The profits are not the result of someone else's loss, but the reward of everyone's success and hard work. When investments profit, so does everyone at the company. The same cannot be said of gambling.

Summary

- Gambling is not approved by God. We are to work for financial gain, not try and win other people's lost money.

189

- Millions of dollars will not solve all of your problems, but can even make more problems in your life. Rather, God is the answer to all of our problems.
- You are more likely to be struck by lightning several times than win the lottery once. Casinos make a profit off of people's gambling. Gambling is essentially throwing your money away.
- Casting lots, insurance, and investments are not the same as gambling as they have different purposes.

CHAPTER EIGHT

HOMOSEXUALITY

Introduction

It is a mournful day when things that were once obviously unnatural to all are now considered normal. The thought of a man or a woman romantically involved with a member of their own gender used to be rejected in America. That is not the case any longer. Our culture has arrived at the place where homosexuality is not only tolerated but pushed to the point where it *must* be accepted by everyone. Anyone who does not accept it is tagged as prejudiced and cruel. It has come so far that even many Christian groups ask, "What's so wrong with it? Two people love each other. Jesus is all about love. This is good, isn't it?" No, it is wrong and will always be so. It pollutes and mocks God's idea of marriage. It is referred to as abominable in the Bible. Even natural science by itself clearly speaks against it, but people will not hear. They have stopped their ears to the truth and common sense so that they may have their evil passions.

Some, should they hear of this book's speaking out against homosexuality, will accuse me of hate and bigotry. For those who think that, I do not hate you. I am not looking down on you. My sin is no more excusable than yours, nor is it really worse than yours. However, there is a plague in America, yea, the world. Homosexuality has seized most cultures today and violently twisted them into accepting homosexuality as being its own race of people. Homosexuality is not a race; it is a lifestyle. If homosexuals were their own race, would not alcoholics deserve to be their own race as well? Last I checked, we all belong to *one* race: the human race. We are all human, regardless of our beliefs, skin color, upbringing, or ethnicity.

For those who do treat homosexuals as lesser people, *you* are wrong as well. We are all sinners, and all need to come to Jesus' feet in repentance. No matter which part of God's law you've broken (or how often you've broken it). Homosexuals are not worse than the average person. They need to be treated with love, respect, kindness, equality, and acceptance.[58] We ought never condone their sin, but we must always love them as people. Now, some may wonder, "If it's no worse than any other sinful lifestyle, why have an entire chapter set aside for it?" Because of how people view it. The sin of murder doesn't need to be expounded on because everyone knows that murder is wrong. The same goes for thievery, lying, and other such things. These are still known by most of the world as bad things, so they need not be addressed

---

58. Just to be crystal clear, I am talking about the person, not their sin. Show love, respect, kindness, equality, and acceptance to the *person*. We do not show those same attributes to the *sin*. Simpler way of stating it: love the sinner, hate the sin.

here, but multitudes of people have fallen under Satan's deception that homosexuality is not wrong. More so, that it is even good, and that cannot go unaddressed. God never intended for the same gender to share the sacred bond of marriage. Marriage was only ever designed to be between one man and one woman.

What Does the Bible Say?

The First Case of Homosexuality in the Bible

Homosexuality is not a new thing. In my opinion, I believe it was present in the days of Noah, before the flood. I have no concrete scriptural backing, but Genesis 6:5 does say that "the wickedness of man *was* great in the earth, and *that* every imagination of the thoughts of his heart *was* only evil continually," which I think could very easily mean homosexuality as well. However, the first undeniable mention of homosexuality in the Bible comes several chapters later in Genesis:

"But before they lay down, the men of the city, *even* the men of Sodom, compassed the house round, both old and young, all the people from every quarter: And they called unto Lot, and said unto him, Where *are* the men which came in to thee this night? bring them out unto us, that we may know them. And Lot went out at the door unto them, and shut the door after him, And said, I pray you, brethren, do not so wickedly."

(Genesis 19:4 – 7)

In this passage, Lot had just received two angels into his household. These angels were disguised as men and were sent by God to bring judgment to the cities of Sodom and Gomorrah, but God was merciful to have them first warn Lot and his family of the coming doom. When the angels abode with Lot, throngs of homosexual rapists surrounded Lot's house in order to sexually violate these new "men" that came into their city. The word "know" in this passage does not mean to understand or to meet. It is a term that is used often throughout the Old Testament, meaning "to have sexual relations with." Another example of this can be found in Genesis 4:1 – "And Adam knew Eve his wife; and she conceived, and bare Cain, and said, I have gotten a man from the LORD."

Now, I do recognize that there are two sins here, and they do not always go together. Homosexuality and rape are not always involved with each other. They can be, but they are each their own sins and are not to be automatically roped together. Furthermore, I do not believe that Sodom and Gomorrah were destroyed simply for the sin of homosexuality. The Lord said "their sin is very grievous" in Genesis 18:20, which no doubt referred to the rampant homosexuality but other evils as well. That being said, this is where the term "sodomite" comes from. They committed all sorts of evil acts, yes, but they were *known* by this sin: The sin of homosexuality. For those who believe homosexuality is acceptable in the eyes of God (which we will discuss that in

194

greater degree further on), note what Lot calls it here: "Do not so wickedly." Some may say that Lot could have been referring only to the rape. He wasn't, but if you believe that, consider our next passage.

What God Said in the Law

"Thou shalt not lie with mankind, as with womankind: it *is* abomination."
(Leviticus 18:22)

"If a man also lie with mankind, as he lieth with a woman, both of them have committed an abomination: they shall surely be put to death; their blood *shall be* upon them."
(Leviticus 20:13)

I have never seen more straight-forward passages that people have tried to explain away. I have been told dozens of things from people that are trying to make these verses, among others, disappear. One of the more popular ones is that when it says "mankind," it is actually referring to young boys. Hence, the verses would be saying, "Thou shalt not lie with children as thou lie with women." Now, having sexual relations with children is very wrong as well, but that isn't what this verse is saying. The Hebrew word for "mankind" in Leviticus 18:22 and 20:13 is "זָכָר" (pronounced "zaw-kawr"), which is translated "male." Young

195

boys fall into that category, yes, but the verse is saying that men ought not have sexual relations with other men.

Another idea I have heard, though more ridiculous than the previous, is that these verses do not refer to sexual relations, but that the word "lie" is actually meaning "bearing false witness." Ergo, they were saying that Leviticus 18:22 and 20:13 were essentially saying, "Thou shalt not bear false witness to men as men bear false witness to women. For a man to lie to another man is an abomination." Firstly, this does not match up with the context. Two verses prior to this one, the Bible says, "Moreover thou shalt not lie carnally with thy neighbour's wife, to defile thyself with her," while 18:23 says, "Neither shalt thou lie with any beast to defile thyself therewith: neither shall any woman stand before a beast to lie down thereto: it *is* confusion." The context deals with sexual prohibitions, not bearing false witness. Secondly, this argument doesn't make sense, for God condemned lying in general in the Ten Commandments. Lying is wrong no matter what gender you lie to. Thirdly, the Hebrew word for "lie" here is "שָׁכַב" (pronounced "shaw-kab"), which means "to lie down for rest, sexual connection, or death." The only one applicable for these verses would be the sexual. Put in contemporary terminology, this verse is saying this: "Men shall not have sexual relations with men as they do with women. It is abomination." To be clear, the same goes for women with women. In the context of these passages, Moses was speaking God's law

196

to the authorities of the households, which would be the men. Hence, it is why the romantic relationship of men with men alone is condemned. For anyone who thinks that lesbianism is permitted, Paul makes it clear that lesbianism is just as unnatural in Romans, but we'll get to that later. The point is, these verses are very clearly saying that it is forbidden by God for men to have sexual relations with men and women to have sexual relations with women.

Now, there are other things that have been said or will be said that will attempt to nullify these verses' relevance, but the truth is here: homosexuality is not okay with God. The Lord Himself called it an abomination.[59] One would think that only one "Thou shalt not" would be needed, but two were given. Additionally, they are not written in some complicated jargon. They are very plain. But people have gone to extremes to explain away something that is very clear and uncomplicated. Furthermore, these two verses are not the only passages that discuss homosexuality, and none of those said passages are shown in a positive light.

---

59. Note: God is not calling homosexuals abominable. God is calling the *act* of homosexuality abominable. That must not be confused. God loves all humanity. We are all His creation. No person is seen as an abomination in His eyes. It is the sin that is disgusting and abhorrent to God.

What about David and Jonathan?

One of the most popular arguments that the homosexual crowd uses today in an attempt to justify their sinful lifestyle is the theory that David, the son of Jesse, and Jonathan, the son of Saul, had a homosexual relationship. This is, of course, completely false. However, many good Christian men and women today are also being found stumped at these allegations, not being able to refute them. There have been more than a few Bible commentaries that have stated nothing more than something along the lines of: "Jonathan and David were simply close friends and nothing more." That is a true statement, but with so many accusations about these two being a homosexual couple, further reasoning and explanation is needed. Without it, many who are for the homosexual theory simply scoff in response, believing that they have just proven themselves correct because of such a poor rebuttal. Plus, those who are seeking more logic as to why Jonathan and David weren't a couple are left feeling deflated, realizing the inadequacy of the answer they were given. This issue *must* be addressed, but in a godly manner. Why? Because if David truly had a romantic relationship with Jonathan and was still called the man after God's own heart, not only would the homosexual crowd be able to justify their sin, but the world would be able to say that the Bible does indeed contradict itself; and if the Bible contradicts itself, then who can trust it?

Bible-believing Baptists need to be better equipped in order to combat these slanders against God's Word. There are a few select Bible passages to which are said to be in favor of the homosexual theory: 1 Samuel 18:1, 18:3 – 4, 20:30, 20:41 – 42, and 2 Samuel 1:26. Those who condone homosexuality use these verses to back four arguments. We will look at each of them in turn and refute each.

1. When David and Jonathan Met:

"And it came to pass, when he had made an end of speaking unto Saul, that the soul of Jonathan was knit with the soul of David, and Jonathan loved him as his own soul…Then Jonathan and David made a covenant, because he loved him as his own soul. And Jonathan stripped himself of the robe that *was* upon him, and gave it to David, and his garments, even to his sword, and to his bow, and to his girdle."

(1 Samuel 18:1, 3 – 4)

According to the homosexual crowd, this was an unmistakable gesture of love from Jonathan. The Bible does state that Jonathan loved David as his own soul and that he generously gave David of his own weapons and royal apparel. In our day and time, this would seem like something a man would do to demonstrate romantic feelings. After all, being the crown prince, Jonathan's possessions would have been of incredible worth. How could this be anything but homosexual desires from Jonathan

199

toward David? Well, loving someone as your own soul does not indicate romantic love.

Let's look at the big picture of what had taken place around chapter 18. First, Jonathan was a man of war. He had done some great things in battle. He was the man that the Lord had begun to bring defeat to the Philistines in 1 Samuel 14. However, when it came to Goliath, we do not find any Hebrew stand up to him except David. This included Jonathan. Jonathan, it would appear, was afraid to face Goliath as well. When he saw a young shepherd boy take down the giant Philistine, I can assure you that Jonathan was deeply impressed. Perhaps not only impressed, but convicted. For Jonathan should have been out on that battlefield rather than a teenager. Additionally, because of David's actions and words, it was clear that this boy had a close walk with the Lord, as Jonathan did. They had a similar spirit, and Christian brothers who walk closely with the Lord tend to have a connection. Not a romantic connection, but a connection of Christian brotherhood that is deeper and more tender than many other connections. In today's world, men are often embarrassed to show it because it is often ridiculed as a gay or girly attitude. Because of this, men, even Christian men, tend to try and be more "manly" by keeping their tender feelings hidden inside. In older times, godly men were not as fearful to show these feelings. Not only that, but the Hebrew culture was/is much more intimate than ours is and men could show deep feelings between each other without being accused with sodomy.

Furthermore, Jonathan was not giving his valuable possessions to David because he was displaying romantic affection. Rather, Jonathan clearly recognized that David did not have any weapons of war. David had a sling that he slew Goliath with, but was forced to take Goliath's sword in order to behead the giant. Given David's age and Goliath's stature, David was probably not able to wield Goliath's sword proficiently. Therefore, Jonathan bestowed a sword to him that would be more appropriate. He replaced David's sling with a bow, which was a far better ranged weapon. This was to equip David for further military escapades. As for the robes, this was to honor what David had done. Since Jonathan himself had refrained from taking Goliath's challenge, Jonathan was basically saying "You deserve these, not me." For David had done something that the crown prince should have been willing to do.

2. Jonathan Defending David:
"Then Saul's anger was kindled against Jonathan, and he said unto him, Thou son of the perverse rebellious *woman,* do not I know that thou hast chosen the son of Jesse to thine own confusion, and unto the confusion of thy mother's nakedness?"
(1 Samuel 20:30)
201

This has been the experience of many homosexuals when they told their parents of their lifestyle. When Jonathan chose to defend David against his father, the homosexual crowd claims that Saul realized of Jonathan's romantic love for David and hated Jonathan for it because Saul was like all of us "closed-minded" Baptists. However, the context completely blows that out of the water.

First, look at Saul. Saul was being oppressed by a demonic spirit. He was also consumed with jealousy when it came to David's popularity. Thirdly, he was suspicious that David was the new king that had been appointed by the Lord. Rather than accepting this honorably, Saul fought tooth and nail to keep his throne. Saul was trying to murder David so as to protect his own kingdom and name. So, when Jonathan defended David's life, Saul said those things not because Jonathan was homosexual, but because Jonathan had chosen to protect David's kingdom more so than Saul's kingdom. This is further backed up by Saul's next words: "For as long as the son of Jesse liveth upon the ground, thou shalt not be established, nor thy kingdom" (1 Samuel 20:31). If David lived, he would be king instead of Jonathan, and Saul was trying to rally Jonathan to his side with that fact. Choosing to defend David meant that Jonathan was willing to give up his father's throne.

Secondly, realize that this passage is talking about a man's life being snuffed out. Jonathan was, beyond a doubt, a godly man. This is shown throughout most passages that he is in. Therefore, we can believe that if any other innocent life was on the line, Jonathan would still defend that person as he did David. Jonathan does not state here, "But I love David!" or something of the like. No, he questions the reasoning behind David's death. He says, "Wherefore shall he be slain? What hath he done?" If the homosexual relationship was present between Jonathan and David, why would Jonathan even need to ask this question? He would know full well why Saul would call for David's life. It was demanded in the law for those who committed sodomy (Leviticus 20:13). On that note, if it was a question of Saul realizing that Jonathan and David being a homosexual couple, Saul would have called for *both* of their deaths. For those who say, "But Jonathan was his son. Saul wouldn't kill his own son," I refer you to 1 Samuel 14:44 –

"And Saul answered, God do so and more also: for thou shalt surely die, Jonathan."
(1 Samuel 14:44)

However, Jonathan was asking this because he had no clue as to what ill thing David had done. Why? Because David hadn't done anything worthy of death. It was all centered around Saul's

203

jealousy for the throne, not a romantic relationship between David and Jonathan.

3. Jonathan and David's Parting:

"*And* as soon as the lad was gone, David arose out of *a place* toward the south, and fell on his face to the ground, and bowed himself three times: and they kissed one another, and wept one with another, until David exceeded. And Jonathan said to David, Go in peace, forasmuch as we have sworn both of us in the name of the LORD, saying, The LORD be between me and thee, and between my seed and thy seed for ever. And he arose and departed: and Jonathan went into the city."
(1 Samuel 20:41 – 42)

According to the homosexual crowd, after Jonathan realized Saul would never approve of their romantic relationship, Jonathan and David mourned that they would never be able to be together. And so, they shared a "long-yearned-for" kiss and essentially promised each other that their families would be one. Basically, the homosexual crowd argues that Jonathan and David married themselves to each other in the only way they could. This is far from the reality, however. Whoever fashioned this idea does not understand the Hebrew culture of that time period. It is absolutely essential to first understand the culture before making any sort of allegations of this sort.

In America, kissing is usually seen as romantic. True, there are families that share kisses between each other, like a parent to a child, but there is a drastic difference between a romantic make-out kiss and a peck on the cheek. In many other cultures, however, kissing is used far more frequently than it is in the United States. Kissing in other cultures is also a way to greet someone. It was and, if I'm correct, still is a large part of Hebrew culture. It is a form of greeting and fellowship. This is evident throughout the Bible: Genesis 27:26, 29:13, 33:4, 45:15, Exodus 4:27, 18:7, Ruth 1:9, 1 Samuel 10:1, 2 Samuel 15:5, 19:39, Proverbs 24:26, Song of Solomon 8:1,[60] Matthew 26:48, Luke 7:45, Acts 20:37, Romans 16:16, 1 Corinthians 16:20, 2 Corinthians 13:12, 1 Thessalonians 5:26, 1 Peter 5:14. David and Jonathan kissing, though still very peculiar to us, was common and unromantic.

Furthermore, the covenant between David and Jonathan was in no way a "marriage" between them. Jonathan knew that the Lord was with David and that he was going to become king. He had made a covenant with him earlier in chapter 20 to show David that he would not betray him to Saul, but there might have been other things on Jonathan's mind. Jonathan's family for instance. At this point in time, Saul sat on the throne. If Saul was to pass away, the throne would naturally pass to Jonathan, then pass to

---

60. Note: Though this passage is talking about a romantic couple (Solomon and the Shulamite woman), the point I want to focus on is that she says she wishes she could kiss Solomon publicly like she could her brother. Ergo, brothers and sisters had this same kind of unromantic kiss.

Mephibosheth, and so on and so forth; but Saul had been rejected as king and David was to be the next king. Now there's a problem because Saul had no intention of resigning his throne to David. Moreover, the Lord was not with Saul any longer; the Lord was with David, whom Saul was fighting against. Saul was therefore fighting against God. Who knew how long God would be patient with Saul's rebellion? Jonathan certainly didn't. At any moment, God could have sent in anything to strike down Saul and his family: a miraculous event, an enemy nation, or even David himself. With these ideas possibly on Jonathan's mind, Jonathan required David to promise kindness to his house when he eventually became king. This covenant was more about the preservation of Jonathan's family than any "marriage."

Another thing to note is that the transfer of a kingdom from one family to another was not typically a friendly exchange. When one king took over the kingdom of another king, all of the relatives of the previous king were slaughtered in order to prevent an attempt to establish one of the relatives as king in rebellion. If David was going to become king, it would undoubtedly come up in Jonathan's mind that every member of his family might have been in danger. After all, Saul was the *first* king of Israel. There had been no previous precedence of how a godly Hebrew king would act when taking over another Hebrew king's kingdom. All they had to go off of was what the surrounding nations did, and they were not godly in the slightest. Though Jonathan may have known in his heart that David would never slay any member of his family (David was, after all, married to Jonathan's sister), his mind might have told him otherwise. For instance, Saul was trying to kill David. What if David fought back? So, in this moment of making a covenant with David, Jonathan decided to add in that David would promise to uphold kindness to Jonathan and his family forever. In return, Jonathan would do the same for David.

4. David's Lament of Jonathan and Saul:
"I am distressed for thee, my brother Jonathan: very pleasant hast thou been unto me: thy love to me was wonderful, passing the love of women."
(2 Samuel 1:26)

For the homosexual crowd, this verse is undeniable to David and Jonathan's relationship. If David loved Jonathan more than women, that is stating in no uncertain terms that he wanted to be with Jonathan as a husband and wife would be. It seems to be a perfect defense for the homosexual theory. I would, however, like to point out various holes in it. For example, Jonathan just died. A life had been lost. A life that was very special and dear to David.

In the summer of 2019, I lost a close friend named Dillon. He had unexpectedly passed away. He was only twenty-three years old. We had grown up together. We were close friends from fourth grade up until long after we were out of high school. We had spent many of our school days hanging out constantly. We often made videos together when we weren't at school, thinking that we would one day become movie directors or something of the like. On August 1st, 2019, I had lost a good job while in Oklahoma City. It was a very frightening and tense time because I was about to be heading back to college and I desperately needed money. I was at a local library, using the public computer to apply for new jobs, when I got a message from my sister. Dillon had died just a few days prior. The impact was astronomically more devastating than my job issues. It blasted a hole through my being that still has yet to heal, even though it has been years since his death.

If someone has not experienced the death of a very dear friend, I don't know if they can really understand David in this passage. David had just learned of Jonathan and Saul's death. The explosion of emotional turmoil was still very much fresh. To honor both of them, David composed a song for them:

"The beauty of Israel is slain upon thy high places: how are the mighty fallen! Tell *it* not in Gath, publish *it* not in the streets of Askelon; lest the daughters of the Philistines rejoice, lest the daughters of the uncircumcised triumph. Ye mountains of Gilboa, *let there be* no dew, neither *let there be* rain, upon you, nor fields of offerings: for there the shield of the mighty is vilely cast away, the shield of Saul, *as though he*

had not *been* anointed with oil. From the blood of the slain, from the fat of the mighty, the bow of Jonathan turned not back, and the sword of Saul returned not empty. Saul and Jonathan *were* lovely and pleasant in their lives, and in their death they were not divided: they were swifter than eagles, they were stronger than lions. Ye daughters of Israel, weep over Saul, who clothed you in scarlet, with *other* delights, who put on ornaments of gold upon your apparel. How are the mighty fallen in the midst of the battle! O Jonathan, *thou wast slain in thine high places.* I am distressed for thee, my brother Jonathan: very pleasant hast thou been unto me: thy love to me was wonderful, passing the love of women. How are the mighty fallen, and the weapons of war perished!"

(2 Samuel 1:19 – 27)

Now, look closely at this song. First off, it's not just about Jonathan. It's about Jonathan **and** Saul. He deeply cared for both. Think about that for a second. David said that Jonathan and Saul were both mighty, lovely, pleasant, undivided, swift, and strong. The same praises David gave his best friend, he also gave to his would-be murderer and greatest nemesis. David further speaks of Saul's achievements while leaving out his failures. David requested, in his lament, for the daughters of Israel to weep over the one who had "clothed you in scarlet, with other delights, who put on ornaments of gold upon your apparel." This was referring to how Saul spoiled all the enemies around Israel. Saul was a man of war and fought very valiantly during his reign. So much so, that 1 Samuel 14:47 recorded him vexing enemy nations. Yet, nothing in David's song was said about Saul's disobedience to God, his attempt to murder David, his slaughter of the priests, etc. David did not lie and claim that Saul was a pure and righteous man, but he also didn't talk about Saul's great mistakes. If David had exaggerated with Saul in his lament, it is not hard to think that he would exaggerate with Jonathan as well. Now, that argument by itself doesn't hold much water, but I have more.

Let us consider what Jonathan was to David when it came to status. David was a shepherd from Bethlehem that was anointed as the next king of Israel. David was a nobody that rocketed to the very top. Jonathan was the one who should have inherited Saul's throne, but was rejected because of his father's sins. Of all the people in all of Israel, Jonathan should have been the first and foremost person to envy, be bitter against, or even hate David. Jonathan could have considered David to have stolen something that was rightfully his. Given human nature, Jonathan should have been right at Saul's side saying, "Kill him, father! Ensure that my kingdom is established!"

Now, let's take it down a notch and give Jonathan a little bit more credit. Imagine, Jonathan's been preparing his entire life to take his father's throne. He's godly; he's strong; he's good with leadership and strategy. He would make a good king. Then, from nowhere, David is found to be the next king of Israel. All of Jonathan's preparation meant nothing. He would never be king. At the very least, we can suppose that Jonathan was either bitter, jealous, or depressed, right? We can believe that every time he saw David, something inside would just hurt because Jonathan knew, "*He's* the one that will be king. Not me." Even if Jonathan wasn't out to kill David like Saul was, we could see Jonathan being disappointed that he was being robbed of the throne, right?

Here's the thing: Jonathan wasn't; Jonathan wasn't out to kill David to assure that he would be king; Jonathan wasn't upset, bitter, or jealous that David would be king and not him. In fact, Jonathan became the closest companion to David, and I do mean the *closest*. Michal, David's own wife, didn't even support David as much as Jonathan did. We know this because both Michal and Jonathan prevented their father from killing David. When confronted, Michal selfishly lied, saying David had threatened her instead of telling Saul the truth (1 Samuel 19:17).[61] However, Jonathan stood his ground and defended David selflessly (1 Samuel 20:32). Saying that Jonathan's love passed the love of women is just as much a condemnation to Michal as it is a praise to Jonathan. Michal should have loved David more than anyone, supported him more than anyone. Michal should have placed

---

61. This was very foolish because it very well could have made Saul's murderous intentions all the more fierce against David. His little girl had been threatened. Many fathers would have been just as livid if someone threatened their daughter.

David as the #2 priority of her life (#1 being the Lord), but she didn't. She put herself above David by protecting herself from her father's anger. Jonathan didn't. Jonathan's bond to David was so strong that it surpassed the love of Michal. Hence, Jonathan's love passed the love of women.

Along with the four verses that the homosexual crowd uses to back their theory, I would like to add in some extra reasons that further disprove the homosexual theory:

5. David's Relationship with the Lord:

It is certainly no secret that David loved God very deeply. Observe:

"I will love thee, O LORD, my strength."
(Psalms 18:1)

"I love the LORD, because he hath heard my voice *and* my supplications."
(Psalms 116:1)

"And David danced before the LORD with all *his* might; and David *was* girded with a linen ephod...And David said unto Michal, *It was* before the LORD, which chose me before thy father, and before all his house, to appoint me ruler over the

people of the LORD, over Israel: therefore will I play before the LORD."

(2 Samuel 6:14, 21)

"Then went king David in, and sat before the LORD, and he said, Who *am* I, O Lord GOD? and what *is* my house, that thou hast brought me hitherto? And this was yet a small thing in thy sight, O Lord GOD; but thou hast spoken also of thy servant's house for a great while to come. And *is* this the manner of man, O Lord GOD? And what can David say more unto thee? for thou, Lord GOD, knowest thy servant. For thy word's sake, and according to thine own heart, hast thou done all these great things, to make thy servant know *them.* Wherefore thou art great, O LORD God: for *there is* none like thee, neither *is there any* God beside thee, according to all that we have heard with our ears."

(2 Samuel 7:18 – 22)

Now, most homosexuals do not have that kind of fervent reverence towards the Lord. Why? Because God calls their lifestyle an abomination. If someone approached me and said, "I think that the love you have for your wife is repulsive," I'd probably not be too happy with him. In like manner, many homosexuals either hate, are conflicted towards, or altogether reject God because of what He says about homosexuality. That or they deceive themselves into thinking that God approves of

213

homosexual relationships. So, what does that have to do with David? Well, he knew God's law. He was reared up under the law. He would have known what God said about sodomite practices, and if he was of that mindset, would he really have had such an admiration towards God? Furthermore, David's fierce love for the Lord wouldn't be real if David didn't do everything in his power to keep God's law. For, like Jesus said in John 14:15 – "If ye love me, keep my commandments."

Secondly, let's look at it from another perspective: God chose, blessed, protected, and honored David throughout his life. He spoke highly of David after David passed away. The Lord, through Samuel, titled David "the man after God's own heart" (1 Samuel 13:14). Paul also referenced this title in Acts 13:22. It was to basically say that God and David had a similar way of looking at life, both in thoughts and feelings. This was not because David was some incredibly spiritual super-human, but because he was submitted to the Lord. When one submits himself or herself to the Lord, God will change that person's heart to match His. Moving on, once David died, the way he lived was the bar of godliness that was set for future kings. Observe:

"And if thou wilt walk in my ways, to keep my statutes and my commandments, as thy father David did walk, then I will lengthen thy days."

(1 Kings 3:14)

"And if thou wilt walk before me, as David thy father walked, in integrity of heart, and in uprightness, to do according to all that I have commanded thee, *and* wilt keep my statutes and my judgments:"

(1 Kings 9:4)

"And it shall be, if thou wilt hearken unto all that I command thee, and wilt walk in my ways, and do *that is* right in my sight, to keep my statutes and my commandments, as David my servant did; that I will be with thee, and build thee a sure house, as I built for David, and will give Israel unto thee."

(1 Kings 11:38)

"Go, tell Jeroboam, Thus saith the LORD God of Israel, Forasmuch as I exalted thee from among the people, and made thee prince over my people Israel, And rent the kingdom away from the house of David, and gave it thee: and *yet* thou hast not been as my servant David, who kept my commandments, and who followed me with all his heart, to do *that* only *which was* right in mine eyes;"

(1 Kings 14:7 – 8)

"Because David did *that which was* right in the eyes of the LORD, and turned not aside from any *thing* that he commanded him all the days of his life, save only in the matter of Uriah the Hittite."

(1 Kings 15:5)

"Now it came to pass in the third year of Hoshea son of Elah king of Israel, *that* Hezekiah the son of Ahaz king of Judah began to reign…And he did *that which was* right in the sight of the LORD, according to all that David his father did."

(2 Kings 18:1, 3)

The Lord would *NEVER* speak this way of someone who would live so contrary to what His law said. If David practiced homosexuality, God would have condemned it. Because the Bible never flatters its heroes. David's other sins were certainly not overlooked. If David believed and lived the wicked practice of sodomy, God would have never been able to say that David was a man after His own heart.

6. Other Points Against this Theory:

There are other reasons that show David and Jonathan were never more than best friends. For instance:

1. Both of them were already married, and David was married to Michal, Jonathan's sister. This made David and

216

Jonathan brothers-in-law. Jonathan's wife is never mentioned, though we know he had one, for he had a son, Mephibosheth. If David and Jonathan were a couple, they also would have been adulterers,[62] which is also condemned by God's law. The seventh of the Ten Commandments (Exodus 20:14). The penalty for committing adultery was death, just as sodomy was (Leviticus 20:10).

2. David pursued women. From Michal to Bath-sheba, David went after multiple women. He was not known for his self-control when it came to his love life. After all, he had somewhere between ten to eighteen wives. Of the ones we know by name, there is:

- Michal, the daughter of Saul (1 Samuel 18:20 – 27, 2 Samuel 3:13 – 15).
- Abigail the Carmelitess, Nabal's wife (1 Samuel 25:39 – 42).
- Ahinoam the Jezreelitess (1 Samuel 25:43).
- Maacah/Maachah, the daughter of King Talmai of Geshur (2 Samuel 3:3, 1 Chronicles 3:2).
- Haggith (2 Samuel 3:4, 1 Chronicles 3:2).
- Abital (2 Samuel 3:4, 1 Chronicles 3:3).
- Eglah (2 Samuel 3:5, 1 Chronicles 3:3).
- Bath-sheba, the wife of Uriah (2 Samuel 11:26 – 27).

---

62. David later became an adulterer with Bath-sheba and it was heavily noted and condemned.

- Abishag[63] (1 Kings 1:1 – 4).

That's nine of David's wives of whom we can find names, but ten concubines are mentioned in 2 Samuel 15:16, though their names are not given. So, if David was a homosexual, why did he chase after so many women? Some might argue that it was to keep up appearances. If that was so, one wife would have been enough. Another argument is that David was trying to produce children in order to establish his throne. To that theory, he already had six sons (and probably daughters as well, though they are not mentioned) in 2 Samuel 3. There would be no need to pursue after Bath-sheba or the other concubines if it were simply to reproduce. Also, God told David that He would establish David's throne in 2 Samuel 7. David trusted the Lord and would not have tried to secure his lineage himself through the gathering of wives. All in all, we see ample evidence of David as a lover of women.

3. David never pursued men. The above point shows David constantly going after women. If David were a true homosexual, would not he have tried to have at least one male concubine when he was king? People might argue, "Well, he didn't because he

---

63. Now, Abishag may not count because the Bible never indicates that they were married, nor did David ever have sexual relations with her (1 Kings 1:3 – 4). However, she is still considered a concubine because Adonijah seeks to take her as his wife after David's death in order to usurp the throne from Solomon (1 Kings 2:13 – 25). In the culture of that time, if someone married or slept with the king's concubine, he was stating in no uncertain terms that the throne belonged to him. Abner did something similar with Saul's concubine in 2 Samuel 3:6 – 8.

didn't want to get caught." That, by itself, would not have been enough to stay David's sexual appetite. David was also forbidden to multiply wives to himself (Deuteronomy 17:17), but he did that anyway. David was also forbidden to have Bath-sheba, but he did that anyway. If David wanted a relationship with a man, he would have done so.

For those who are willing to listen to reason, this shows too many arguments against it for the homosexual theory of Jonathan and David to be valid. At the end of the day, however, there will be those who steel their minds and stubbornly say, "Well, that's what *you* think. *I* see David and Jonathan as a homosexual couple." Now, you can do that. Do I agree with you? Absolutely not. Does the Bible give plenty of evidence that says David was not a homosexual? Yes, it does. So, though you are unquestionably wrong, you have the free will to decide what you are going to believe, whether it be truth or falsity. Given the arguments I have presented today, I would like to imagine that logic would show itself strong and convince those of the opposing side. If not, I have said my peace.

Now, others might wonder, "Why did you devote so much effort and time to this section? It's just one point of the whole." True, but a very significant point. If the homosexual crowd can prove David and Jonathan were a sodomite couple, then the entire Bible is shown to be untrustworthy because of a contradiction.

And if no one can trust the Bible, then Satan has won a major victory. Plus, it angers me when someone horrendously slanders two of my favorite Bible characters by saying they were romantically involved.

I myself have had a few dear friendships that I could liken to David and Jonathan's. We were like close brothers, and, yes, because of the backwards culture today, we were thought to be a homosexual couple at times, but people ought to have close friendships with others without living in fear of being seen as homosexual. Did not Solomon say that there is a friend that sticks closer than a brother (Proverbs 18:24)? God intended for friends to love, confide in, pray for, and share their hearts with each other without it being romantic. Too often today, those kind of friendships are avoided because of the pressure of what others might say or think. Who is bettered by that? No one. In fact, nearly all are made worse. Back to the subject at hand, let no one ever proclaim that the Bible promotes homosexuality as anything decent. Homosexuality is sin. It is evident that David, one of the greatest champions in the Bible, was never affiliated with it.

Associated with Other Wickedness

Back to the subject of homosexuality as a whole, American media has gone to great lengths to make homosexuality appear good, normal, and just as wonderful as a heterosexual relationship. The Bible does not do this. In fact, many passages in the Bible that reference a homosexual also reference other vile sins. Observe:

"*Now* as they were making their hearts merry, behold, the men of the city, certain sons of Belial, beset the house round about, *and* beat at the door, and spake to the master of the house, the old man, saying, Bring forth the man that came into thine house, that we may know him. And the man, the master of the house, went out unto them, and said unto them, Nay, my brethren, *nay,* I pray you, do not *so* wickedly; seeing that this man is come into mine house, do not this folly."
(Judges 19:22 – 23)

"Know ye not that the unrighteous shall not inherit the kingdom of God? Be not deceived: neither fornicators, nor idolaters, nor adulterers, nor effeminate, nor abusers of themselves with mankind, nor thieves, nor covetous, nor drunkards, nor revilers, nor extortioners, shall inherit the kingdom of God."
(1 Corinthians 6:9 – 10)

"Knowing this, that the law is not made for a righteous man, but for the lawless and disobedient, for the ungodly and for sinners, for unholy and profane, for murderers of fathers and murderers of mothers, for manslayers, for whoremongers, for

221

them that defile themselves with mankind, for menstealers, for liars, for perjured persons, and if there be any other thing that is contrary to sound doctrine;"
(1 Timothy 1:9 – 10)

"Even as Sodom and Gomorrha, and the cities about them in like manner, giving themselves over to fornication, and going after strange flesh, are set forth for an example, suffering the vengeance of eternal fire."
(Jude 1:7)

First, just to clarify for 1 Corinthians and 1 Timothy, the words that are referencing homosexuality in these verses would be "abusers of themselves with mankind" and "them that defile themselves with mankind." I reckon everyone can understand the references in Judges and Jude. In 1 Corinthians and 1 Timothy, these two phrases both come from the Greek word "ἀρσενοκοίτης" (pronounced "arsenokoitēs") which means "sodomite." Looking deeper, (if that's not enough for you) this word is made up of two other Greek words. The first one is "ἄῤῥην" or "αρσην" (pronounced "arrhēn" and "arsēn") which both mean "male." The second word is "κοίτη" (pronounced "koitē") which means "couch." "κοίτη" also greatly implies the sexual nature, for this word is also used in Romans 9:10 – "And not only *this;* but when Rebecca also had <u>conceived</u> by one, *even* by our father Isaac;" and Hebrews 13:4 – "Marriage *is* honourable

222

in all, and the <u>bed</u> undefiled: but whoremongers and adulterers God will judge." "κοίτη" is used for the words conceived and bed in those verses. So, these two Greek words, when put together, essentially mean "men on a couch together" with sexual implications. It doesn't get much clearer than that.

Now that that's been established, let's look a little closer at the original verses that were listed. Judges 19:22 – 23, 1 Corinthians 6:9 – 10, 1 Timothy 1:9 – 10, and Jude 1:7 all show very serious crimes that are listed alongside homosexuality: rape, murder, adultery, theft, drunkenness, prostitution, kidnapping, rampant fornication, and others. If homosexuality is good, why is it listed with other wickedness? If homosexuality is acceptable to God, does that mean that murder is too? On the flip side, if homosexuality is a good thing, why is it never listed with other deeds that please the Lord? Frankly, because it doesn't please the Lord. Satan may be puppetteering some in this world to say that homosexuality is a very good thing, but there is not one passage at all where a homosexual is seen in a positive light. Not a single passage from Genesis 1:1 to Revelation 22:21 shows homosexuality as good.

The Explanation in Romans

Many people try to argue that condemning homosexuality is only an Old Testament thing. Of course, the previous section just blew that out of the water. However, one of the easiest and well-known passages against homosexuality in the New Testament is the passage in Romans:

"For the invisible things of him from the creation of the world are clearly seen, being understood by the things that are made, *even* his eternal power and Godhead; so that they are without excuse: Because that, when they knew God, they glorified *him* not as God, neither were thankful; but became vain in their imaginations, and their foolish heart was darkened. Professing themselves to be wise, they became fools, And changed the glory of the uncorruptible God into an image made like to corruptible man, and to birds, and fourfooted beasts, and creeping things. Wherefore God also gave them up to uncleanness through the lusts of their own hearts, to dishonour their own bodies between themselves: Who changed the truth of God into a lie, and worshipped and served the creature more than the Creator, who is blessed for ever. Amen. For this cause God gave them up unto vile affections: for even their women did change the natural use into that which is against nature: And likewise also the men, leaving the natural use of the woman, burned in their lust one toward another; men with men working that which is unseemly, and receiving in themselves that recompence of their error which was meet. And even as they did not like to retain God in *their* knowledge, God gave them over to a

reprobate mind, to do those things which are not convenient; Being filled with all unrighteousness, fornication, wickedness, covetousness, maliciousness; full of envy, murder, debate, deceit, malignity; whisperers, Backbiters, haters of God, despiteful, proud, boasters, inventors of evil things, disobedient to parents, Without understanding, covenantbreakers, without natural affection, implacable, unmerciful: Who knowing the judgment of God, that they which commit such things are worthy of death, not only do the same, but have pleasure in them that do them."
(Romans 1:20 – 32)

A long passage, I admit, but the context is needful. This passage not only reveals the truth about homosexuality, but it also shows the digression to it. Whatever people may say about it, homosexuality is not natural. It is not something people are born with. It – like with other unnatural sins – is a place people go to after they have either:

1. Been greatly deceived that this is good and it should be enjoyed.

2. Rejected God and pursued their own lusts until they have spiraled down from the natural realm to the unnatural.

1. The Deceived: Now, I have to say that we will cover the first reason rather briefly, because this Bible passage doesn't really cover it, but it's like this: cigarrette smoking has been medically proven to be destructive to one's health. Yet, decades after that discovery, smoking is still disgustingly common throughout the world. Why? One of the reasons is because people portray it to be good. Movies and television often display smoking as something that is tough, cool, mysterious, fancy, sophisticated, or even elegant. Young people get snagged into this and try out smoking for themselves. Once they get addicted, they pressure their other peers into trying them as well. Though cigarettes are evil and harmful, they are portrayed as good and desirable. The same goes with homosexuality.

As stated previously, homosexuality is portrayed as good everywhere nowadays. It used to be seen as unnatural, weird, shocking, and appalling. However, the homosexual crowd (and their leader, Satan) has been working very diligently to transform that image from hideous into enchanting. With constant buffeting from the homosexual crowd that these unnatural relationships are normal, wonderful, attractive, etc., there are many people that have been duped into believing the lies. They have, if I may, been deceived that the cigarette isn't truly harmful and they have begun to smoke it themselves; but that doesn't change the fact that smoking is deadly. No opinion or feeling has ever been able to change a scientific fact. Gravity doesn't care about your opinions.

226

It will throw you down every time, as it always has. Friction cannot be negotiated with. If you rub your hands together, heat will generate. Time will not stop because of your feelings. It will keep moving forward, regardless of everyone's emotions. The same goes with moral fact, and the billions of people who condone homosexuality will never be able to alter the fact that it is wrong.

2. Those who Reject God: This is the reason that is thoroughly talked about in Romans 1. I would like to take this opportunity to simply go through what Paul wrote and break it down a little bit.

First, Paul tells us that God is clearly seen in His Creation. No one can look at Creation and not see that there was a masterfully artistic Creator behind it. Majesty doesn't come from explosions, for all of those evolutionists out there, and dirt doesn't appear from nowhere. This universe was fashioned by God's powerful hand, but some people deny this because they don't want to have to answer to God. If God is real, that means we have to one day stand before Him and give an account of our life. That means that He is our ruler. That means that we have to live how He dictates. If God isn't real, then everyone can do whatever they want to. That's what verse 21 gets into. These people Paul talks of knew who God was, but they rejected Him and began worshipping the creation rather than the Creator. They denied their own conscience, so darkness grew within them. They pursued their own desires and, because sin's nature is to consume, they only ever grew worse and worse. And God, because He never forces anyone to follow Him, allowed them to do this.

There are five digressions within this passage. First, their foolish heart was darkened (1:21), then they became fools (1:22), then they were given up to uncleanness (1:24), then they were given up to vile affections (1:26), until finally they were given over to a reprobate mind (1:28). Somewhere in that digression, they went from the natural realm to the unnatural: Women with women and men with men. Not only doing it because they were curious, but eventually committing it because they loved it.

Now, for those who may consider homosexuality a God-approved lifestyle, look through this passage. Analyze it well and then point out to me anything good mentioned about homosexuality. Can't? Neither can I. Rather, I find words like "vain," "foolish," "fools," "uncleanness," "lusts," "dishonour," "vile," "unseemly," "error," and "reprobate." Homosexuality is a result of debauchery. It is what happens when one's mind is opened to darkness, not enlightenment.

Other Points

Reproduction

Nature by itself shows that homosexuality isn't a viable option for any species that wishes to continue its existence. Put more simply, homosexual couples cannot reproduce. Just imagine what would have happened if God truly made Adam and Steve instead of Adam and Eve. Well, it would have just been those two until they died. Simple logic showing that homosexuality is unnatural. On the flip side, it is natural for couples to come together and have children; that is God's design. Marriage is God's idea, sex is God's idea, and children are God's idea. They ought to be done God's way since He is the author of them.

Furthermore, children need a father and a mother. Living in a sin-cursed world, that doesn't always happen. Parents die, one parent may leave the other to raise the children alone, divorce happens, etc. Having a mother and a father doesn't always work out, but it is always to be the method by which children should be raised. Those who don't have a mother and a father tend to develop emotional problems in life. We usually refer to these as "Daddy Issues" or "Mommy Issues," depending on which parent was absent. It can be emotionally taxing, even scarring, for a child to have to be raised by only one gender. Why? Because something did not go according to God's plan. God fashioned parenthood to consist of a mother and a father because they both represent a different part of His relationship with His children. As stated in the Abortion section, the mother is the nurturer and comforter, while the father is the provider and protector. Both are teachers, but in different ways because God made men and women different. These differences allow children to learn various aspects of life that they wouldn't with only one type of parent. Mothers often help establish kindness and gentleness, while fathers often help establish confidence and courage. Both are needful in life. Both should be available as God intended.

Sinners Sin

One thing I would also like to point out is that no Christian should ever try to reform a lost homosexual. If a person is lost, that person is subject to the evils of sin and Satan. They can't do anything else; they are *lost*. As I have heard many a pastor say: "You can clean a pig up, make it look nice, and even dress it up all fancy. At the end of the day, though, it's still a pig and it will eventually go back to the mud."[64] The same is true with sinners. You can tell someone that their vice is terrible and wrong and that they should change; you can try and help them avoid their sin; you can do anything you like, but as long as that person has not accepted the salvation of Jesus Christ, they will not have the power nor the desire to abstain from sin. A lost homosexual would not be able to change the way he or she is because they are

---

64. I'm not calling people pigs, just to be clear. I'm just using an analogy to make a point.

spiritually dead. Reformation is not the way, nor should it be the aim for Christians today. Salvation of souls should be what Christians are striving for. After one is saved, then they ought to be more like Christ. After a person is saved, then they will have the power of God to be changed from their wicked ways.

Now, while we're on the subject, does this mean that all homosexuals are lost individuals? I don't believe that is always the case, necessarily. Just like there are saved liars, saved adulterers, saved thieves, saved blasphemers, etc. Being a Christian does not mean someone is no longer a sinner and triumphant over temptation. If someone had homosexual desires before they were saved, it may be that they will still have those tendencies after salvation.[65] Just like someone saved out of a life of drinking still has a temptation for the bottle, someone who has accepted Christ out of a life of homosexuality may still long for their sinful desires.

I have such people in my life that I care about. People who I genuinely believed are saved, but under the deception that

---

65. Now, let's be clear: people who are genuinely saved will not relish in committing sin. The Bible points out that if someone is constantly living in sin and enjoying it/not feeling guilty about it, odds are they are not a child of God (1 John 1:6, 2:4 – 6, John 14:23 – 24, Matthew 7:15 – 20). If people have the Holy Spirit within them, He will alert their conscience when they are doing wrong. When a believer trespasses, they feel guilty. So, though someone with homosexual desires can be saved, they will not be able to commit that sin and still have peace if they are truly born again. Now, believers can shove down the calls from the Spirit and purposely sin anyway. However, a true believer *CANNOT* do this without internal turmoil (2 Peter 2:7 – 8).

because they are tempted by homosexual desires, those desires are okay. We must still love them and show them grace but not forsake truth while doing it. Show them what the Bible says. If they will not hear you, you have said what you needed to. If they truly are saved, God will either get a hold of their heart or they will stubbornly refuse to move and the Lord will have to chasten.

A Final Point

Now, for all of those people who are reading this book to combat the ideology of a homosexual that believes God is okay with his or her lifestyle, I urge great caution. It is one thing to defend what the Bible says. It is another thing to attack someone with the Bible. Apologetics must be done with compassion and wisdom. If done wrong, your words could push a homosexual further away from God instead of drawing that person nearer. Please see the final chapter of this book for further explanation.

Summary

- Homosexuality is not acceptable with the Lord. Multiple Bible passages in both the Old and New Testament show this to be the case (Leviticus 20:13, Romans 1:26 – 27).
- Romans 1 shows that homosexuality is a moral digression from rejecting God.

- Seek to see homosexuals saved before trying to get them to change their homosexual practices. A lost individual will not have the power nor the desire to abstain from their sin.
- Always show compassion and kindness without condoning the sin. Homosexuals see enough hatred and anger. Showing them the love of God, yet without saying their sin is okay, is the best way to go.

CHAPTER NINE

MODESTY

Introduction

Just to let you all know right off the bat, this is going to be a long introduction. I apologize for that, but I feel that it's needful. Now, what does modesty mean? Boiled down, it can be described as "appropriate." Allow me to explain. Say someone is in charge of remodeling a church. It gets completed quickly and efficiently. Furthermore, it looks wonderful. Doubtless, countless church-goers shower this individual with compliments for how much better the church looks, how well done the remodeling was, and so forth. There are a few ways this person could respond:

A. Overly Proud – "Yeah, I did such an awesome job, didn't I?"

B. Overly Humble – "I had nothing to do with it."

C. Modest – "Thank you. It was a team effort, and God is
ultimately the One who made this possible."

Option C would be the appropriate response. For Option A, no one likes people who are high on themselves. This person was simply the one in charge of the remodel. The entire church certainly wasn't single-handedly remodeled by that person alone. There were others involved, and lifting up yourself rather than giving God the glory is sinful. Now, why is Option B not appropriate? Nothing is wrong with humility, but sometimes people take it too far. If you did a good work and someone praises you for it, you ought not go to the extreme like some do and say "It really wasn't me at all." First off, that's lying. Lying's a no-no. Secondly, if you had a part in some achievement, it is not wrong to accept praise as long as you give the glory that is due to God. Moreover, if someone does a great work and takes absolutely no credit, there is a question of whether they are truly being humble or if they are putting up a guise of humility to shadow their pride. It sounds backwards, but it does happen. I know this because I've done it in my own life. I rejected compliments in order to seem super humble, thus being praised more and being thought of even better. At the end of the day, it's best to simply be modest.

Now that I've gone over that aspect of modesty, I must confess that we'll actually not be going over this kind of modesty. Why? Firstly, because modesty, when it comes to your accomplishments, can really be summed up with this: Everything you do, you can do it because God enabled you to do it. You won first place in a cross country marathon? Ask yourself who gave you the legs to run that marathon. You achieved the highest grades in your class? Ask yourself who gave you the brain to get such

235

good grades. No matter what you do, God gave you the ability to do it. One might say, "Yes, but I did the work," and that's valid. You studied to get the good grades, or you trained to run that marathon. That deserves some accolade, but that doesn't negate the fact that you are able to do what you do because you have an Almighty Creator who built you. At the end of the day, we all have to realize that God didn't have to give us life. So, it's not all about you and it's not all about me. That is why it's okay to take some praise for accomplishments, but not without giving due glory to God. Taking compliments appropriately. Not overly proud. Not overly humble.

As I said before, however, the majority of this chapter will actually not deal with that kind of modesty. The modesty that I'm more concerned within our world deals with being modest with clothing. Even in Christian circles, people think that dressing less than appropriate is acceptable. They don't understand what kind of danger they put themselves in or what kind of stumbling block they are to other people.

Before I go anywhere with this, let me just say that this subject is *not* just for women. Let me say that again: modesty is not just for women, but men as well. Let me say that one more time, just for good measure: modesty is for *both* men and women. Men have a tendency to think that women need to keep themselves appropriately clothed, but that they themselves aren't bound to such morals. That thinking is false. A man exposing his body is just as wrong as a woman exposing hers.

However, being a man myself, I do believe I must encourage women more strongly as to why modesty is so vital. When it comes to sexuality, men tend to be more affected by what they see. The more exposure a woman shows, the more tempting it is for a man to stare and lust after her. That is not necessarily the case when it comes to a man's immodesty. Now, again, I'm not saying that women are not affected by an immodest man. There have been many a Hollywood actor with abs that have caused women to stare and dwell on impure thoughts. So, yes, it is right for a man to properly clothe himself just as much as a woman. Men do not have any right to be more naked than women should be. However, when it comes to sexuality, women are not as much affected by what they see as they are with what they *feel*. A woman is more often attracted to a man that makes her feel beautiful, special, admired, and loved. That is why modesty is typically urged more towards women. Modesty is to be for both, but the greater danger comes from an indecently clothed woman.

Another tendency that I have found is that not all women understand men when it comes to modesty. I have heard more than a few women believe that only perverts stare at an immodest woman. They believe that gentlemen will have more integrity and resist such urges. Allow me to burst that bubble: all men are

237

perverts, according to that logic. First off, men are designed by God to have a sexual attraction towards the female body. It is natural. So, if a woman starts flaunting herself in front of a man, regardless of that man's integrity, he will be tempted to lust.

Now, don't misunderstand. I'm not saying that wearing immodest clothing makes a woman responsible for a man's actions, not in any way, shape, or form. Here's what I am saying: women wearing immodest clothing emphasizes the sexuality of their bodies; but what does modesty do for a woman? What does dressing appropriately do for a woman? First off, those who are looking to feast their eyes on immodesty will veer off from you. A man who is looking to lust after women will not want to work hard for it. Moreover, if a man is looking at you, what will his attention be more likely to be directed to? Your face. Your eyes. Your smile. Much better places to look than what immodesty offers.

Speaking to the men for a moment, we as Christians should do everything to avert our eyes from that which would make us lust. A man ought not stare if that woman is not his wife. He ought to turn his eyes away if an immodest woman should cross his path. If you are married, remember that your eyes should only look upon your wife with that kind of desire. If you're not, remember that you are saving your eyes for the woman that God has for you in the future. If both men and women do their part, everyone is made better. If women dress modestly, a man is not so tempted to view her impurely.[66] If men purpose to view women with a godly mind, women are respected and treated rightly.

Now, I realize this is some heavy material for the introduction to Modesty, but some people see modesty as just a mild suggestion in the realm of Christianity. Rather, it's a serious issue, and not just when it comes to the danger it might have in the sexual arena. It also shows your heart attitude. Many who wear immodest clothing do it to be noticed, having an attitude of "look at me!" That deals with pride and vanity. Two things that should not be a part of a Christian's lifestyle, but purposing to be modest is easier said than done in our day and time. Modesty seems to be completely forsaken in our world today. In certain places, people go so far as to be completely nude in movies, television shows, social media, and even public, yet they are praised for it. Immodest apparel is seen as normal or even a good thing. This is not how it is supposed to be. Now, I know full well that I cannot keep the world from dressing the way they do. They are lost. They know no better, neither do they want to hold themselves to such standards, but when it comes to Christians, we ought to hold ourselves to higher standards. That means being appropriately clothed. Your naked body is to be a gift for your wife or your husband alone. It is not to be shared with anyone

66. I do understand that it can be somewhat difficult for women to find appropriate clothing to wear in our modern times. More will be spoken on this in the "Was It Made to Cover or Expose" section.

else. If you are not married, you are to be saving it for your future wife or husband; but don't just take my word for it.

What Does the Bible Say?

The Origins of Clothing

The first thing we need to analyze when it comes to modesty is the original purpose behind clothing. In the beginning of Creation, there was no clothing. It was not a part of the original design. Adam and Eve were both naked, but neither were ashamed. That's how it was before sin entered into the world. When they sinned however, the shame of nudity came upon them and God instituted clothing:

"Unto Adam also and to his wife did the LORD God make coats of skins, and clothed them."
(Genesis 3:21)

A rather short verse, but it establishes something very important. Though nudity was how humanity was originally designed to be before the fall into sin, exposure of skin is *no longer right*. There are certain sects and groups of people, institutions, and even churches, that hold to the belief that nudity is how they should live their everyday lives. They cling to this belief for various reasons, though their reasoning is not very substantial.[67] Let me be clear: when everything was perfect, nudity was fine because sin was not a part of this world. Had humanity continued in perfection, nakedness probably still would be a thing today. However, Adam and Eve sinned, so God Himself made coats for them. God does not do anything without purpose.

Another aspect to think over is this: Adam and Eve lived in a perfect world. The world had no seasons:

"And God said, Let there be a firmament in the midst of the waters, and let it divide the waters from the waters. And God made the firmament, and divided the waters which *were* under the firmament from the waters which *were* above the firmament: and it was so."[68]

(Genesis 1:6 – 7)

---

67. According to White Tail Chapel in Ivor, Virginia, all of Jesus' most important moments in life were when He was naked: when He was born, when He hung on the cross, and when He rose from the grave (He left His grave clothes behind). Of course, Jesus was naked when He was born. That's a given. An argument can be given that He was naked on the cross (Matt. 27:35), but if He was, it was because the Romans wanted to *shame* Him. It was not to be a good thing. Thirdly, Jesus did leave His grave clothes behind, but He did not appear to His disciples naked. Jesus was in perfect fellowship with His Father, and God condones clothing.

68. These verses point to the fact that, in the beginning of Creation, the world had a layer of water that surrounded the Earth. This caused the world to be like a greenhouse, for the sun's rays would hit this layer of water and it would warm the entire world equally. Hence, there were no climate differences, nor seasons. This ended after the Flood, when this canopy of water above the Earth fell. After that, climates originated and seasons began because of the way the Earth rotated on its axis.

There was no winter, nor cold climates. I believe that everything was at the perfect temperature. Also, it never rained:

"And every plant of the field before it was in the earth, and every herb of the field before it grew: for the LORD God had not caused it to rain upon the earth, and *there was* not a man to till the ground. But there went up a mist from the earth, and watered the whole face of the ground."
(Genesis 2:5 – 6)

Nowadays, we have rain and cold. People, if they waltzed about in their birthday suits, would have myriads of problems due to the weather. The human body is not meant to be completely naked in 50 degree weather or below. The only place people would be able to constantly be naked without eventually freezing their tail off would be in tropical climates; but in tropical climates, there's not only a large amount of rain and seasonal storms, but there are dangerous plants and animals that you don't want to touch with your bare skin. This brings me to my next point. In Adam and Eve's day, the animal kingdom lived in perfect harmony with humanity. There was no such thing as animal attacks. However, after the Flood, God told Noah that the fear of man would come upon all animals (Genesis 9:2) which is why animals usually either flee from us or attack us when we encounter them. Two of the most common attackers are snakes and bugs, if you ask me. In tropical climates, snakes and bugs are

242

often very dangerous. Exposure of bare skin can mean death if a venomous reptile bites you. So, not only is nudity a very big moral problem, but a practical problem as well.

Vashti's Integrity

Many things are said about Queen Vashti. Most of them are speculative, simply because we do not know much about her. She's only in one chapter in the entirety of the Bible and she never actually speaks in it. But I have found that her most notable action speaks greater than any words she could have said:

"On the seventh day, when the heart of the king was merry with wine, he commanded Mehuman, Biztha, Harbona, Bigtha, and Abagtha, Zethar, and Carcas, the seven chamberlains that served in the presence of Ahasuerus the king, To bring Vashti the queen before the king with the crown royal, to shew the people and the princes her beauty: for she *was* fair to look on. But the queen Vashti refused to come at the king's commandment by *his* chamberlains: therefore was the king very wroth, and his anger burned in him."
(Esther 1:10 – 12)

Now, I know what readers might be thinking: "We've already gone through this verse." That's true, but it was discussing the evils of alcohol on the part of Ahasuerus. We are revisiting this verse to show the firm stand against immodesty on the part of Vashti. In the beginning of the chapter, Ahasuerus had orchestrated a massive banquet to display his greatness before he went off to war against Greece. This was for all of his princes, generals, and other such important people. On the last day of this huge party, Ahasuerus got an idea in his drunk state that he would show off his wife before all of these people.

Now, it is not necessarily confirmed that Ahasuerus commanded her to come naked. However, Ahasuerus was very much intoxicated. Ahasuerus was also seen throughout history to be a very wicked man. Ahasuerus once ordered one of his own soldiers to be cut in half simply because the soldier's father, Pythias, requested that he be relieved of his military obligation.[69] This was a man who was not foreign to vulgarity and obscenity. Not only that, but the women of Persia were not required to wear veils, so Vashti's face was known throughout Shushan. No, I believe that Ahasuerus wanted Vashti to appear before them in her crown and only her crown. Yet, the message that was sent back was "No."

This was not a light thing. Vashti knew who she was standing up to. Ahasuerus was known for his fits of anger, *plus* he was drunk. Vashti said "No" to the most powerful man on planet Earth

69. Hodsdon, Edd. *"King Xerxes I: 9 Facts About His Life And Rule."* The Collector. 26, February, 2021. thecollector.com/king-xerxes-i/.

at that time. Her life could have very easily been forfeit. Now, let's just take a moment to think about that. Ahasuerus had commanded Vashti to show up at his party unclothed. This was not a hard thing to do. This was not something she couldn't do. It would have been very simple for her to do this, but she refused. Her motives were not given, though I do believe it was more than just embarrassment. It could have been pride that forbade her from stripping before a massive crowd of men. She was a queen, after all. However, I would like to think that she had enough self-respect for herself to stand up for her dignity, and what did she receive for it? Was she praised? Did Ahasuerus ask for her forgiveness for this terrible request? No, she was banished – removed of her title. She went from being queen to being an outcast. She did something right and was rewarded with punishment; but she retained her honor and her modesty.

Many female celebrities give out the message to young girls today that exposing more skin or being sexy is the way to be noticed, to be valued, to be important, etc. What message did Vashti give? She stood up to a very dangerous man in order to keep her body free from strangers' eyes. Now, am I saying that Vashti was a godly individual? No. She was the wife of a heathen and terrible man. Odds are that she was heathen as well. Of course, Esther, Ahasuerus' next queen, believed in Jehovah, so I suppose we can't be too dogmatic. But her message is one that is better than many female celebrities today. Numerous female celebrities expose their bodies not only to just a crowd of men, but broadcast it over television or magazines to the entire world that can be viewed over and over again. Have some respect for yourself, reader. Keep your body to yourself and your spouse alone.

Uncovering the Thigh

The Bible doesn't often go into the details of what is specifically immodest and what isn't. This passage happens to be an exception:

"Come down, and sit in the dust, O virgin daughter of Babylon, sit on the ground: *there is* no throne, O daughter of the Chaldeans: for thou shalt no more be called tender and delicate. Take the millstones, and grind meal: uncover thy locks, make bare the leg, uncover the thigh, pass over the rivers. Thy nakedness shall be uncovered, yea, thy shame shall be seen: I will take vengeance, and I will not meet *thee as* a man."
(Isaiah 47:1 – 3)

This passage is a prophecy against Babylon, although we won't necessarily be focusing on that. What we will be focusing on is what this passage says is nakedness: making bare the leg and uncovering the thigh. Exposing the area above the knee to the hip is immodest, by Bible standards. This would be why many churches and biblical institutions forbid shorts. I personally don't believe that shorts are automatically immodest, so long as they are the right kind of shorts. Shorts that don't cover all the way to the knee would fall under the category of immodest, such as short-shorts and most swim suits.

Demonic Association

"And they come to Jesus, and see him that was possessed with the devil, and had the legion, sitting, and <u>clothed</u>, and in his right mind: and they were afraid."
(Mark 5:15)

"Then they went out to see what was done; and came to Jesus, and found the man, out of whom the devils were departed, sitting at the feet of Jesus, <u>clothed</u>, and in his right mind: and they were afraid."
(Luke 8:35)

These two passages are about the same story: the demoniac of Gedara. Both of them show that this man, who had been driven insane by the amount of devils that possessed him, was not clothed (or at least not properly clothed), but once Jesus freed him from the demons, he desired to be clothed again.

Many people don't realize the association that nudity has with demonic forces. As stated earlier, once sin entered the world, nudity was no longer acceptable. God clothed Adam and Eve. Satan, ever wishing to do the opposite of everything God does, promotes nakedness. After all, exposing skin usually leads to other sins, like lust and pride.

The Negativity of "Naked"

The word "naked" is used in a couple of ways in the Bible. It is either stating a historical fact:

"And there followed him a certain young man, having a linen cloth cast about *his* naked *body;* and the young men laid hold on him:"
(Mark 14:51)

Showing how financially destitute someone is:

"If a brother or sister be naked, and destitute of daily food, And one of you say unto them, Depart in peace, be *ye* warmed and filled; notwithstanding ye give them not those things which are needful to the body; what *doth it* profit?"
(James 2:15 – 16)

Or is tied to a bad connotation:

"Because thou sayest, I am rich, and increased with goods, and have need of nothing; and knowest not that thou art wretched, and miserable, and poor, and blind, and naked:"

(Revelation 3:17)

Exposure of the body is never shown in a positive light after the first sin.[70] Aside from just stating a historical fact or depicting poverty, nudity is always associated with either shame or sinfulness:

"And the LORD God called unto Adam, and said unto him, Where *art* thou? And he said, I heard thy voice in the garden, and I was afraid, because I *was* naked; and I hid myself. And He said, Who told thee that thou *wast* naked? Hast thou eaten of the tree, whereof I commanded thee that thou shouldest not eat?"

(Genesis 3:9 – 11)

"And Moses said unto Aaron, What did this people unto thee, that thou hast brought so great a sin upon them?...And when Moses saw that the people *were* naked; (for Aaron had made them naked unto *their* shame among their enemies:)"

(Exodus 32:21, 25)

---

70. With the exception of it being between a husband and wife.

"For the LORD brought Judah low because of Ahaz king of Israel; for he made Judah naked, and transgressed sore against the LORD."
(2 Chronicles 28:19)

"And I will also give thee into their hand, and they shall throw down thine eminent place, and shall break down thy high places: they shall strip thee also of thy clothes, and shall take thy fair jewels, and leave thee naked and bare."
(Ezekiel 16:39)

"And they shall deal with thee hatefully, and shall take away all thy labour, and shall leave thee naked and bare: and the nakedness of thy whoredoms shall be discovered, both thy lewdness and thy whoredoms."
(Ezekiel 23:29)

"Lest I strip her naked, and set her as in the day that she was born, and make her as a wilderness, and set her like a dry land, and slay her with thirst."
(Hosea 2:3)

"And *he that is* courageous among the mighty shall flee away naked in that day, saith the LORD."
(Amos 2:16)

"Pass ye away, thou inhabitant of Saphir, having thy shame naked: the inhabitant of Zaanan came not forth in the mourning of Bethezel; he shall receive of you his standing."
(Micah 1:11)

Now, for those who defend their immodesty, I would ask them to find a verse or a passage in the Bible that shows nakedness as a good thing. Better yet, let me help you out – there isn't one. However, some might point to the passage where Isaiah the prophet walks around "naked and barefoot" to show Israel a sign of what is going to happen:

"At the same time spake the LORD by Isaiah the son of Amoz, saying, Go and loose the sackcloth from off thy loins, and put off thy shoe from thy foot. And he did so, walking naked and barefoot."
(Isaiah 20:2)

If you use this as your defense, it doesn't hold water. First, read the next two verses:

"And the LORD said, Like as my servant Isaiah hath walked naked and barefoot three years *for* a sign and wonder upon Egypt and upon Ethiopia; So shall the king of Assyria lead away the Egyptians prisoners, and the Ethiopians captives,

young and old, naked and barefoot, even with *their* buttocks uncovered, to the shame of Egypt."
(Isaiah 20:2 – 4)

This was a sign to show coming judgment and shame that was coming to Egypt and Ethiopia. It was not to broadcast liberation, exaltation, or any other venerable notion. Bondage and humiliation were associated with Isaiah's demonstration. I don't imagine many people would want to purposely associate themselves with those ideals.

Secondly, I don't believe Isaiah was actually naked. As Matthew Henry states, "Isaiah has orders given him to *loose his sackcloth from his loins,* not to exchange it for better clothing, but for none at all – no upper garment, no mantle, cloak, or coat, but only that which was next to him, we may suppose his shirt, waistcoat, and drawers; and he must *put off his shoes,* and go barefoot; so that compared with the dress of others, and what he himself usually wore, he might be said to go *naked.*"[71]

All in all, there is no good that's associated with nakedness or being improperly clothed, and, all too often, it is just a stepping point for more sin.

71. Henry, Matthew. 2008. "*Matthew Henry's Commentary on the Whole Bible.*" Hendrickson Publishers.

Too Much

"In like manner also, that women adorn themselves in modest apparel, with shamefacedness and sobriety; not with broided hair, or gold, or pearls, or costly array;"
(1 Timothy 2:9)

This verse is the only place in the Bible where the word "modest" is actually used. And, humorously enough, it's referring to how women were putting on *too much* rather than not having enough on. Remember, boiled down, modest basically means "appropriate." Too much can also be inappropriate. The same attitude that many not-dressed-enough individuals have of "look at me!" is found in this passage, but just at the opposite end of the spectrum. In 1 Timothy 2:1 – 8, Paul emphasizes that all are loved and equal in the eyes of God. Then, he suddenly switches to talking about the women adorning themselves modestly instead of having these gaudy accessories draped over them. What's the connection? As we established earlier, the attitude that the women had in this passage is "look at me!" The heart of that attitude is "I'm better than everyone else." Paul was trying to point out the fact that they weren't. No one is better than anyone in God's eyes, and modesty reflects that.

Of course, there's nothing wrong with wanting to look our best, but there's a difference between looking nice and trying to show off. In the context of the passage, the women that Paul was referring to were wearing very expensive ornaments, likely to display the wealth they had. This is a very common thing in our time as well. People buy sleek cars, million dollar homes, name designer clothing, and other such things to show off just how wealthy they are.[72] With the world and the lost, that's going to happen, but that ought not be God's people. Let's look at the reasons why, shall we?

1. God and pride do not mix: Flaunting your money in this fashion just screams the messages "I have better stuff than you," "I have a better life than you," and a whole bunch of "I, I, I, I, me, me, me, me." But just think for a moment what God thinks of that mindset. Twice in the Bible does it say that "God resisteth the proud, and giveth grace to the humble" (James 4:6, 1 Peter 5:5). Let us not forget pride was the very first sin to be committed. It is what caused Lucifer to fall, and pride has greater consequences than people realize. Solomon also said that God hates a proud look in Proverbs 6:16 – 17, as well as the classic "Pride *goeth* before destruction" in Proverbs 16:18. There are innumerable accounts where someone was lifted up with pride, but eventually fell because of it. It's even a classic plot device in movies and

---

72. I feel that I should add that not everyone who has those things is actually incredibly wealthy but wants to put forth that idea. Some people who have those things have obtained them by drowning themselves in enormous debt. It is far better to live peacefully within your means than look fancy while paying through the nose to debt collectors.

books, usually referred to as "comeuppance." Why then would we devote ourselves to such a terrible thing as pride? Jesus Christ, our example, never did such things and neither should we.

2. It's not even your money: If you are a Christian, you need to acknowledge that the money and possessions you have truly belong to God and you are simply a steward of them. And speaking of stewards, we are to use what God gave us in order to further His mission while we are still on Earth.[73] Instead of using the money that God has given us to stock up on desirable fashion, it would be better used to purchase needed items for your church or missionaries. That is how we end up more like the wise steward that gained five more talents rather than the foolish steward that only buried his talent (Matthew 25:14 – 29).

3. The message it sends to others: People watch you. If they know you're a Christian, they will scrutinize everything you do and see if it matches up with what a Christian should be in their minds. If you pursue appearance in this manner, whether you intend to or not, people will assume wrong things about you and, therefore, about Christianity as a whole. Jesus did not attract crowds to Him by money or spectacular clothes He wore; He attracted people to Him by His character, His compassion, and His words. That is what we should do.

---

73. Providing for ourselves and our family is included in that. If you die of starvation, you can't really continue the mission that God has for you.

Just remember to dress appropriately. Like so many things, dress is a balance. Don't go overboard, but definitely cover up. If you aren't sure, ask someone who has your best intentions at heart and will give you an honest answer, like your parents, your spouse, or godly friends. Let us glorify God by dressing in a way that shows the world that we have something different.

Other Points

Practical Parameters for Clothing

Before going too far into the various other points of modesty, I felt that it would be helpful to layout what is and is not acceptable when it comes to contemporary clothing. Now, note that this is *my opinion*. This isn't inspired of God. There is nowhere in the Bible where it says what all should be covered up, possibly due to how much clothing has changed and will continue to change. However, I am a man and I know what tempts me when it comes to women. My wife has also contributed to this section, telling me what she finds distracting when it comes to what some men wear. If you take issue with this section, I would advise you consult your pastor with how he believes God would have us all dress. The way I see it, it's rather simple to keep both genders under the same restrictions:

Torso: The general rule of thumb is covering *everything* from the waist to the collar bone, including the shoulders as well.

256

The only skin that should be seen when it comes to the upper body is one's neck, and one's arms (from the elbow to the fingers. Where the upper arm meets the shoulder should also be covered). This means no low-cut shirts that expose the chest, no tank-tops or sleeveless shirts that expose the shoulders or rib cage, no no-back dresses that expose the back, and no half-shirts that expose the stomach and hips. All of these can incite lust and are not fit for the children of God. Tightness should also be considered. Even if your body is covered, your clothes shouldn't be so tight that everyone can see the shape of your torso. On the other end of the spectrum, your clothes shouldn't be too loose that your shirt is slipping down your shoulders. A balanced medium is encouraged.

Legs: Legs ought to be at least covered from the waist to the knee and everything in between. Below the knee to the feet is a safe area to expose. Now, I know that there are some places/people that discourage certain types of clothing altogether, such as women wearing pants and men wearing shorts. I am not going to say that either of those are right or wrong to wear. I will, instead, say this: if the type of clothing you wear portrays your body in a way that God would not be pleased with, you ought not wear it. If the jeans you wear (whether male or female) show off your legs or rear, you shouldn't wear them. If you wear shorts that expose too much, you shouldn't wear them. Again, tightness should be considered. The clothes that cover your legs ought not hug your rear and thighs to a point where everyone can ogle them.

The same goes for being too loose. Wear clothes that will actually fit around your waist. Where a belt or suspenders if need be. Skinny jeans and holey jeans are not an option. Neither of those are modest. Neither of those are worth any money. They are only worthy of the trash bin.

Church: When it comes to a church's dress code, they vary exponentially throughout the world. Some have very high standards while others have no dress standards at all. My thoughts are this: church is where you come to learn about the Lord and have fellowship with fellow Christians. This is the place where people come to meet with God. Why, then, would you wear something that causes those around you to be distracted or uncomfortable? Church is the place where people get away from worldly influences, such as provocative dress. If your attire at church causes someone to think inappropriately about you, you should change the way you dress at church. Immodest, tight, distracting, or revealing clothing do not belong there. Moreover, why would you wear something that makes you look like you just rolled out of bed? On the contrary, don't put on too much that it attracts everyone's attention to you (refer back to the "Too Much" section). Dress appropriately for your God. Wear your best, but don't over-exaggerate. Wear what God would approve of, because He is our only audience. Cover the danger areas. Men, wear a suit and tie (or at least a button-up shirt with dress pants). Ladies, wear a dress or a nice shirt with a skirt (in my opinion, ladies wearing pants to church is not appropriate. Take that however you will).[74]

What's the Big Deal?

Now, I know that there may be some readers that are arguing with me in their minds. After all, most of the passages we've been looking at deal with nudity, not necessarily modesty. So, I can bet some people are saying, "Yeesh! I don't walk around naked, but I'm certainly not going to follow these guidelines you've given. I live in Texas, for crying out loud! It's way too hot for that!" And there's probably thousands of other excuses someone could come up with concerning what they want to wear. They're all essentially saying, "What's the big deal?"

Well, the big deal is God. As it was asked in the very first chapter of this book: are you wishing to please Him or are you just trying to do what *you* want to do. News-flash: Christianity is not about what you want. Christianity is about how you submit your life to Christ. God is not pleased about showing off skin or showing off gaudy apparel. It's not good for lost people, it's not good for saved people, and it's ultimately not good for you. Wear what's appropriate so you send the right message to others. The lost are constantly looking at Christians with judgmental eyes,

---

74. These suggestions are coming from an American culture. I realize and understand that other cultures around the world might wear something different to church that is still very appropriate and God-honoring.

259

watching for us to slip up. A lot of lost people have higher standards of what a Christian should be than most Christians do. They see you wearing something that doesn't match up with godliness and they'll say to themselves, "Aren't they not allowed to wear that?" For saved people, immodesty is just asking to make someone stumble. Christian men and women still have the sin nature of lust within them. As I said before, it's more common for men to lust at what they see than women, but it does happen for both. So, don't trip up your brother or sister in Christ by wearing something revealing. Paul talks about not being a stumbling block for a fellow Christian in 1 Corinthians 8:7 – 13.[75]

Dressing immodestly doesn't bring many benefits to you. The main ones I find is the following:

1. "These clothes are comfortable" (whether in how they fit or temperature-wise).

2. "I'm noticed when I wear these/I look attractive in these."

3. "I fit in with my friends."

There may be others, but these are the most common ones that I know of. Addressing reason 1, there is plenty of comfortable

75. Now, Paul talks about the subject of eating meat that was offered to idols, but the principle is still there of purposely withholding things from self so as to not hurt the brethren.

clothing out there that isn't immodest. God isn't requiring you to dress up in a tuxedo or ball gown every time you go outside.

Addressing reason 2, that just deals with pride, and God hates pride. Moreover, showing off your body or wearing extra-expensive clothing may attract the eyes of people you do not want, such as lechers and thieves.

Addressing reason 3, if you have to dress immodestly in order to fit in with your friends, you may not have the friends that God would want you to have. If you have many lost friends, dressing modestly may be one of the first steps that points them to Christ.

Breast-Feeding in Public

This category is always a can of worms. Always. There are those who are completely against breast-feeding a baby in public and loudly shame anyone who does it. There are also those that believe mothers ought to be able to throw off their shirt at McDonald's with pride because their child is hungry. Hate me if you wish, but *both* are wrong.

Let me make this clear: I am a parent. Yes, a father, but my wife has had to feed our children in public before. The baby is hungry and that baby will cry until he or she is fed. For us parents that have already endured hours upon hours of screaming baby, we just want some peace, and it isn't right to keep one's child from feeding at those incredibly young stages. Not to get too into it, but the mother will also have issues with her breasts if she doesn't feed the baby at consistent intervals. So, yes, I am for feeding the baby in public, but I stress this: it must be done appropriately and properly. Exposing her chest for everyone to see is not the right avenue. No real good comes of it except for convenience. Those around you are either made uncomfortable or, as for us men, tempted to stare. I don't care what all of those young mothers out there say about it. They may argue, "It's natural! Nothing is wrong with it!" but guess what? Pooping is natural, too. Does that mean I have the right to take a dump right before your eyes? Not in the slightest.

First off, there are plenty of ways to still breast-feed a baby in public without exposing one's chest. How many products and clothing have been designed for modest breast-feeding? If one only searches, they can find a very acceptable alternative to simply going bare-chest in front of hundreds of people.

Secondly, plan ahead. I know from experience that those first couple days with a newborn are incredibly stressful and new. Before our kids, Marissa and I were used to just having to worry about each other (and our dog and cat), but when we left the hospital in the summer of 2020, we had a wrinkly little girl with us. Our lives were completely flipped upside down. Now, that being said, we eventually got into a rhythm. We knew when she needed to eat (with just a few exceptions) and we planned accordingly. I urge everyone to do the same. If you have a newborn, don't leave the house without a feeding plan. If you're unable to get some sort of covering for when you're out and about, you can quietly excuse yourself to the bathroom or a mother's lounge for more privacy.

The "Right" to Be Shirtless

One thing that is terribly common today is men who strut about in public without wearing a shirt. There is some sort of old, passed down belief that men have a right to be shirtless. I don't know where this idea originated (nor does it really matter), but men ought to cover their bodies just as much as women should. Why? Because it affects women. It either makes them uncomfortable (most of us guys don't exactly have six-pack abs), or it causes them to dwell on impure thoughts. Women can have just as much a problem with lust as men, and men need to cover up their chest just as much as women do.

"What about when swimming or at the beach?" Wear a shirt. It's not the end of the world to have your torso covered when in the water. "What about when exercising?" Wear a shirt. They make breathable clothing that goes well with exercising. That, or exercise at your own house. "What about when working outside in the hot sun?" Wear a shirt. I've worked at a construction company in Oklahoma in the middle of summer. The temperature easily got above 90 degrees every day while we worked on concrete for hours. I didn't die because I was wearing a shirt. Neither will you. If you're in public, be courteous to others and submissive to your God. Wear a shirt.

Was It Made to Cover or Expose?

Shortly after I was married, I learned that my wife is much more zealous about clothing than I am. Now, granted, she's not crazy like some people I know, but she's informed me how things ought to match, how certain outfits go with certain shoes, how some clothes are strictly for specific seasons, etc. I am not that way. Especially if I'm not going somewhere where I have to wear a suit. I open my drawers, pick out a random selection of essential clothing (usually the comfy kind), get dressed, and go. Now, if I'm going to church or someplace else where I should look my best, it takes me a little longer to get something that really looks nice.

Now, I say all this to point out the fact that women tend to be more fashionable and like "cute" clothing. Men, on the other hand, typically care much less, and our culture has exploited that. How? Well, just look through Wal-Mart's clothing department some time. When it comes to the men's/boy's sections of clothing, it's easy to find shirts and pants that are modest, but when looking through the women's/girl's section, many of the shirts are cut low to expose the chest. Many of the pants are made in such a way to show off the legs. One of the first times I went shopping with my wife for clothes, this conversation came up. She said something along the lines of, "I like this shirt, but it's too low." and, "This dress is really cute, but I wouldn't be able to wear it without a jacket because it has no back." Then, she turned to me and said, "It must be easy to shop for clothes for you. For us ladies, it's so hard to find stuff that's both cute and modest."

After seeing all of the outfits that were made to be immodest, I had to agree with her. It's shameful how the clothing departments of so many stores make it difficult for women to dress appropriately. But the world is the world, and it constantly feeds both men and women the lie that they should show off their bodies. To be seen. To be gawked at. To attract others of the opposite gender. To allow their vanity to be validated. That is the way of the world. But we Christians are not of the world, and if we are not of the world, *we* need to be the ones to take the initiative and take the extra effort to be clothed rightly. That means sometimes wearing a jacket with an immodest dress in order to make it modest. That may mean not buying that "super cute" outfit. That could mean shopping at thrift stores like Goodwill or even start learning how to make some of your own clothes instead of buying them. But, at the end of the day, we need to put God first. And God wants modesty from His children.

<u>Summary</u>

- Modesty is not only for women. It is just as important for men as well. However, since men lust over what they see, modesty is more urged with women.
- The sexual nature of the body is reserved for your husband or your wife alone. It is not to be displayed publicly.
- Honoring God with modesty is worth the cost of comfort or fashion.
- Putting on too much can be just as immodest as putting on too little.

CHAPTER TEN

MUSIC

Introduction

Music is a part of everyone's daily lives. It plays at grocery stores and restaurants. We listen to it in our car. We sing in the shower. Music is a beautiful and amazing aspect of life. It was designed by God to be a part of our very core. Everyone is drawn to some kind of music.

But therein lies the rub. Not all music is good. It depends on two things: the words and the melody. The words are a little more obvious: What is the song saying? Are there curse words? Blasphemies? Does the song praise or encourage sin? Does it condemn godly things? Etc. Most people can easily discern if a song is good or not when it comes to the words. The melody, however, is a little more tricky with some people. There are those who believe that every kind of instrumental music is amoral and, therefore, is not bad. This is not true, because every kind of melody makes someone feel something. Soft, soothing, violin music tends to make people calm or sad. Intense, blaring, electric guitar music tends to make people feel excited or angry. Music, even wordless music, appeals to the emotions. If you don't believe me, just watch a movie. During a sad scene, does the movie play peppy, upbeat music? No. They play music that makes people feel sad and somber. During a fight scene, exhilarating music is played to keep us on edge. During a suspenseful scene, edgy music is played to incite anxiety. Music influences emotions; emotions influence thoughts; and those thoughts influence actions.

The question is this: is the music you are listening to bringing about godly emotions or worldly? An emotional influence can take someone a long way and we Christians ought not be influenced in the way of the world. When listening to your favorite tunes, ask yourself if it appeals to your flesh or your spirit. Music can be dangerous if you're pumping the wrong kind into your head. Is it a sin? Not necessarily.[76] But it's not wise at all, and it could lead to a sinful mindset, which in turn could lead to sinful actions. Whether there are words or not, music will influence you. Endeavor to listen to music that God would approve of. But what music does God approve of and what music does God reject? We'll try and look at that through this chapter.

---

76. Listening to bad music can be considered sinful if it causes you to dwell on evil thoughts: "The thought of foolishness *is* sin: and the scorner *is* an abomination to men." – Proverbs 24:9.

What Does the Bible Say?

War Music

> **"And when Joshua heard the noise of the people as they
> shouted, he said unto Moses, *There is* a noise of war in the
> camp. And he said, *It is* not the voice of *them that* shout for
> mastery, neither *is it* the voice of *them that* cry for being
> overcome: *but* the noise of *them that* sing do I hear."**
> **(Exodus 32:17 – 18)**

This is the first Bible passage that hammers home that just
the tune of music can make someone think/feel a certain way. In
this passage, Moses and Joshua are up on Mount Sinai while the
children of Israel are at the base of the mount, sinning by
worshipping the golden calf:

> **"And when the people saw that Moses delayed to come down
> out of the mount, the people gathered themselves together
> unto Aaron, and said unto him, Up, make us gods, which shall
> go before us; for *as for* this Moses, the man that brought us up
> out of the land of Egypt, we wot not what is become of him.
> And Aaron said unto them, Break off the golden earrings,
> which *are* in the ears of your wives, of your sons, and of your
> daughters, and bring *them* unto me. And all the people brake
> off the golden earrings which *were* in their ears, and brought
> *them* unto Aaron. And he received *them* at their hand, and**

fashioned it with a graving tool, after he had made it a molten calf: and they said, These *be* thy gods, O Israel, which brought thee up out of the land of Egypt. And when Aaron saw *it,* he built an altar before it; and Aaron made proclamation, and said, To morrow *is* a feast to the LORD. And they rose up early on the morrow, and offered burnt offerings, and brought peace offerings; and the people sat down to eat and to drink, and rose up to play."

(Exodus 32:1 – 6)

Now, when they were celebrating and worshipping the golden calf, they decided to play some music and to sing. Joshua, who was halfway up the mount, heard it. After hearing it, he concluded that a battle was taking place in the camp. The music that the sinning Hebrews were orchestrating influenced Joshua in a way of violence. Much like rock music does today. I'm not entirely sure how well Joshua would have heard the music, being halfway up Mount Sinai, but I figure it was more faint than clear. After all, we know that it took him some time before he realized that people were singing. Regardless, his initial thought was "war" when it came to his ears. Only by Moses' logical reasoning ("It is not the voice of them that shout for mastery, neither is it the voice of them that cry for being overcome") was his mind swayed from that.

This goes to show that instrumental music is not amoral. Joshua did not originally hear the singing. He just heard the melody of the music and said, "There is a noise of war in the camp." So, this would most certainly fall under the category of bad music. Nowadays, there are video games, T.V. shows, movies, books, etc. that glorify war. Many children (mostly boys) think that war is cool and a thing to be envied. Growing up, I, too, thought that, but any veteran who has been through war will tell you that it is not a good thing. War can be used *for* good things, such as the Revolutionary War. It was the fight for the United States of America's independence from Great Britain. That was good, but war, in of itself, is terrible. It is unnatural to humanity. It has caused millions of people to develop major mental and emotional issues after what they have seen and experienced. In Moses' day, I dare say it would have been even worse. Today, wars are fought by people shooting at each other with guns, missiles, and bombs. In ancient times, wars were fought by two armies crashing into each other, each warrior whipping around a sword, axe, spear, or some other kind of weapon of the sort. It was up close and personal. The blood would have been everywhere. Screams of agony would have been deafening. Constant terror was exploding in everyone on the battlefield, pushing each fighter to kill first instead of being killed. After the battle was over, the count of the dead would take place. People came to the realization that friends and loved ones had perished in the fight. Families would be forever incomplete.

I want you to take all of that in, dear reader. Joshua experienced this kind of war. He had led the Israelites into battle against the Amalekites in Exodus 17, and the music he had heard made him think of all of that horrible, unnatural, traumatizing war. If there is music that you listen to that makes you think of such things, it is not of God.

Expelling Turmoil

"And it came to pass, when the *evil* spirit from God was upon Saul, that David took an harp, and played with his hand: so Saul was refreshed, and was well, and the evil spirit departed from him."

(1 Samuel 16:23)

Before we get into this verse, I recognize that there is some controversy over this passage. Did God **send** a demon to oppress Saul or simply **allow** the demons to oppress him? Was this a demon at all or an angel that was accomplishing a specific mission for God to try and bring Saul to repentance?[77] For that, I will allow you, dear reader, to study it out. Mostly because, regardless of which situation it was, it's not all too pertinent to the subject at hand. Also, I'm frankly not entirely certain of which it was myself.

---

77. The backing behind the idea that this was a heavenly angel is the fact that the Hebrew word for "evil" here doesn't just mean morally evil, but can mean "calamity," "ruin," or "distress." Meaning that this could have been an angel that brought "calamity" upon Saul, not that the spirit itself was evil.

272

Moving on, Saul was oppressed by some sort of spirit. So much so that Saul's servants could easily observe it (1 Samuel 16:15). Whether this was a demonic spirit or not, David's playing refreshed him and the spirit left him. Now, to me, this makes more sense that the spirit that was oppressing Saul was a demonic spirit.[78] Because why would a heavenly angel leave at David's playing? But I digress. This shows the power of music. Saul was noticeably under affliction from this spirit, and David's harp was able to help him feel refreshed. Have we not all been there? Where some tranquil, soothing music was able to help a sour mood? I can tell you that playing soft, instrumental music has made my kids behave less chaotically when I needed them to.

So, at the most, this shows that music has the power to expel demons. At the least, it shows that it can be a tool to bring us out of a troubled spirit. That is why we must be very careful as to what kind of music we listen to. David, having a harp, was not rocking out with it. If you've ever heard harp playing before, you would know that it is calming and appeasing.

---

78. If this was the case, what likely would have happened is God simply allowed the demon to torment Saul. The demon's oppression would be all the more incentive for Saul to turn back to the Lord, but Saul did not and rather sought band-aid solutions.

Good Music is Associated with Praising God

"Make a joyful noise unto the LORD, all ye lands. Serve the LORD with gladness: come before his presence with singing."
(Psalms 100:1 – 2)

"I will sing unto the LORD as long as I live: I will sing praise to my God while I have my being."
(Psalms 104:33)

"Sing unto Him, sing psalms unto Him: talk ye of all His wondrous works."
(Psalms 105:2)

"Sing, O ye heavens; for the LORD hath done *it:* shout, ye lower parts of the earth: break forth into singing, ye mountains, O forest, and every tree therein: for the LORD hath redeemed Jacob, and glorified himself in Israel."
(Isaiah 44:23)

"Speaking to yourselves in psalms and hymns and spiritual songs, singing and making melody in your heart to the Lord;"
(Ephesians 5:19)

I feel like these verses speak for themselves. Does this mean that every song you listen to or like has to be a song that praises

God. No, but be careful what you cling to. As Christians, we should want to listen to music that glorifies God.

Dwelling on Good Things

"Finally, brethren, whatsoever things are true, whatsoever things *are* honest, whatsoever things *are* just, whatsoever things *are* pure, whatsoever things *are* lovely, whatsoever things *are* of good report; if *there be* any virtue, and if *there be* any praise, think on these things."
(Philippians 4:8)

Referring back to how music influences feelings and how feelings influence thoughts, we need to safeguard our mind. We need to ensure that, as Paul states, we think on the things that are profitable for us. Thinking on things such as sin, temptations, or wicked things are not only not beneficial but straight up dangerous. Satan is after your mind and he will use any window he can to gain access. So often, he uses music.

Other Points

Other Aspects That Show Music is Not Amoral

1. History tells us that culture follows the arts. That includes music, and if our culture is influenced by music then so are we.

2. When on a date, countless people have put on romantic music. Much of that music doesn't have words so it can play in the background without distracting the couple. If music can give a sense of romance, it is not amoral.

3. Take any video of people just walking down the street. Partner that with several different types of music and then show it to different people. Then, stop the video and ask them what they think is about to happen. The results should differ depending on what music you partnered with the video because the differing music made people feel different things. If patriotic music is playing, people will think it's a documentary on America. If horror music is playing, they'll think someone is about to die or a monster is about to appear, etc.

Music in Church

Most of this chapter has been focused on the personal side of things. As in, what someone should personally abstain from when it comes to music and whatnot. However, music in the church is a big topic of discussion nowadays. There are churches that are adamant to be hymns only, there are churches that allow for new age music, and there are churches that think basically anything is acceptable when it comes to music. Taking all of what was previously discussed in this chapter, I would say that we must be incredibly careful as to what music is sung and listened to while at church.

Perhaps you have your own personal preferences when it comes to music, and you decide that you're going to stick to those regardless of what I say. That's between you and God. However, we cannot have that kind of attitude when it comes to God's house. Church is a time for worship, for the preaching of the Bible, for honoring God, for praise, for prayer, and for fellowship with other believers. It is a time dedicated so that we may get away from worldly influences that might be at our schools and work places. That being said, music that honors God and promotes godly feelings and thoughts is the only music that should be played or sung in church. What is the point of any other music in that setting? If we are trying to get closer to God at church, why would we listen to music that promotes evil or influences us in ungodly ways. It just doesn't make sense and it is incredibly counter-productive.

What is Good and What is Bad

Clarification: I'm not going to list all of the music categories that are good and bad. That would be tiresome and, honestly, I don't think I know all of the music genres. However, someone may be legitimately wondering which music is permissible and which isn't. For that, I go back to one of the core questions: "Are you really trying to please the Lord or are you simply justifying your sin?" If you are genuinely trying to please the Lord, you will take an honest approach at the music you listen to. If you realize that it's junk, get rid of it. Seek God on it. The Holy Spirit will let you know what is beneficial for you and what isn't.

Also, it's good to consider the messenger of the music you listen to. Now, good music can come from worldly singers. All the same, singers who are known for raunchy and ungodly music should not be favorites on our playlists. Furthermore, should another believer see that you listen to ungodly artists, that may become a stumbling block for him or her. Especially if you're a role model or leader in the church. As Paul says:

"As concerning therefore the eating of those things that are offered in sacrifice unto idols, we know that an idol *is* nothing in the world, and that *there is* none other God but one...But take heed lest by any means <u>this liberty of yours become a stumblingblock to them that are weak</u>. For if any man see thee which hast knowledge sit at meat in the idol's temple, shall not the conscience of him which is weak be emboldened to eat those things which are offered to idols; And through thy knowledge shall the weak brother perish, for whom Christ died? But when ye sin so against the brethren, and wound their weak conscience, ye sin against Christ. <u>Wherefore, if</u>

meat make my brother to offend, I will eat no flesh while the world standeth, lest I make my brother to offend." (1 Corinthians 8:4, 9 – 13)

Paul is saying here that the Corinthian believers had the liberty to eat meat offered to idols. It wasn't a sin because idols are just pieces of stone and wood. However, if that became a stumbling block to weaker believers, Paul said not to do it for their sake. We can take the same principal for music. If certain music makes another believer stumble, don't listen to it for that individual's sake.

Summary

- Music, even wordless music, is not amoral. It will influence you in some fashion.
- Listen to music that influences you towards God and godly thoughts. Discard music that does the opposite.
- Listening to bad music is not necessarily a sin, but it can *lead* you to sin. It is therefore unwise and should not be done.
- Music can be used to expel inner turmoil and refresh one's self.
- Satan is after your mind and thoughts and will use music to get in.

- Only truly godly music should be used in church since it is God's house and the place where we try to draw closer to Him.
- Affiliation and association with certain music or artists may be a stumbling block for other believers.

CHAPTER ELEVEN

SALVATION

Introduction

Before we really begin, I would like to say something to those of us who have been bought by the blood of Christ. Our God suffered and died for us. Let that truly sink in. Jesus Christ, who is perfect, took on your punishment. My punishment. What we rightfully deserved when He had no obligation to.

Imagine it this way: there is a wasp's nest outside of your house. Not a regular wasp's nest, either. These wasps are the biggest, filthiest, nastiest, most violent, and wicked wasps that have ever been found on the planet. They have stingers that are twice the size of thumb tacks. Every time you step out of your house, they do nothing but charge at you, sting you, do everything they can to hurt you in every way possible; and they do this to everyone you know. Your parents, your siblings, your spouse, your friends, your neighbors, everyone. They are nothing but murderous, demonic, slimy insects that have never done anything good for you. One day, the exterminator comes to destroy them. He has a five gallon bucket full of insect killer to wipe them from existence, but when he is about to spray the poison, you pick up that five gallon bucket and gulp down every last bit of poison. None is left and the wasps are allowed to live. You, however, suffer for several agonizing hours until the poison does its work and kills you. You gave your life for insects that brought you nothing but pain. That is exactly what Jesus did for us.

It's incredible, isn't it? The One who is everything wonderful, beautiful, righteous, and majestic...came down to be among humanity – humanity, who is corrupt, rotten, blind, naked, abominable, and lost. When Jesus sacrificed Himself for us, He never gained anything. We brought no benefits to the table when He bought our redemption. What Jesus did was done solely out of love for us, which makes it all the more amazing. After all, humanity by itself never seeks after God. It's not that we were begging for His salvation. Humanity naturally runs from God. If left without God's spirit working in us, we would relish in our condemnation. We would endlessly pursue our lusts and our selfishness until it consumed us, but God loved us too much to stand idly by and let that happen. He gave His life for wretched wasps, so to speak. We need to remember that and not take it for granted. Remember every day that Jesus died for **YOU**.

Now that we've established that to reflect on, let us go over what salvation is. Each faith has a kind of salvation. Only one is true, but each faith has a promise of salvation. Boiled down, it comes down to three:

1. Works: This would be doing good things (or things that the religion says is good[79]) to essentially earn one's way to redemption. Religions with these kind of ideals would include Catholicism, Islam, Mormonism, Buddhism, Hinduism, and others. They must constantly do good things to make up for their sin or in order to attain higher enlightenment. This causes believers of such religions to have consistent unrest in their spirit, unsure if they've done enough good to outweigh their evil. Either that or they live in toxic arrogance, as the Pharisee of Luke 18:

"The Pharisee stood and prayed thus with himself, God, I thank Thee, that I am not as other men *are,* extortioners, unjust, adulterers, or even as this publican. I fast twice in the week, I give tithes of all that I possess. And the publican, standing afar off, would not lift up so much as *his* eyes unto heaven, but smote upon his breast, saying, God be merciful to me a sinner. I tell you, this man went down to his house justified *rather* than the other: for every one that exalteth himself shall be abased; and he that humbleth himself shall be exalted."

(Luke 18:11 – 14)

---

79. I say this because there are certain religions that promote evil things as good. An easy example would be radical Islam and how they believe killing non-Islamic people pleases Allah.

Biblical Christianity is *not* a works based faith.[80] And here are some verses that support that:

"For if Abraham were justified by works, he hath *whereof* to glory; but not before God. For what saith the scripture? Abraham believed God, and it was counted unto him for righteousness."
(Romans 4:2 – 3)

"Knowing that a man is not justified by the works of the law, but by the faith of Jesus Christ, even we have believed in Jesus Christ, that we might be justified by the faith of Christ, and not by the works of the law: for by the works of the law shall no flesh be justified."
(Galatians 2:16)

"For by grace are ye saved through faith; and that not of yourselves: *it is* the gift of God: Not of works, lest any man should boast"
(Ephesians 2:8 – 9)

---

80. Also consider the thief on the cross: "And he said unto Jesus, Lord, remember me when Thou comest into Thy kingdom. And Jesus said unto him, Verily I say unto thee, To day shalt thou be with Me in paradise." (Luke 23:42 – 43). First off, this man had done wicked works previously. We knew that he was a thief. Furthermore, there was no more opportunity for him to do good works. He was on the cross. His life would be over in a matter of hours. He could not get baptized or give money to the poor, yet Jesus still told him that he would be with Him in paradise.

284

2. Godlessness: What I mean by this is that certain people believe there is no such thing as God, sin, heaven, or hell. If there are none of those things, there is no need to be saved. Though it really is the antithesis of salvation, it is a form of salvation in of itself. It ultimately gives people the deception that they are free to live however they wish with no eternal consequence. This way of thinking belongs to those who embrace atheism, agnosticism, and evolution. If there is no ultimate Judge to answer to, there is no right and wrong. If there is no absolute truth, then whatever I claim as truth *is* truth. Though they believe they are freeing themselves from religious shackles, they are utterly opening themselves up to hopelessness, emptiness, hollowing dissatisfaction, despair, and, should they continue in these beliefs, an eternal home in hell. Solomon said it best in Ecclesiastes when he was living life without God:

> **"Therefore I hated life; because the work that is wrought under the sun *is* grievous unto me: for all *is* vanity and vexation of spirit."**
> **(Ecclesiastes 2:17)**

Solomon had everything. Riches, authority, wisdom, pleasures. Anything he desired, he could have; but without God, life was miserable. That is what await those who pursue a life without God.

Furthermore, we all *know* there is a God. That knowledge is bestowed inside us. We may not know who exactly He is without the Bible, but every person on Earth knows that there is a Creator. Those who say they do not believe there is one are purposely rejecting the fact that they know. Creation itself proclaims that there is a God:

"The heavens declare the glory of God; and the firmament sheweth His handywork."
(Psalms 19:1)

But we all know this within our minds as well:

"For the wrath of God is revealed from heaven against all ungodliness and unrighteousness of men, who hold the truth in unrighteousness; <u>Because that which may be known of God is manifest in them; for God hath shewed *it* unto them</u>. <u>For the invisible things of Him from the creation of the world are clearly seen</u>, being understood by the things that are made, *even* His eternal power and Godhead; so that <u>they are without excuse</u>: Because that, when they knew God, they glorified *Him* not as God, neither were thankful; but became vain in their imaginations, and their foolish heart was darkened. Professing themselves to be wise, they became fools,"
(Romans 1:18 – 22)

3. Rescue: I call it "rescue" because this would be the form of salvation where the person does absolutely nothing outside of accepting the salvation. This would be the form of salvation that biblical Christianity adheres to. Christ already did everything for us. Like a victim trapped in a burning building, all we have to do is call for help and our Saviour will come and bring us out of the fire.

No good works are needed to be saved. Rather, salvation is offered to us freely. In a world where everything has a price or a catch, many find that awfully suspicious, but it is true. God is love, and He does love His creation, and so He went to great lengths to provide a way of salvation with no work on our part required. But God is also perfectly just, which means the price of sin had to be paid. So, God paid the price through Jesus Christ. Jesus Christ, who is all man and all God. He had to be both. In order to pay mankind's price, it had to be paid by a man, but only God could pay the price fully for everyone. If a human lived a perfectly sinless life (which no one can) and paid the penalty of sin with his or her death, that would provide salvation for only one individual. No more. Since God sacrificed Himself, He took on the sins of all time upon Himself. Each sin you've ever committed or will commit. All of my sins. All of everyone's sins from Adam and Eve to the end of the world. All people of all generations. But there is one requirement for people: Repentance.

Repentance can be defined as "a change of mind that results in a change of action." A very simple analogy for that is driving. Say you live in Kansas and want to drive to Florida. If you start driving northwest, however, you are not going to get to Florida. So, what needs to happen? First, you need to realize you're going the wrong way, which would most likely be the signs that say, "You're heading to Washington." After realizing you're going the wrong way, you need to turn around and go the right way. That is repentance in a nutshell. We all began life on the path of sin that leads to destruction, but then God led someone into our lives that pointed out the signs that say "destruction ahead." We realized we were going to perish in our sins if we continued living this way. So, we repented. We admitted we were wrong and in need of salvation, and we turned around. We changed our mind that resulted in a change of action.

<u>What Does the Bible Say?</u>

<u>You Can't be Found until You're Lost</u>

There is only one sin that cannot be forgiven: the sin of unbelief or utmost rejection of God. Jesus touched on this in passages like the following:

"And whosoever shall speak a word against the Son of man, it shall be forgiven him: but unto him that blasphemeth against the Holy Ghost it shall not be forgiven."

(Luke 12:10)[81]

Unbelief or rejection of God comes from several different mindsets, but the most prominent one typically boils down to: "I'm fine without God." So, the first step in salvation, whether you are trying to witness to a lost individual or you are the lost individual, is to realize that we are not fine without God. That is crucial to the salvation process.

Imagine a man is swimming out in the ocean. It's a beautiful day, the water is lovely, and he's quite enjoying himself. Suddenly, a woman comes out of nowhere, frantically swimming towards this man. The man is alarmed at this approach, but concludes that there must be a valid reason she's trying to get to him. Once she gets to him, however, she says nothing. She simply grabs him and starts pulling him to shore. She drags him all the way back to the beach and leaves him in the sand.

Now, this man is probably very confused as to what just happened. Irritation would likely set in with the woman who interrupted his pleasant swim, and eventually, the man will simply

---

81. A lot of confusion and controversy surround this verse and the others like it. People take it as that if you curse the Holy Spirit's name, you will not be able to have your sins forgiven. That doesn't match up with the rest of Scripture. Rather, this verse reflects upon the Holy Spirit's ministry of first leading people towards salvation. If you reject the Holy Spirit's leading, you cannot be saved because you are rejecting being saved. God cannot wash away the sins of those who refuse to come to Him in repentance.

swim out again. However, the whole situation would have been drastically different if the woman would have said one thing: "Shark." Then, everything makes sense. She's desperately trying to reach him and pull him out of the water because there is danger lurking nearby.[82] The man would be grateful rather than confused and irritated, and he would have stayed on the beach instead of swim back out to where the danger was.

When trying to lead people to salvation, a similar instance can easily occur. Many people are not aware of the situation that they are in. They realize that we Christians are trying to get them saved, but they don't understand that they need to be saved. They don't see the shark, and, honestly, who wants to be saved that doesn't think he or she needs saving? That is why people cannot be saved until they are first lost. A good way to start this revelation to the lost would be going through the Ten Commandments in Exodus 20:1 – 17:

1. Thou shalt have no other gods before Me.
2. Thou shalt not make unto thee any graven image.
3. Thou shalt not take the name of the LORD thy God in vain.
4. Remember the sabbath day, to keep it holy.

---

82. Just for clarification, this analogy was only to demonstrate a point. If you are swimming in the ocean and actually see a shark, **don't** frantically swim towards shore. Sharks are attracted to panicked swimming and splashing since it's something their prey does. Instead, slowly and gently swim towards shore, keeping your eyes on the shark. This will make it less likely for a shark to pursue you.

5. Honour thy father and thy mother.

6. Thou shalt not kill.

7. Thou shalt not commit adultery.

8. Thou shalt not steal.

9. Thou shalt not bear false witness against thy neighbour.

10. Thou shalt not covet.

My personal favorite ones to go through would be #9, #7, and #6. You start off with "Have you ever told a lie before?" Someone has to be pretty delusional to say he or she has never lied and mean it. Most people cave at that one. Moving on to the next one, "Have you ever committed adultery?" Most respond with a resounding "NO," at which you can jokingly add "Come on, you just admitted to me that you're a liar."[83] If they persist that they've never done something like that, add in the fact that Jesus raised the standard in Matthew 5:28 so that if someone looks upon another with lust, they've committed adultery in their heart. You can do the same with how Jesus raised the standard with anger in Matthew 5:22. At that point, you can tell them that, after going through just *three* of the ten, they are a lying, adulterous murderer. At this point, they'll either reject what you're trying to show them, or they'll start to realize that they're not okay with God.

---

83. May not be suitable for all witnessing situations. Read the room and do not use if you feel it would not be beneficial.

There are a multiplicity of ways to show someone that he or she is in need of saving. The best ways, however, come from the Bible, the Law, specifically. For Paul states the following:

"What shall we say then? *Is* the law sin? God forbid. Nay, I had not known sin, but by the law: for I had not known lust, except the law had said, Thou shalt not covet. But sin, taking occasion by the commandment, wrought in me all manner of concupiscence. For without the law sin *was* dead. For I was alive without the law once: but when the commandment came, sin revived, and I died."
(Romans 7:7 – 9)

"*Is* the law then against the promises of God? God forbid: for if there had been a law given which could have given life, verily righteousness should have been by the law. But the scripture hath concluded all under sin, that the promise by faith of Jesus Christ might be given to them that believe. But before faith came, we were kept under the law, shut up unto the faith which should afterwards be revealed. Wherefore the law was our schoolmaster *to bring us* unto Christ, that we might be justified by faith."
(Galatians 3:21 – 24)

Paul is stating that the purpose of the Law was to show that we cannot keep it. We are not righteous, but sinful. If we could
292

keep every single aspect of the Law perfectly from the day we are born until the day we die, we could save ourselves, but none of us can do that. Even if we messed up in just *one* area, we would still be worthy of condemnation:

"For whosoever shall keep the whole law, and yet offend in one *point,* he is guilty of all."
(James 2:10)

Upon realizing that we could never keep the whole Law, it drives us to Christ because we realize that we need a Saviour. We need Jesus, who did keep the Law perfectly and then sacrificed Himself for us.

Only One Way

Another false idea that has become quite prominent today is the idea that there are many ways to salvation. It goes something along the lines of this: "As long as people are sincere in their beliefs, God will just let them into heaven anyway because He recognizes their genuinity." The Bible does not support this. Consider the following:

"Again, the devil taketh Him up into an exceeding high mountain, and sheweth Him all the kingdoms of the world,

and the glory of them; And saith unto Him, All these things
will I give Thee, if Thou wilt fall down and worship me.
Then saith Jesus unto him, Get thee hence, Satan: for it is
written, Thou shalt worship the Lord thy God, and Him only
shalt thou serve."
(Matthew 4:8 – 10)

"Jesus saith unto him, I am the way, the truth, and the life: no
man cometh unto the Father, but by Me."
(John 14:6)

"Neither is there salvation in any other: for there is none other
name under heaven given among men, whereby we must be
saved."
(Acts 4:12)

"For *there is* one God, and one mediator between God and
men, the man Christ Jesus;"
(1 Timothy 2:5)

Furthermore, if God accepted other religions as long as they
were sincere, what would be the point of the Great Commission?
Rather, it would make more sense for Jesus to command us to go
out and compel people to be sincere in their religion, since God
would accept that. There is no indication throughout Scripture that

God accepts any other faith. I mean, it's even in the Ten Commandments:

"Thou shalt have no other gods before Me. Thou shalt not make unto thee any graven image, or any likeness *of any thing* that *is* in heaven above, or that *is* in the earth beneath, or that *is* in the water under the earth: Thou shalt not bow down thyself to them, nor serve them: for I the LORD thy God *am* a jealous God, visiting the iniquity of the fathers upon the children unto the third and fourth *generation* of them that hate Me;"
(Exodus 20:3 – 5)

The thought that you can believe whatever you want as long as you're genuine comes from no one other than Satan. Certainly not a message from the Bible.

The Steps of Salvation

Salvation is supposed to be simple, and much in depth discussion on it can sometimes make it seem more complicated than it really is. So, I wanted to provide the simplicity of the steps of salvation right here:

1. God is holy and cannot tolerate sin

These first two steps would be for those who need to realize that they actually need a Saviour. So, in essence, you could call the first two steps the pre-steps to salvation. Because, as stated before, someone cannot be found until they're aware that they are lost. Because a man will not call out for Jesus' salvation unless he sees that he needs it.

Moving on, God absolutely cannot mix with sin. He is pure light and sin is darkness. Just like with light and darkness in our world, the two cannot mingle. They cannot warp together. When light shines, darkness must flee from it. The same is true for God and sin. Sin cannot be in the presence of God and vice versa. Here are some verses for your consideration:

"But the LORD of hosts shall be exalted in judgment, and God that is holy shall be sanctified in righteousness."
(Isaiah 5:16)

"But as He which hath called you is holy, so be ye holy in all manner of conversation; Because it is written, Be ye holy; for I am holy."
(1 Peter 1:15 – 16)

"This then is the message which we have heard of him, and declare unto you, that God is light, and in Him is no darkness at all."

(1 John 1:5)

The word "holy" means "separate," "sanctified," "blameless," or "pure." That which is clean cannot be amongst filth and still call itself clean. In order for God to be holy, He cannot be with the filth of sin.

2. We are sinners and are worthy of God's judgment

We have established that God cannot tolerate sin. So, since we are sinners, God cannot abide us as we are. We cannot be in His presence as we are. And the Bible states this over and over again:

"Behold, I was shapen in iniquity; and in sin did my mother conceive me."

(Psalms 51:5)[84]

---

84. Though this Psalm was written by David, it applies to us as well. If you think you're closer to God than the one who was called the man after God's own heart (1 Samuel 13:14, Acts 13:22), you must be very spiritual indeed.

297

"If <u>ye then, being evil</u>, know how to give good gifts unto your children, how much more shall your Father which is in heaven give good things to them that ask him?"
(Matthew 7:11)[85]

"For all have sinned, and come short of the glory of God;"
(Romans 3:23)

"If we say that we have no sin, we deceive ourselves, and the truth is not in us."
(1 John 1:8)

Also refer back to the "You Can't be Found until you're Lost" section when it comes to going through the Ten Commandments and the purpose of the Law.

3. Jesus paid the price for salvation by dying on the cross

God didn't have to do *anything* for us. We need to understand that. Not a thing. We are owed nothing from God. Some people can get it in their minds that they are entitled to things. We're really not. When it comes to God's goodness, we *certainly* are not. Yet, Jesus still died for us:

---

85. This is Jesus, talking to His disciples. It's just a brief point in the verse, but it does establish that the Apostles were sinful. The word for "evil" here is "πονηρός" (pronounced "pon-ay-ros'") can mean "guilt," "devil," or "sinner."

"He is despised and rejected of men; a man of sorrows, and acquainted with grief: and we hid as it were *our* faces from Him; He was despised, and we esteemed Him not. Surely He hath borne our griefs, and carried our sorrows: yet we did esteem Him stricken, smitten of God, and afflicted. But He *was* wounded for our transgressions, *He was* bruised for our iniquities: the chastisement of our peace *was* upon Him; and with His stripes we are healed."
(Isaiah 53:3 – 5)

"But God commendeth His love toward us, in that, while we were yet sinners, Christ died for us."
(Romans 5:8)

"In whom we have redemption through His blood, the forgiveness of sins, according to the riches of His grace;"
(Ephesians 1:7)

Think on this – really think on this: Jesus *died* for us. We don't often feel the true weight of that. Jesus, who is God, *died* for us. Just leaving heaven for us is something that we did not deserve, but He *died* for us. We're talking death. Death is terrifying. It is the antithesis of life. The One who brought all life into existence had to experience death. Death was never brought into existence by God. It is the firstborn of sin. So, Jesus had to experience something that was totally foreign to His nature. Not just death, but the worst death imaginable. The death of the cross. The death of suffocation while going through excruciating agony of the scourging on His back, the nails through His wrists, and the nails through His ankles. Worst of all, Jesus took all the sin of the world upon Himself. He took the very first sin of Eve, all the way to the very last sin that will ever be committed upon Himself. Because of this, He was separated from God the Father. Remember, God cannot tolerate sin. So God the Father had to turn His back on God the Son.

He did that for us, and it paid the price for redemption. Jesus was a man, so He could pay a debt that was for mankind; but He was also God, so He could pay all of the sin debt and not just one person's. I don't fully understand all of how that works, but none of us have to understand it to accept it. You don't have to understand all of how electricity works to be able to flip a light switch. You don't have to understand all of how aeronautics work to fly in an airplane. You just have to trust it.

4. Repent
"And saying, The time is fulfilled, and the kingdom of God is at hand: repent ye, and believe the gospel."
(Mark 1:15)

"And they went out, and preached that men should repent."
(Mark 6:12)
300

"I tell you, Nay: but, except ye repent, ye shall all likewise perish."

(Luke 13:5)

"Repent ye therefore, and be converted, that your sins may be blotted out, when the times of refreshing shall come from the presence of the Lord;"

(Acts 3:19)

As stated before, repentance is changing your way of thinking that will result in a change of action concerning your sin. Going back to the driving example, you're not going to get to Florida from Kansas by driving towards Washington. If you're going to ever get to Florida, you need to repent. You need to change your way of thinking that will result in a change of action. You need to think to yourself, "this way is not working, I need to turn around" and then turn around. That is what repentance essentially is in our spiritual lives. We all started our lives with heading down the road of destruction and hell. Once we realize the fact that we're going down a bad road, we need to change our mind about how we're living our lives and turn around to Jesus.

Another example is this: you're trapped in a cement room. There are no windows and there is only one door. No matter how much you try, you will not get out of that room unless you go through the door. You can kick, punch, claw, and even headbutt that cement wall (none of that is recommended), but you will not get out of that room that way. You need to repent and realize you are doing this wrong and turn to the right way.

5. Place faith in Jesus Christ

Repentance and faith go hand in hand, and they often happen in the same moment or very close to it. Once someone realizes they are going the wrong way, spiritually speaking, they need to turn to Jesus; but in order to truly get saved, they need to place faith in who He is and that He is able to save them. See, because someone can technically repent to another wrong way. People can realize that they are going a wrong direction, change their way of thinking that results in a change of action, and go down another wrong way. An example of this? An atheist converting to Islam. Atheism is a wrong way, but so is Islam. Using the driving analogy one more time, the driver might realize, "Oh, I'm not heading towards Florida!" and then start heading towards Arizona instead. Still a wrong way and that person will never reach Florida by heading to Arizona from Kansas. So placing faith in Jesus Christ is vital to becoming a saved believer. The following Bible verse demonstrate how someone does this:

"For God so loved the world, that He gave His only begotten Son, that whosoever believeth in Him should not perish, but have everlasting life."

(John 3:16)
302

"And it shall come to pass, *that* whosoever shall call on the name of the Lord shall be saved."

(Acts 2:21)

"Then Philip opened his mouth, and began at the same scripture, and preached unto him Jesus. And as they went on *their* way, they came unto a certain water: and the eunuch said, See, *here is* water; what doth hinder me to be baptized? And Philip said, If thou believest with all thine heart, thou mayest. And he answered and said, I believe that Jesus Christ is the Son of God."

(Acts 8:35 – 37)

"And brought them out, and said, Sirs, what must I do to be saved? And they said, Believe on the Lord Jesus Christ, and thou shalt be saved, and thy house."

(Acts 16:30 – 31)

"That if thou shalt confess with thy mouth the Lord Jesus, and shalt believe in thine heart that God hath raised Him from the dead, thou shalt be saved."

(Romans 10:9)

"For whosoever shall call upon the name of the Lord shall be saved."

(Romans 10:13)

"Whosoever shall confess that Jesus is the Son of God, God dwelleth in him, and he in God."
(1 John 4:16)

Another passage I would like to touch on is when Peter was walking with Jesus on the water. <u>**Not**</u> because it shows Peter's salvation, but it's a very good picture of how are lives are when we get saved. Observe:

"But when he saw the wind boisterous, he was afraid; and beginning to sink, he cried, saying, Lord, save me. And immediately Jesus stretched forth *His* hand, and caught him,"
(Matthew 14:30 – 31a)

Again, just to make sure we're all on the same page, we're just looking at this passage to get an idea of what salvation is like portrayed in a physical analogy. Because none of us see any physical reaction when a person gets saved. To clarify, <u>**Peter was already a saved man in this instance**</u>.[86] He was only in physical danger.

Now that we've established that, imagine yourself in Peter's place. You are on the unstable and boisterous waves of life, and you're sinking. You're drowning in sin. You desperately need help. You will die if someone doesn't bring you aid. You know

---

86. See Luke 5:8 – 11

who to turn to in this moment. You cry out to Jesus, "Lord, save me!" And just like that, Jesus reaches out and catches you. He pulls you back up out of the waters that were about to overwhelm you. In this analogy, Peter knew Jesus could save him. He believed that Jesus was able to save him, and he cried out for salvation. That, dear reader, is all we have to do as lost sinners.

We don't need to do any grand works. We don't need to become some religious brainiac. All we need to do in order to be saved is first believe and then call out for it. See, because you won't cry out for help to someone who you know can't help you. Peter did not call out to any of the other Apostles for help. He knew they wouldn't be able to help him. Instead, he was convinced that Jesus could and Jesus did.

So, call out to God. Ask for His cleansing salvation. It doesn't need to be a certain prayer. It doesn't need to have spiritual jargon in it. It doesn't need to be done in a church or in a specific place. God makes this incredibly simple and easy for us. All we need to do is believe and call out.

6. Follow Jesus' Teachings

This is not a step of salvation. By step 5, a person is saved, but I felt that this needed to be added to show what someone does after salvation. So this is more of a post-step of salvation. What we do after salvation is follow the commands that Jesus gave us:

"Then said Jesus unto His disciples, If any *man* will come after Me, let him deny himself, and take up his cross, and follow Me."
(Matthew 24:16)

That first means that we have to know what the Bible says, because, "All scripture *is* given by inspiration of God, and *is* profitable for doctrine, for reproof, for correction, for instruction in righteousness:" (2 Timothy 3:16). So, read your Bible. And they are many things that Jesus said, so we'll just elaborate on the major one:

"Go ye therefore, and teach all nations, baptizing them in the name of the Father, and of the Son, and of the Holy Ghost: Teaching them to observe all things whatsoever I have commanded you: and, lo, I am with you alway, *even* unto the end of the world. Amen."
(Matthew 28:19 – 20)[87]

"But ye shall receive power, after that the Holy Ghost is come upon you: and ye shall be witnesses unto Me both in Jerusalem, and in all Judaea, and in Samaria, and unto the uttermost part of the earth."
(Acts 1:8)

---

87. For confusion on this verse concerning whether or not someone has to be baptized in order to be saved, see "Chapter Four: Baptism – Salvation and Baptism."

If we had no further purpose after getting saved, one might think we would just "poof" into heaven after salvation, but we're not because we have a mission. Our mission is really two-fold but they go hand in hand:

1. Glorify God.

2. Witness to the lost so that they may get saved.

Glorifying God is a far more generic mission, but it is commanded in the Scriptures:

"Let us hear the conclusion of the whole matter: Fear God, and keep His commandments: for this *is* the whole *duty* of man."[88]
(Ecclesiastes 12:13)

"For ye are bought with a price: therefore glorify God in your body, and in your spirit, which are God's."
(1 Corinthians 6:20)

However, the more specific mission for the Christian would be reaching out to the lost to bring them to Jesus. This, in turn, also glorifies God, and it's always good motivation to remember

---

88. The Hebrew word for "fear" here is "יָרֵא" (pronounced "*yaw-ray*"), which means "revere."

where you would be had not the message of salvation reached your ears. People are needing to hear the Gospel. You cannot tell the wrong person. If the person is lost, they need to hear it. If the person is saved, they need to be reminded of it.

Eternal Security

Another highly debated topic – "Does salvation last forever or do you need to continually get saved after you sin?" First off, the words "eternal" and "everlasting" in verses such as John 3:16 and Romans 6:23 in of themselves connote that salvation cannot be lost. However, for those who aren't fully certain of that, allow me to provide the Bible verses that support the fact that once a person is saved, that person is always saved:

"My sheep hear My voice, and I know them, and they follow Me: And I give unto them eternal life; and they shall never perish, <u>neither shall any _man_ pluck them out of My hand</u>. My Father, which gave _them_ me, is greater than all; and <u>no _man_ is able to pluck _them_ out of My Father's hand</u>."
(John 10:27 – 29)

"In whom ye also _trusted,_ after that ye heard the word of truth, the gospel of your salvation: in whom also after that ye believed, <u>ye were sealed with that holy Spirit</u> of promise,

Which is the earnest of our inheritance until the redemption of the purchased possession, unto the praise of his glory."
(Ephesians 1:13 – 14)

Imagine you catch a fly in your hand. A measly, little housefly. One of its fly buddies sees what happened and latches onto your hand. It, through sheer force, pries your hand open to set his friend free. Does that ever happen? Of course not! That's laughable! No fly would be able to take another fly out of a human hand. How much more so could a human being forcibly take someone else out of God's hand? Including *one's self*. Going back to the fly analogy, imagine that you catch a fly. And then, all of a sudden, that fly pushes against your fingers and muscles its way out by itself! Is that possible? No. It's ridiculous and comical to even think about it. We have less chance of taking ourselves out of the God's hand than that fly does, and that's just considering one hand.[89] Jesus mentions His hand, the Father's hand, and then being sealed with the Spirit. Going back to the fly example one last time, imagine you catch a fly in one hand. Then, you cover that hand with your other hand and then someone comes up and wraps duct tape all around both hands. Is that fly getting out? No, and neither are we getting out of God's hand, Jesus' hand and the sealing of the Spirit once we are saved.

---

89. I understand that Jesus' hand *is* God's hand, but for the sake of the analogy, please humor me.

A further question concerning those who say you can make yourself unsaved is why would you *want* to? Why would you want to take yourself out of God's hand? Why would you want to lose your salvation? Those who say, "I was saved, but I don't want to be saved anymore" may not have been saved in the first place. Because once you are saved, you have the Holy Spirit inside you, confirming that the Bible is truth and that faith in Jesus Christ is the only true way.

Some people like to use the following verses to "disprove" eternal security:

"But he that shall endure unto the end, the same shall be saved."
(Matthew 24:13)

"But wilt thou know, O vain man, that faith without works is dead?"
(James 2:20)

Allow me to explain what these verses are really referring to. In Matthew 24:13, Jesus is talking about the Tribulation. This is shown by the beginning of the chapter:

"And as He sat upon the mount of Olives, the disciples came unto Him privately, saying, Tell us, when shall these things

be? and what *shall be* <u>the sign of Thy coming, and of the end</u>
<u>of the world</u>?"
(Matthew 24:3)

Then, Jesus expounds on how death for Christians will be
very prominent:

"Then shall they deliver you up to be afflicted, and shall kill
you: and ye shall be hated of all nations for My name's sake."
(Matthew 24:9)

So, with the context of the verse, Jesus is simply saying that
those who make it to the end of the Tribulation will be saved, as in
physically saved. Not spiritually in this sense.

As for James 2:20, James is not saying that you have to add
works to faith in order to be saved. What he's saying is that faith
will produce a desire in you to do good works. So, if you do no
good works or have no desire for them after having faith in Jesus,
it shows that perhaps there was no faith to begin with. Your faith
gets you saved; your works reveal that you got saved.

Furthermore, it's always good to have Scripture interpret
Scripture. By that I mean if there is a certain way you can take a
verse that doesn't match up with the rest of the Bible, that means

that it doesn't mean that. The Bible doesn't contradict itself. We just often times are not understanding it correctly.

Other verses that back eternal security:

"All that the Father giveth Me shall come to Me; and him that cometh to Me I will in no wise cast out."
(John 6:37)

"For I am persuaded, that neither death, nor life, nor angels, nor principalities, nor powers, nor things present, nor things to come, Nor height, nor depth, nor any other creature, shall be able to separate us from the love of God, which is in Christ Jesus our Lord."
(Romans 8:38 – 39)

"Now He which stablisheth us with you in Christ, and hath anointed us, *is* God; Who hath also sealed us, and given the earnest of the Spirit in our hearts."
(2 Corinthians 1:21 – 22)

"He that hath the Son hath life; *and* **he that hath not the Son of God hath not life. These things have I written unto you that believe on the name of the Son of God; that ye may know that ye have eternal life, and that ye may believe on the name of the Son of God."**
(1 John 5:12 – 13)

"Whosoever"

Anyone can come to salvation. Anyone. It doesn't matter on gender, age, ethnicity, types of sin, or anything else you can think of. Anyone can be saved by coming to Jesus. It is not based on a certain elect group of people that God chooses. Any prejudiced reason you can fathom in your mind does not disqualify anyone from getting saved. Observe:

"Whosoever therefore shall confess Me before men, him will I confess also before My Father which is in heaven."
(Matthew 10:32)

"That whosoever believeth in Him should not perish, but have eternal life. For God so loved the world, that He gave His only begotten Son, that whosoever believeth in Him should not perish, but have everlasting life."
(John 3:15 – 16)

313

"Jesus said unto her, I am the resurrection, and the life: he that believeth in Me, though he were dead, yet shall he live: And whosoever liveth and believeth in Me shall never die. Believest thou this?"
(John 11:25 – 26)

"I am come a light into the world, that whosoever believeth on Me should not abide in darkness."
(John 12:46)

"And it shall come to pass, *that* whosoever shall call on the name of the Lord shall be saved."
(Acts 2:21)

"For the scripture saith, Whosoever believeth on Him shall not be ashamed. For there is no difference between the Jew and the Greek: for the same Lord over all is rich unto all that call upon Him. For whosoever shall call upon the name of the Lord shall be saved."
(Romans 10:11 – 13)

"Whosoever believeth that Jesus is the Christ is born of God: and every one that loveth Him that begat loveth Him also that is begotten of Him."
(1 John 5:1)

The word for "whosoever" here is "πᾶς" (pronounced "pas") means "all," "any," and "every." Given the amount of verses that state this, it's rather surprising at the amount of people who are convinced that there are some people in the world who can't be saved, even if they want to be.

Other Points

<u>Praying for the Lost's Salvation</u>

This may be a no-brainer, but we ought to pray for those who have not accepted Jesus Christ as their Saviour. Yes, we should actively work to witness to others, but prayer should be partnered with that. It is ultimately the Holy Spirit that draws the lost to Christ. We are just tools to assist in that. For that person that is on your heart, whether it be a family member, friend, co-worker, classmate, teacher, or any other relationship, you ought to keep them in your prayers regularly. Jesus commanded this and Paul demonstrated this:

"Therefore said He unto them, The harvest truly *is* great, but the labourers *are* few: pray ye therefore the Lord of the harvest, that He would send forth labourers into His harvest."
(Luke 10:2)

"Brethren, my heart's desire and prayer to God for Israel is, that they might be saved."
(Romans 10:1)

The Bible does not encourage praying for someone after they have died, however. Once someone has passed from this life, their opportunity is up. Either they were saved or they were lost and they will meet God with that status:

"And as it is appointed unto men once to die, but after this the judgment:"
(Hebrews 9:27)

Summary

- A person must first realize they are in need of Christ's salvation in order to want salvation. Use the Ten Commandments to demonstrate how we miss the mark. (Exodus 20:1 – 17, James 2:10)
- The Bible teaches there is only one way to salvation, not multiple. (John 14:6, Acts 4:12, 1 Timothy 2:5)
- The steps of salvation are these:
  - 1. God is holy and cannot tolerate sin. (Isaiah 5:16, 1 Peter 1:15 – 16, 1 John 1:5)
  - 2. You are a sinner and worthy of God's wrath. (Romans 3:23, 1 John 1:8)

- 3. Jesus paid our sin debt on the cross. (Isaiah 53:3 – 5, Romans 5:8, Ephesians 1:7)
- 4. Repent; change your thinking that results in a change of action. (Mark 1:15, Luke 13:5)
- 5. Place faith in Jesus Christ. (John 3:16, Acts 2:21, Romans 10:9)
- 6. Follow Jesus' Teachings and witness to the lost. This is not a requirement for salvation, just what you ought to do after being saved. (Matthew 28:19 – 20)

- Once you're saved, you're *eternally* saved. You cannot lose it. (John 10:27 – 29, Ephesians 1:13 – 14)
- *Anyone* can be saved as long as they accept Jesus' gift of salvation. (Romans 10:11 – 13, 1 John 5:1)
- We ought to pray for those who are not saved, but after they die, praying for them is useless. Praying for the dead is not a biblical teaching. (Luke 10:2, Romans 10:1, Hebrews 9:27)

CHAPTER TWELVE

TATTOOS, PIERCINGS, AND CUTTINGS

Introduction

I'll not spend too much time on this topic. A good rule of thumb is to talk much about what the Bible talks much about and to talk little what the Bible talks little about; and in the Bible, tattoos, cuttings, and piercings are not addressed very often. But it does have something to say, so I'll get right to it.

What Does the Bible Say?

The Direct Command

"Ye shall not make any cuttings in your flesh for the dead, nor print any marks upon you: I *am* the LORD."
(Leviticus 19:28)

Here it is, clear and plain. Nothing obscure or complicated about it. I know what everyone is thinking, though: "Why?" And it's not wrong to ask why. Now, I don't know all of what was in God's mind when He gave this commandment to Moses, but I do have a theory.

You're wonderful as you are. Many people don't like how they look for various reasons. Just think of this when those negative thoughts hit you: you are a creation of God. Now, are you perfect? No. You're a sinner that lives in a sinful world. The curse of sin brings negative aspects upon our bodies, such as deformities, physical ailments and imperfections, wear with age, degenerate features, etc. So, no, you are not perfect. You will never be perfect in this life. But there are many lessons we can find when it comes to being content with our appearance and not trying to "improve" ourselves. Think of all the people in the Bible that God used who weren't picture perfect:

- **Leah**. Leah is called "tender eyed" in the Bible (Genesis 29:17). Tender eyed basically means "weak to the eyes," ergo she was more on the ugly side. However, Rachel was beautiful, and with both of them having the same husband, Leah was certainly the lesser liked of the two.[90] However, it was through Leah that came most of Jacob's children. She gave birth to Reuben, Simeon, Levi, Judah, Isaachar, Zebulun, and Dinah. It was through Leah that Judah, the kingly line of Israel came. David came from the line of Judah, and our Lord, Jesus Christ, came from the line of Judah, Leah's son.

---

90. This is not necessarily just because Rachel was more beautiful. Jacob loved Rachel from the very beginning and never intended to marry Leah. Laban had tricked Jacob into marrying both Leah and Rachel (Genesis 29:18 – 28).

- **Paul**. Paul was believed to have some sort of physical ailment. Most people attribute it as a problem that dealt with his eyesight, but there are some beliefs that Paul was balding, shorter than the average person, or even bow-legged. Of course, he may have been none of these things, but if he did deal with such things, God still greatly used him to spread the Gospel throughout the world.

- **Jesus**. Now, I know that many people are probably thinking "That doesn't count. Jesus probably chose how He looked," but that's not necessarily true. See, Jesus continually relied on His Father for everything. When Jesus robed Himself in human flesh, He temporarily put off certain of His attributes so that He might be our example in that we must rely constantly on God for everything. That being said, Jesus' looks probably originated from Mary's genetics, being born from her. If there was any choosing of what He looked like, I doubt Jesus Himself did so. Rather, it would have been God the Father who deemed what God the Son looked like.[91] One thing we know for certain is that no one ever looked at Jesus and, from His appearance, immediately thought "This has to be the Messiah." Meaning that Jesus was probably very average looking. For you and I, that's no big deal, but for the Almighty Creator of the universe that existed before time did,

---

91. I know it's confusing. We, as finite beings, are unable to fully understand the Trinity of God.

that's quite the humility. Jesus should have been someone quite spectacular to see, but He humbled himself to a lowly, regular appearance at best. Yet, He did extraordinary things. He did the greatest works in all of history. All while having an average appearance. Some go so far as to say that Isaiah 53:2 describes the actual physical appearance of Jesus:

"For He shall grow up before Him as a tender plant, and as a root out of a dry ground: He hath no form nor comeliness; and when we shall see Him, *there is* no beauty that we should desire Him."
(Isaiah 53:2)[92]

Other Points

Their Origins and Affiliations

Tattoos, piercings, and cuttings in the skin have been around since ancient times. In those days, they always were a result of pagan religious practices or tribal affiliation. Even today, tribal affiliation is still very much a part of tattoos. How many street gangs have their members get tattoos in order to show their association? Or just consider the cast from The Lord of the Rings.

---

92. Now, Isaiah may not have been speaking about the literal appearance of Jesus. To be perfectly candid, I have trouble with the book of Isaiah sometimes and I'm altogether unsure if he's speaking about Jesus' literal appearance or using some sort of poetic language for a picture of something else. I would urge you to study it out for yourself.

Ian McKellen (Gandalf), Viggo Mortensen (Aragorn), Orlando Bloom (Legolas), Elijah Wood (Frodo), Sean Astin (Sam), Dominic Monaghan (Merry), Billy Boyd (Pippin), Sean Bean (Boromir) and Brett Beattie (Gimli's stunt double)[93] all got matching tattoos since they were the members of the Fellowship of the Ring. Why did they do this? Out of affiliation of what they were all a part of.

That being considered, we as Christians ought to be associated with Christ. Rather than taking a mark in our skin, Christ would rather that we don't mark ourselves and show our affiliation through something that speaks much louder than a bunch of ink: living the Christian life.

Their Focus

When it comes to art, the main aspect is to look at it. Painters want you to *look* at their art; sculptors want you to *look* at their art; sketch-artists want you to *look* at their art; and when it comes to people with tattoos, piercings, and whatnot, they typically consider it all to be art on their body like they are a canvas to be painted on. That's the thing. What is the message they are sending? "Look at me, look at me, look at me." As we discussed in "Modesty," this mindset has the essence of pride and

---

93. John Rhys-Davies, the actor that played Gimli, declined to get a tattoo, so his size double/stunt double got one instead. John Rhys-Davies has not spoken much as to why he did not get one, but he has reportedly joked that Brett was more worthy of getting one since he did all the dangerous things.

selfishness about it. Of course, God has no association with either of those attributes. The Christian is always to direct attention to Christ and not to one's self. This applies with more than just tattoos, piercings, and cuttings, because we can try to get everyone to look at us rather than look at our God. However, with the subject at hand, this tends to be the thing that comes to mind the most when people say that they want to make themselves a work of art.

<u>Summary</u>

- God commanded against marking or cutting one's skin (Leviticus 19:28).
- You are made wonderful as you are and don't need to "improve" yourself with markings.
- They deal with affiliation and not the affiliation of God.
- They come from a "look at me!" mindset.

CHAPTER THIRTEEN

TEMPTATION

Introduction

In this book, there are a slew of sins that could be crippling temptations in someone's life. Sometimes it's not necessarily enough to know something is wrong. There are many of us that are enticed into committing sins while we're very aware that they're wrong. So, I felt it was necessary and appropriate to elaborate on how to combat temptation when those times come.

What Does the Bible Say?

Our Perfect Example

"Then was Jesus led up of the Spirit into the wilderness to be tempted of the devil. And when He had fasted forty days and forty nights, He was afterward an hungred. And when the tempter came to Him, he said, If Thou be the Son of God, command that these stones be made bread. But He answered and said, It is written, Man shall not live by bread alone, but by every word that proceedeth out of the mouth of God. Then the devil taketh Him up into the holy city, and setteth Him on a pinnacle of the temple, And saith unto Him, If Thou be the Son of God, cast thyself down: for it is written, He shall give

His angels charge concerning thee: and in *their* hands they shall bear thee up, lest at any time thou dash thy foot against a stone. Jesus said unto him, It is written again, Thou shalt not tempt the Lord thy God. Again, the devil taketh Him up into an exceeding high mountain, and sheweth Him all the kingdoms of the world, and the glory of them; And saith unto Him, All these things will I give Thee, if Thou wilt fall down and worship me. Then saith Jesus unto him, Get thee hence, Satan: for it is written, Thou shalt worship the Lord thy God, and Him only shalt thou serve. Then the devil leaveth Him, and, behold, angels came and ministered unto Him."

(Matthew 4:1 – 11)

There are many things in this passage that I'd love to go over, but I'm going to focus just on the temptation aspect. When it comes to the nature of Satan and his tactics, that will be covered more heavily in Volume Two of Baptist Apologetics.

Satan threw at Jesus all of the things that Jesus wanted. First, it was simply food because of Jesus' lengthy fast. Secondly, Satan went a little deeper and waved acceptance in front of Jesus' face. It was true that Jesus wanted acceptance of the people, though that was not His mission. His mission was to start the first New Testament church, fulfill the Old Testament Law, die on the cross for our sins, and rise from the dead. If He had been accepted by chief priests and scribes, it could have been that He would not

325

have gone to the cross. Thirdly, Satan offered Jesus the world. He offered Jesus a ceasefire of the constant war that had been between them for millennia. Satan would willingly give over all of the kingdoms of the Earth and Jesus would not have to go to the cross. We know that Jesus wanted to avoid the cross:

"And He went a little further, and fell on His face, and prayed, saying, O my Father, if it be possible, let this cup pass from Me: nevertheless not as I will, but as Thou *wilt*."
(Matthew 26:39)

Honestly, who wouldn't want to avoid the cross? It was a horrible way to die. So, these temptations were real with Jesus,[94] but look at what He did to combat them:

"But He answered and said, It is written, Man shall not live by bread alone, but by every word that proceedeth out of the mouth of God."
(Matthew 4:4)

"Jesus said unto him, It is written again, Thou shalt not tempt the Lord thy God."
(Matthew 4:7)

---

94. That is not to say that Jesus could have sinned. He was all God and therefore, could not have existed with sin. His nature was impeccable.

"Then saith Jesus unto him, Get thee hence, Satan: for it is written, Thou shalt worship the Lord thy God, and Him only shalt thou serve."

(Matthew 4:10)

These are all passages from Deuteronomy. Deuteronomy 8:3, 6:16, and 6:13. So, in those dire moments of temptation, Jesus went back to the Bible. If our Saviour, who could not sin, quoted Scripture in the face of temptation, how much more should we? This is why it is important to memorize Bible verses that help us against our besetting sins.

Our Way of Escape

"There hath no temptation taken you but such as is common to man: but God *is* faithful, who will not suffer you to be tempted above that ye are able; but will with the temptation also make a way to escape, that ye may be able to bear *it*."

(1 Corinthians 10:13)

This verse has been a particular help to me throughout my life. It points out truths that are very beneficial to know:

1. **Others have faced the very temptation you struggle with.**
    ("There hath no temptation taken you but such as is common to man...")

One of the tactics of Satan is to make you feel like you're alone or that you are different from everyone. This is to lead you to the idea that no one can help you with this. Many predators in the animal kingdom try to get their prey to separate from the rest of the herd. A few lionesses can't take down a herd of water buffalo, but one? Much more doable. The same is true of Satan. If he separates you from the help of other Christians, you're far easier to take down. Realize that you are not alone and that you can get help from other Christians. Another good verse to reference would be Proverbs 11:14.

2. **God will not allow a temptation come your way that you will not be able to handle.** ("...God *is* faithful, who will not suffer you to be tempted above that ye are able...")

There is a wonderful truth that Satan cannot do *anything* without first getting permission from God. We know this from the first two chapters of Job. So, every temptation that Satan throws at you has first been stamped with God's approval. That means that He's not going to give you a test that you absolutely cannot pass. Now, this is not to say that God will allow temptations that you can handle all by yourself. No, He will allow temptations that you can handle *with His help*.

3. **<u>God always gives a way to escape.</u>** ("...but will with the temptation also make a way to escape, that ye may be able to bear *it*.")

Whenever in the trouble of temptation, God always gives a way to get out of it. Joseph did this by literally getting himself out:

"And it came to pass about this time, that *Joseph* went into the house to do his business; and *there was* none of the men of the house there within. And she caught him by his garment, saying, Lie with me: and he left his garment in her hand, and fled, and got him out."
(Genesis 39:11 – 12)

A good rule to live by when it comes to your specific temptations is to not be around them or not be alone with them. I recognize that doesn't apply to every situation or temptation, but if you are addicted to gambling, don't hang around a casino. If you have issues with pornography, don't allow yourself unbridled access to the internet. If you have a drinking problem, don't go to a bar. That's a bit of a side tangent to God's way of escape, but the two are connected. Because many times, in order to find that way of escape, we need to be determined in our minds and hearts to not sin against God *before* the temptation arrives. If we are not, the likeliness of us falling to the temptation increases greatly.

Think of it this way: you are given the opportunity to [insert your given temptation]. It is something you really want. If you're going to decide in that moment, you're very vulnerable to your desires. It's not wise, and it's often time the way that Christians fall. No, you need to make that decision prior to the temptation and then stick to it when it arrives.

Another thing that must be noted about the way of escape is that it takes work on our part. It's not just a "Get Out of Temptation Free" card. Observe:

"But Daniel purposed in his heart that he would not defile himself with the portion of the king's meat, nor with the wine which he drank: therefore he requested of the prince of the eunuchs that he might not defile himself. Now God had brought Daniel into favour and tender love with the prince of the eunuchs. And the prince of the eunuchs said unto Daniel, I fear my lord the king, who hath appointed your meat and your drink: for why should he see your faces worse liking than the children which *are* of your sort? then shall ye make *me* endanger my head to the king. Then said Daniel to Melzar, whom the prince of the eunuchs had set over Daniel, Hananiah, Mishael, and Azariah, Prove thy servants, I beseech thee, ten days; and let them give us pulse to eat, and water to drink. Then let our countenances be looked upon before thee, and the countenance of the children that eat of the

portion of the king's meat: and as thou seest, deal with thy servants. So he consented to them in this matter, and proved them ten days. And at the end of ten days their countenances appeared fairer and fatter in flesh than all the children which did eat the portion of the king's meat. Thus Melzar took away the portion of their meat, and the wine that they should drink; and gave them pulse."[95]

(Daniel 1:8 – 16)

Daniel could have easily said "Well, I tried" after being told no from the prince of the eunuchs and then follow along with eating the king's meat that was forbidden by the law, but he didn't. He persevered and went the hard route rather than just give in to what was easy, and the Lord blessed and provided a way of escape.

Prayer

I love it when my kids ask for my help. When they quietly and pleadingly ask for me to get a certain toy down from some high place that they can't reach, and I love the gratitude that comes afterwards. Big smiles and "thank you!"'s. I love it. I'm sure that our Lord does, too, when we come and ask Him for help.

---

95. I recognize that this may not have been as much of a temptation situation for Daniel. After all, he had been forbidden from the law to eat this meat for his entire life, so he didn't exactly know what he was missing; but there certainly was pressure on Daniel to not make a fuss and do what everyone else was doing, as well as other tempting factors involved in this.

Help to resist temptation. Help to have victory over temptation. When we do triumph over it, I'm sure God enjoys the big smiles and "thank You!"s that come His way. We need help from our Father to reach that which we cannot, to use the analogy. Go through these verses about prayer with the mindset of going to God for help in the midst of temptation:

"*The righteous* cry, and the LORD heareth, and delivereth them out of all their troubles."
(Psalms 34:17)

"Ask, and it shall be given you; seek, and ye shall find; knock, and it shall be opened unto you: For every one that asketh receiveth; and he that seeketh findeth; and to him that knocketh it shall be opened. Or what man is there of you, whom if his son ask bread, will he give him a stone? Or if he ask a fish, will he give him a serpent? If ye then, being evil, know how to give good gifts unto your children, how much more shall your Father which is in heaven give good things to them that ask Him?"[96]
(Matthew 7:7 – 11)

_____

96. This does not mean that God will give you everything you ask for. Just like a normal parent won't give his or her child everything the child asks for.

"And forgive us our sins; for we also forgive every one that is indebted to us. <u>And lead us not into temptation; but deliver us from evil.</u>"[97]

(Luke 11:4)

"Be careful for nothing; but in every thing by prayer and supplication with thanksgiving let your requests be made known unto God."

(Philippians 4:6)

As we spoke of earlier, God gives a way of escape. Going to Him in prayer while you are being tempted may in of itself be the escape. Let us not be so proud to think that we can handle temptations ourselves (we can't) or to think that we ought not involve God in our problems. He is willing and eager to help. He only waits for you to ask.

Summary

- Jesus used Scripture to combat temptation. We should do likewise (Matthew 4:1 – 11).
- You've never dealt with a temptation that no one else has. Seek godly individuals for help in overcoming (Proverbs 11:14).

---

97. This was in Jesus' model prayer for His disciples. This is not to say that God leads us into temptation. James 1:13 says "Let no man say when he is tempted, I am tempted of God: for God cannot be tempted with evil, neither tempteth He any man:"

- God will not allow a temptation to come your way that you cannot triumph over. However, you need His help to do so. God also provides a way of escape through every temptation (1 Corinthians 10:13).
- When in the midst of temptation, pray to the Lord for help (Psalms 34:17, Matthew 7:7 – 11).

CHAPTER FOURTEEN

THE TRIUNE GOD

Introduction

I must be transparent, you and I will not understand everything about I AM THAT I AM; but that makes sense, doesn't it? God, who is above all earthly knowledge and wisdom, created things we don't understand in ways that we don't understand. For instance, space. Our world just floats in space, revolving around the sun. How? I don't know. Or consider the water cycle. Water, in liquid form, evaporates into vapor form until it rains back down into liquid form again. How? Again, I don't know. The same could be said of the human mind, cellular structure, conception, the vastness of space, etc. I know there is probably some scientific explanation that someone could give to point out each step and how they happen. But how did that water get there in the first place for the water cycle? How did the world start revolving around the sun in the first place? Just because we can't fully understand something doesn't mean it doesn't exist. The same is true of God. Just because we can't logically explain every attribute about Him does not mean that they're not true. The need for proof for everything about God in order to believe it shows a disturbing lack of faith, and may I remind the reader:

"But without faith *it is* impossible to please *Him:* for he that cometh to God must believe that He is, and *that* He is a rewarder of them that diligently seek Him."
(Hebrews 11:6)

Attempting to be a Christian while replacing faith with human logic is not only unwise, but impossible. It's what leads people to come up with things like theistic evolution, which contradicts so much of what the Bible says. Trying to add worldly logic to the mix of Christianity only makes it harder to believe because God sometimes does things that don't add up. For instance, the feeding of the five thousand with just five loaves and two fishes. Every calculator on the planet will say that does not compute, but it did happen because God does the miraculous.

What Does the Bible Say?

The Trinity

God is three in one. God the Father, God the Son, and God the Holy Spirit. They are not three different Gods. Just one God, yet, at the same time, all three are fully God and not just a part of God, which makes our brains hurt a bit, but that's just how it is. It is above our mental capacity to understand how God can be three distinct persons, yet still just be one God. But we are not made to understand everything. As one man once said: "We are made to be followers, not understanders." Here are some verses to demonstrate that God is three and yet still one:

"And God said, Let Us make man in Our image, after Our likeness: and let them have dominion over the fish of the sea, and over the fowl of the air, and over the cattle, and over all the earth, and over every creeping thing that creepeth upon the earth."
(Genesis 1:26)

"And the LORD God said, Behold, the man is become as one of Us, to know good and evil: and now, lest he put forth his hand, and take also of the tree of life, and eat, and live for ever:"
(Genesis 3:22)

"Hear, O Israel: The LORD our God *is* one LORD:"
(Deuteronomy 6:4)

"I *am* the LORD, and *there is* none else, *there is* no God beside Me: I girded thee, though thou hast not known me:"
(Isaiah 45:5)

"And Jesus, when He was baptized, went up straightway out of the water: and, lo, the heavens were opened unto Him, and He saw the Spirit of God descending like a dove, and lighting

337

upon Him: And lo a <u>voice from heaven</u>, saying, This is my beloved Son, in whom I am well pleased."
(Matthew 3:16 – 17)[98]

"<u>I and *My* Father are one</u>. Then the Jews took up stones again to stone Him. Jesus answered them, Many good works have I shewed you from My Father; for which of those works do ye stone Me? The Jews answered Him, saying, For a good work we stone Thee not; but for blasphemy; and because that Thou, being a man, makest Thyself God."
(John 10:30 – 33)

The trinity of God has been likened to many things. The egg is probably the most popular. An egg has three parts to it, but is one entity. The egg has the shell, the yolk, and the white, but the analogy does fall apart some because the shell isn't also the full egg, whereas the three entities of God are all in themselves fully God. That is why I like using time as an example more often. Time has three parts to it: past, present, and future. Yet, they are all referred to as time. Past is fully time, present is fully time, and future is fully time. All three together are fully time as well.

Now, there are many people, organizations, and faiths out there that believe in God the Father, Jesus Christ, and the Holy

---

98. Jesus the Son on Earth, the Holy Spirit lighting upon Him, and God the Father speaking from heaven.

Spirit, but do not consider Jesus and the Holy Spirit to also be God. Some consider Jesus to be a prophet, a good man, or some kind of divine being, but not God. As for the Holy Spirit, some liken Him more as a force or a sensation, but not a personal being. First off, both were involved with Creation, as shown in Genesis 1:26, which we already looked at. God alone is the Creator. Angels were not involved in it because they were a part of Creation. Furthermore, God says the words, "Let Us make man in Our image, after Our likeness:" This refers to how mankind is made up of three parts – body, soul, and spirit. God was saying that man should be three parts just as He is three parts – Father, Son, and Holy Spirit. That in of itself demonstrates the Godhead of both Jesus and the Holy Spirit. However, for those who are looking for more concrete evidence, consider the following. For Jesus:

"But to us *there is but* one God, the Father, <u>of whom *are* all things, and we in Him</u>; and one Lord Jesus Christ, <u>by whom *are* all things, and we by Him</u>."
(1 Corinthians 8:6)

This verse is stating that both God the Father and Jesus Christ brought about all things. Only God can claim that all things came by Him.

"Looking for that blessed hope, and the glorious appearing of the great God and our Saviour Jesus Christ;"
(Titus 2:13)

The word for "God" here is the Greek word "θεός" (pronounced "theh'-os"), which means "deity" or "supreme divinity." We all recognize that God is the supreme divinity and deity of all Creation. That title is also being applied to Jesus. As for the Holy Spirit:

"But Peter said, Ananias, why hath Satan filled thine heart to lie to the Holy Ghost, and to keep back *part* of the price of the land? Whiles it remained, was it not thine own? and after it was sold, was it not in thine own power? why hast thou conceived this thing in thine heart? thou hast not lied unto men, but unto God."
(Acts 5:3 – 4)

The same word "θεός" is used here for "God." Peter is proclaiming to Ananias that lying to the Holy Spirit is the same as lying to God. Moreover, the Holy Spirit is indeed a person, not just a force or power. Consider these verses:

"And grieve not the holy Spirit of God, whereby ye are sealed unto the day of redemption."
(Ephesians 4:30)

340

"But God hath revealed *them* unto us by His Spirit: <u>for the Spirit searcheth all things</u>, yea, the deep things of God."
(1 Corinthians 2:10)

"The grace of the Lord Jesus Christ, and the love of God, and the <u>communion of the Holy Ghost,</u> *be* with you all. Amen."
(2 Corinthians 13:14)

You cannot grieve an impersonal force, nor does something without consciousness search or commune. If you still are not convinced at this point, I would urge you to search the Scriptures for yourself to find the answers.

Attributes of God

You know, when I first began this chapter, I was overwhelmed. I mean, I was trying to talk about the attributes of God. The eternal, all-knowing, omnipotent Creator and Saviour. How could I do Him justice in my little book? Honestly, I can't. So, I deeply encourage every reader to do his or her own studies of the Bible when it comes to our Lord, but I will do my best to convey what the Bible says concerning Him. Just know that I *cannot* cover everything.

After the previous subject of the trinity, we all might need a mental break to keep our brains from overloading (I know that I need one). So, instead of going really in depth with how each role (the Father, the Son, and the Spirit) has different aspects and attributes, I'm going to just do more of a blanket statement of applying them all to God in general when it comes to these attributes. I thank you for your understanding. Moreover, the attributes we touch on are ones that God has revealed to us. It is possible that God, being infinite, has attributes that we cannot comprehend and, therefore, are not revealed to us. Again, I'm not even going to cover every attribute that has been revealed to us. Just a few of the major ones.

Holiness: There are a great number of verses that proclaim God's holiness. Here are just a few:

"For I *am* the LORD your God: ye shall therefore sanctify yourselves, and ye shall be holy; for I *am* holy: neither shall ye defile yourselves with any manner of creeping thing that creepeth upon the earth. For I *am* the LORD that bringeth you up out of the land of Egypt, to be your God: ye shall therefore be holy, for I *am* holy."
(Leviticus 11:44 – 45)

"*There is* none holy as the LORD: for *there is* none beside Thee: neither *is there* any rock like our God."
(1 Samuel 2:2)

"Glory ye in His holy name: let the heart of them rejoice that seek the LORD."

(1 Chronicles 16:10)

"But Thou *art* holy, *O Thou* that inhabitest the praises of Israel."

(Psalms 22:3)

"But the LORD of hosts shall be exalted in judgment, and God that is holy shall be sanctified in righteousness."

(Isaiah 5:16)

"So will I make My holy name known in the midst of My people Israel; and I will not *let them* pollute My holy name any more: and the heathen shall know that I *am* the LORD, the Holy One in Israel."

(Ezekiel 39:7)

"For such an high priest became us, *who is* holy, harmless, undefiled, separate from sinners, and made higher than the heavens;"

(Hebrews 7:26)[99]

---

99. I didn't put the context, but Hebrews 7:22 makes it evident that this passage is talking about Jesus. I encourage the reader go through the context.

"But as He which hath called you is holy, so be ye holy in all manner of conversation; Because it is written, Be ye holy; for I am holy."
(1 Peter 1:15 – 16)

"And the four beasts had each of them six wings about *him;* and *they were* full of eyes within: and they rest not day and night, saying, Holy, holy, holy, Lord God Almighty, which was, and is, and is to come."
(Revelation 4:8)

Holiness can be defined as "being separate," "pure," "blameless," or "sanctified." It means something that is undefiled or without sin. So, God is completely without evil, but that also means that He cannot be in the presence of sin or evil. He cannot tolerate it or overlook it. It's like a clean, white glove. If you put that clean, white glove in a puddle of mud, it would no longer be clean nor white. God's holiness is a part of His nature. If He associated with sin, He would no longer be God. It would contradict who He is and He cannot do that. It's like someone asking you to turn your leg into a living duck. You can't do it. It contradicts the nature of the cells that make up your leg. It's just downright impossible. The same is true for God mixing with sin.

So, when Adam and Eve sinned, God could no longer fellowship with them and there was separation between them. It

344

has been that way until Jesus paid the price for all sin. The bill has been paid, and it was after that where redeemed sinners were allowed into heaven to fellowship with God once more. Jesus went to Abraham's bosom and led all those that had trusted in the Lord to heaven after He died on the cross.

Now, that explanation clears up some theories people have come up with throughout history, such as the blasphemous idea that God created sin. He did not. He *cannot*. It is completely impossible. The origin of sin began in an angel named Lucifer that later became known as Satan:

"How art thou fallen from heaven, O Lucifer, son of the morning! *how* **art thou cut down to the ground, which didst weaken the nations! For thou hast said in thine heart, I will ascend into heaven, I will exalt my throne above the stars of God: I will sit also upon the mount of the congregation, in the sides of the north: I will ascend above the heights of the clouds; I will be like the most High."**
(Isaiah 14:12 – 17)

This proud proclamation from Lucifer took place before Genesis 3 since he then tempted Eve to eat the forbidden fruit. Lucifer would not have done so until he had first sinned himself. The originator of sin is Satan, who then seduced Adam and Eve to sin as well, which brought sin into the world. God was not involved in sin's inception.

Another thing we can take from God's holiness is that this makes Him absolutely intolerable to sin. Imagine yourself in a restaurant. You order your favorite dish, whether it be a gourmet burger, tortellini soup, chicken a la king, chef salad, sushi, you name it. You wait excitedly for it to be brought out to you, but as the waiter brings you your food, you find a steaming pile of vomit on your plate. Vomit. Human regurgitation. What is your reaction? Something along the lines of "Blereghh! Get that away from me!" It's disgusting. It's putrid. It's abominable. That is probably a pretty good representation of how our sin is to God. Why do we think God would be okay with allowing our sin in His presence? Would you smear vomit all over yourself? No. So why would God? I bring all this up to lead to a couple of things:

1. Your sin is not okay.

No matter what it is. God is not going to overlook "small" sins at the end of your life. If you have *any* sin on your account (and you do), you are worthy to be cast out of His presence and into everlasting darkness. The only way to escape that destination is to be washed by the blood of Jesus Christ. That is when you can become holy in the eyes of the Father.[100]

---

100. More on this in Chapter Eleven: Salvation.

2. We can't define what is sin and what isn't sin

God is not only the Creator of all of existence but also the only holy Judge. As Creator, He made everything, so He gets to set the rules. As the only holy Judge, He defines what is right and what is wrong. We don't because we're fallen creatures. Sin permeates every part of our being now. We easily excuse our own sin as something permissible, while condemning others' sins. We have no right to say what is wrong and what is right because we are corrupt and biased. God is not. So, things that are being lauded as good or noble things nowadays such as abortion, homosexuality, suicide, gambling, sex outside of marriage, etc. are all still wrong, and you cannot make them right.

3. God is good[101]

A highly questioned topic throughout history, but since there is no sin in or with God, that means there is no evil with God. If there is no evil with God, that means that the only thing that God can be is goodness. So whether you love God or hate God, He is good. Not even considering Jesus on the cross and the gift of salvation, God is good (though He is also good because of those things as well). We all honestly know that if we take a look at all that He has given us. For your consideration, God gave you:

- Life

- His Word

---

101. More on this in the Goodness section of Attributes of God, as well as in Chapter Fifteen: Wrath, Love, and Other Enigmas – "Why do Bad Things Happen in Life if God is Good and in Control over Everything?"

- A family
- A body you can move around with
- A mind that you can comprehend complex things with
- Friends
- Food
- Nature and all the beautiful things in it
- Sleep
- A job
- Clothing
- Money

That list could go on forever. These are just a few things, and I know that there are some out there that don't have some of these things. Say someone was born with a broken body and cannot use it like the average person can. That is a result of sin, for with sin came sickness and corruption.

Love: All true, genuine love comes from God. It is our greatest need. Without love, people wither. If someone knows they are loved, they are able to endure anything, aren't they? Have you ever seen newlyweds that are just head-over-heels for each other? They're on top of the world! It's all because of love. There is an absolutely fantastic sermon from Rowland Road Baptist Church by Pastor John Yates titled "You are Always Loved" that really delves into God's love. I would recommend a listen. Observe how the Bible speaks of God's love:

"The LORD hath appeared of old unto me, *saying,* Yea, I have loved thee with an everlasting love: therefore with lovingkindness have I drawn thee."
(Jeremiah 31:3)

"*It is of* the LORD'S mercies that we are not consumed, because His compassions fail not. *They are* new every morning: great *is* Thy faithfulness. The LORD *is* my portion, saith my soul; therefore will I hope in Him."
(Lamentations 3:22 – 24)

"For God so loved the world, that He gave His only begotten Son, that whosoever believeth in Him should not perish, but have everlasting life."
(John 3:16)

"Greater love hath no man than this, that a man lay down his life for his friends."
(John 15:13)[102]

"But God commendeth His love toward us, in that, while we were yet sinners, Christ died for us."
(Romans 5:8)

---

102. The reason I put this in here is because Jesus would demonstrate this very thing in just a few chapters.

"Who shall separate us from the love of Christ? *shall* tribulation, or distress, or persecution, or famine, or nakedness, or peril, or sword? As it is written, For Thy sake we are killed all the day long; we are accounted as sheep for the slaughter. Nay, in all these things we are more than conquerors through Him that loved us. For I am persuaded, that neither death, nor life, nor angels, nor principalities, nor powers, nor things present, nor things to come, Nor height, nor depth, nor any other creature, shall be able to separate us from the love of God, which is in Christ Jesus our Lord."

(Romans 8:35 – 39)

"I am crucified with Christ: nevertheless I live; yet not I, but Christ liveth in me: and the life which I now live in the flesh I live by the faith of the Son of God, who loved me, and gave Himself for me."

(Galatians 2:20)

"Behold, what manner of love the Father hath bestowed upon us, that we should be called the sons of God: therefore the world knoweth us not, because it knew Him not."

(1 John 3:1)

"Beloved, let us love one another: for love is of God; and every one that loveth is born of God, and knoweth God. He that loveth not knoweth not God; for God is love. In this was

manifested the love of God toward us, because that God sent His only begotten Son into the world, that we might live through Him. Herein is love, not that we loved God, but that He loved us, and sent His Son *to be* the propitiation for our sins."

(1 John 4:7 – 10)

We need to reflect on how much God truly loves us. Because it's not like how a little girl has a crush on a boy in her class. It's not like how we love our favorite food. The best comparison to God's love that we can fathom is the love from a parent to a child. Have you ever seen a mother with her newborn baby? She *adores* that child. Her world completely revolves around that little baby. She was, just moments ago, in absolute agony. Yet, as soon as she holds that baby in her arms, she says things like, "It was all worth it" or "I'll take a dozen more." That was love for that child that makes all the pain seem like nothing. Have you ever seen a father who's kid is in danger? There was a story I once heard about a father in either Florida or Louisiana. His son was playing near the edge of a lake[103] and an alligator got a hold of him. His father saw it and, racing to where his boy was, he fought the alligator and was able to save his son from death. This ordinary man fought a large, carnivorous beast that could have easily killed him. He put himself at risk and went to great lengths to save his son because

---

103. Always use caution when playing near or in bodies of water near the gulf, especially with small children. Alligators are known to thrive down there and a great deal of people have been killed by alligator attacks.

351

he loves his child. Now, even the example of a parent's love is still flawed because we are imperfect. Parents don't always love their children as they ought to. And even the parents who love their children over the moon still don't perfectly represent how God feels about us because God's love is so much deeper, broader, and greater than we can ever grasp.

God did not need to do anything for us. Once Adam and Eve sinned, He could have just wiped out the human race, and He would have been just to do so. It would have been much easier that way. Instead, He took the hard road. He showed mercy, patience, kindness when multitudes of people throughout the ages wanted nothing to do with Him. He even died on a cross for us. This was a method of death that is presumed to be the **worst** way to die since it was slow suffocation combined with nails being driven into the wrists and ankles. The excruciating pain would have increased when the victim had to push up on those nails just in order to get a breath in. Now, if someone thinks there is a worse way to die, I won't be so dogmatic as to say there isn't, but this was *God* in the flesh. God did not have to go to such lengths for us. He is God! He shouldn't have to go a day without every luxury and comfort and good thing ever! He did not have to sully His hands with our filth and our wretchedness, but He did! He took all sin upon Himself! Why? Because of love! He loves you! He loves you too much to let you perish without the chance of saving you!

When we start to realize that and think upon that, it makes being His child all the more special. He did this for no other reason than this: He loves you. He loves you so much that He died for you. Never ever think that His love is not amazing. Because if we were in the same position, I promise you that none of us would have gone to such lengths. If we did, it would only be for those who love us in return. Not the ones who scorn us or ignore us or reject us, but God did this for even those who hate Him the most.

Omnipotence: "Omnipotent" comes from two words. "Omni," meaning "all" and "potent," meaning "having great power or effect." So "omnipotent/omnipotence" can be simply defined as "having all power," and God does. He possesses all power. This is demonstrated many times throughout the Bible. Creation is certainly a good place to start:

"In the beginning God created the heaven and the earth."
(Genesis 1:1)

"And God said, Let there be light: and there was light."
(Genesis 1:3)

"And God made two great lights; the greater light to rule the day, and the lesser light to rule the night: *He made* the stars also."
(Genesis 1:16)

"When I consider Thy heavens, the work of Thy fingers, the moon and the stars, which Thou hast ordained;"
(Psalms 8:3)

I would like to ask the reader to perform a little exercise after reading these few passages about God forming Creation. I want you to look around at nature. If you're inside, go to a window or walk outside. Just look around. Look at the sky. The clouds. The stars. Look at the trees, the grass. Feel the wind on your face, the warmth of the sun (***Don't*** look directly at the sun). Look at the ocean if you're near it. Listen to the soothing sounds of rainfall. The beauty of a gentle snowfall. The awe-inspiring brilliance of thunder and lightning. The calm magnificence of mountains. Look at all that God has made. Bask in it. There are many things we can talk about concerning God just from looking from His Creation, but the point I want to make in this section is this: God made all of that from *nothing*. There was nothing in the beginning until God created it. That means everything from the atom to the largest star we know. To bring those forth from nothing is *power*. Power beyond our imagination.

I was always impressed with people who had a great amount of authority over others, like a navy admiral. He tells his men to do stuff, and they do it without hesitation. Without question. That's some pretty impressive power, isn't it. But guess what? God does that with nothingness. He spoke and the nothingness

354

immediately obeyed without hesitation or question and manifested into *somethingness*. That is incredible, next-level power! Even more incredible is the fact that God created life where there was none:

"And the LORD God formed man *of* the dust of the ground, and breathed into his nostrils the breath of life; and man became a living soul."
(Genesis 2:7)

Frankenstein by Mary Shelley is probably one of the most well known stories about a mere man finding the secret to creating life. There's tons of other stories where humanity was finally able to achieve the impossible and create life, whether it was life just like ours or some kind of imitation in the case of AI and whatnot; but those are all fiction. Humanity has never and will never be able to form life. The closest we have come is robotics, but that isn't life. It's puppetry. Programming an object to do exactly what we tell it to. Only God has the power to actually create life. Even Satan, who is a very powerful being, does not have the ability to bring forth life. Only the omnipotent One does. The One who has *all* power.

There are so many other things we could discuss when it comes to God's omnipotence, but I believe the point has been made. Other things that demonstrate God's omnipotence would be salvation, the Flood, the plagues of Egypt, the fire coming down for Elijah on Mount Carmel, and multiple raising of the dead just to name a few. Other verses that demonstrate or speak about God's omnipotence:

"God *is* our refuge and strength, a very present help in trouble."
(Psalms 46:1)

"So shall My word be that goeth forth out of My mouth: it shall not return unto Me void, but it shall accomplish that which I please, and it shall prosper *in the thing* whereto I sent it."
(Isaiah 55:11)

"Ah Lord GOD! behold, Thou hast made the heaven and the earth by Thy great power and stretched out arm, *and* there is nothing too hard for Thee:"
(Jeremiah 32:17)

"And what *is* the exceeding greatness of His power to us-ward who believe, according to the working of His mighty power, Which He wrought in Christ, when He raised Him from the dead, and set *Him* at His own right hand in the heavenly *places,* Far above all principality, and power, and might, and dominion, and every name that is named, not only in this

world, but also in that which is to come: And hath put all *things* under His feet, and gave Him *to be* the head over all *things* to the church, Which is His body, the fulness of him that filleth all in all."
(Ephesians 1:19 – 23)

"For by Him were all things created, that are in heaven, and that are in earth, visible and invisible, whether *they be* thrones, or dominions, or principalities, or powers: all things were created by Him, and for Him: And He is before all things, and by Him all things consist."
(Colossians 1:16 – 17)

Omniscience: "Omniscience" comes from two words. "Omni," meaning "all" and "science," meaning "knowledge." So "omniscient/omniscience" can be simply defined as "having all knowledge." God is all-knowing. He would have to be in order to be God. First off, God made time. That means that He is outside of time. If He is outside of time, that means that there is no past, no present, and no future where He is. First off, we can't even fully comprehend that. Time is a part of our existence, so the absence of it is beyond our understanding. How is God in the past, present, and future all at once? I don't know, but He is. He *can* understand that. He knows and understands everything:

"Shall not God search this out? for He knoweth the secrets of the heart."
(Psalms 44:21)

"O LORD, thou hast searched me, and known *me.* Thou knowest my downsitting and mine uprising, thou understandest my thought afar off. Thou compassest my path and my lying down, and art acquainted *with* all my ways. For *there is* not a word in my tongue, *but,* lo, O LORD, thou knowest it altogether. Thou hast beset me behind and before, and laid thine hand upon me. *Such* knowledge *is* too wonderful for me; it is high, I cannot *attain* unto it."
(Psalms 139:1 – 6)

"He telleth the number of the stars; He calleth them all by *their* names."
(Psalms 147:4)

"For My thoughts *are* not your thoughts, neither *are* your ways My ways, saith the LORD. For *as* the heavens are higher than the earth, so are My ways higher than your ways, and My thoughts than your thoughts."
(Isaiah 55:8 – 9)

"He hath made the earth by His power, He hath established the world by His wisdom, and hath stretched out the heaven by His understanding."

(Jeremiah 51:15)

"Daniel answered and said, Blessed be the name of God for ever and ever: for wisdom and might are His: And He changeth the times and the seasons: He removeth kings, and setteth up kings: He giveth wisdom unto the wise, and knowledge to them that know understanding: He revealeth the deep and secret things: He knoweth what *is* in the darkness, and the light dwelleth with Him. I thank Thee, and praise Thee, O Thou God of my fathers, who hast given me wisdom and might, and hast made known unto me now what we desired of thee: for Thou hast *now* made known unto us the king's matter."

(Daniel 2:20 – 23)[104]

As God has all power to bring forth Creation, He also has all knowledge and wisdom. Going back to the concept of time, can you imagine the intricacies that would go into creating it? Or the water cycle? Or all of the mysteries within the human subconscious? Just take a single cell. That cell contains hundreds of thousands of parts that make up it's anatomy and is more

---

104. These verses, as well as Jeremiah 51:15 are also good verses for God's omnipotence.

complex than a supercomputer. God designed that![105] Which means He knows what makes it tick. The vastness of His knowledge and wisdom could not be contained in the largest galaxy of our universe. By the way, the universe? God knows everything about that, too. We'll never understand everything of what's out there, but He does. He also knows everything about you, as well. Including what you think, say, and do:

"And GOD saw that the wickedness of man *was* great in the earth, and *that* every imagination of the thoughts of his heart *was* only evil continually."

(Genesis 6:5)

"But the LORD said unto Samuel, Look not on his countenance, or on the height of his stature; because I have refused him: for *the LORD seeth* not as man seeth; for man looketh on the outward appearance, but <u>the LORD looketh on the heart</u>."

(1 Samuel 16:7)

"And thou, Solomon my son, know thou the God of thy father, and serve Him with a perfect heart and with a willing mind: <u>for the LORD searcheth all hearts, and understandeth all the imaginations of the thoughts</u>: if thou seek Him, He will be

---

105. That's also a good fact to use when combating evolution simply because the chances of all of those parts just happening to come together by themselves without a creative Designer are maddeningly remote.

found of thee; but if thou forsake Him, He will cast thee off for ever."
(1 Chronicles 28:9)

"And, behold, certain of <u>the scribes said within themselves,</u> This *man* blasphemeth. And <u>Jesus knowing their thoughts said, Wherefore think ye evil in your hearts</u>?"
(Matthew 9:3 – 4)

"And I saw the dead, small and great, stand before God; and the books were opened: and another book was opened, which is *the book* of life: <u>and the dead were judged out of those things which were written in the books, according to their works.</u>"
(Revelation 20:12)

Humbling and sobering, if you ask me. God knows what no one else knows about you. The thoughts you have that you dare not utter. The sins that you keep secret. Words that have never been heard by any human ear. That fact alone may drive many of us to praying for forgiveness, but it can be used in a positive light as well. For God knows your troubles that no one else seems to notice. God knows your pain and your fears and is there for you through them. He understands you when you feel like no one else does.[106] When you really think about it, wouldn't you rather have a God that knows everything more than a God who you have to bring up to speed with everything that's going on? I know I would want the omniscient One. It's a good thing that He is.

Omnipresence: "Omnipresent" comes from two words. "Omni," meaning "all" and "present," meaning "in a particular place." So "omnipresent/omnipresence" can be simply defined as "in all particular places." This one is probably the hardest to mentally grasp. All-powerful? Easy to understand. All-knowing? A simple concept. Everywhere at once?….What? But it is once again true about our Lord. It doesn't quite fully compute that someone's full entity can exist in Tokyo, but also in Shreveport, and also in Antartica, and also on the planet Jupiter, and also in heaven, and even also in hell. All of those places and more all at the same time. These Bible verses back this up:

"Whither shall I go from Thy spirit? or whither shall I flee from Thy presence? If I ascend up into heaven, Thou *art* there: if I make my bed in hell, behold, Thou *art there. If* I take the wings of the morning, *and* dwell in the uttermost

---

106. Note that I said when you *feel* like no one else understands you. Because many times there are plenty of people who do understand us, but it doesn't seem that way. This can often be a tactic of Satan to lure us away from others (especially other Christians), lure us towards people who "do understand us" but are ungodly, or drive us to depression.

parts of the sea; Even there shall Thy hand lead me, and Thy
right hand shall hold me."
(Psalms 139:7 – 10)

"The eyes of the LORD *are* in every place, beholding the evil
and the good."
(Proverbs 15:3)

"*Am* I a God at hand, saith the LORD, and not a God afar
off? Can any hide himself in secret places that I shall not see
him? saith the LORD. Do not I fill heaven and earth? saith
the LORD."
(Jeremiah 23:23 – 24)

"For where two or three are gathered together in My name,
there am I in the midst of them."
(Matthew 18:20)

Going through these verses really show that Jonah's flight
"from the presence of the LORD" was a hopeless cause. But how
many of us try that as well? We use the darkness of night or
solitary rooms to try and hide our sinful actions from God, but
God is right there with us. This, of course, is also a positive thing.
God is there with the Christians in China who are locked up in
prison for their beliefs. God is there for the lonely child whose
parents are going through a nasty divorce. God is right there with

you, no matter how alone you feel. In those times, remember verses such as this:

"For the LORD will not forsake His people for His great name's sake: because it hath pleased the LORD to make you His people."
(1 Samuel 12:22)[107]

Though your colleagues, friends, and even family may abandon you, God will not.

Faithfulness: This happens to be a perfect transition from what we were discussing at the end of Omnipresence. Faithfulness. The Hebrew words often used for "faithful" are "אֱמֶת" and "אָמַן" (pronounced "eh'-meth" and "aw-man'"). "אֱמֶת" can be defined as "stability" or "trustworthiness." "אָמַן" can be defined as "to be true," "to be permanent," or "to have assurance." Those definitions basically sum it all up. You can find stability in what God has said. You can trust God. He is true and permanent and you can have assurance in Him. God is faithful. He keeps His

107. It is true in the context of this verse that Israel is being spoken about, however, it can be applied to Gentile Christians as well. For Paul elaborated to the Galatians (comprised of mainly Gentile believers) that Jesus came to redeem them and that they might receive the adoption of sons (Galatians 4:4 – 7), meaning that they were brought into the family of God. It can be dangerous for Gentile believers to take promises that were spoken to Israel alone. All the same, this is not one of those instances because God is not saying that He will only not forsake Jewish believers, but will forsake Gentile believers. We who have called upon the name of Jesus Christ for salvation are the children of God, whether Jewish or Gentile.

promises, and He doesn't just do that to those who love Him and who follow Him. God is faithful to the unfaithful. Which is good because we are all unfaithful to God at some point in time. But God shows His faithfulness to us through His promise of Jesus' coming:

"And I will put enmity between thee and the woman, and between thy seed and her seed;[108] it shall bruise thy head, and thou shalt bruise His heel."
(Genesis 3:15)

"Therefore the Lord Himself shall give you a sign; Behold, a virgin shall conceive, and bear a son, and shall call His name Immanuel."
(Isaiah 7:14)

"Now the birth of Jesus Christ was on this wise: When as His mother Mary was espoused to Joseph, before they came together, she was found with child of the Holy Ghost. Then Joseph her husband, being a just *man,* and not willing to make her a publick example, was minded to put her away privily. But while he thought on these things, behold, the angel of the Lord appeared unto him in a dream, saying, Joseph, thou son of David, fear not to take unto thee Mary thy wife: for that

---

108. This reference's the fact that Jesus would come of a virgin, because women do not have seed. The seed comes from the man, but Jesus would have no earthly father.

which is conceived in her is of the Holy Ghost. And she shall bring forth a son, and thou shalt call His name JESUS: for He shall save His people from their sins. Now all this was done, that it might be fulfilled which was spoken of the Lord by the prophet, saying, Behold, a virgin shall be with child, and shall bring forth a son, and they shall call His name Emmanuel, which being interpreted is, God with us."
(Matthew 1:18 – 23)

That promise alone was kept for over thousands of years, not that it should be surprising. God is over time, after all. God was also faithful when He promised Abraham and Sarah a son, even when they faltered some:

"For all the land which thou seest, to thee will I give it, and to thy seed for ever. And I will make thy seed as the dust of the earth: so that if a man can number the dust of the earth, *then* shall thy seed also be numbered."
(Genesis 13:15 – 16)

"And Abram said, Lord GOD, what wilt Thou give me, seeing I go childless, and the steward of my house *is* this Eliezer of Damascus? And Abram said, Behold, to me Thou hast given no seed: and, lo, one born in my house is mine heir. And, behold, the word of the LORD *came* unto him, saying, This

shall not be thine heir; but he that shall come forth out of
thine own bowels shall be thine heir."
(Genesis 15:2 – 4)

"Now Sarai Abram's wife bare him no children: and she had
an handmaid, an Egyptian, whose name *was* Hagar. And Sarai
said unto Abram, Behold now, the LORD hath restrained me
from bearing: I pray thee, go in unto my maid; it may be that
I may obtain children by her. And Abram hearkened to the
voice of Sarai."
(Genesis 16:1 – 2)

"And God said unto Abraham, As for Sarai thy wife, thou
shalt not call her name Sarai, but Sarah *shall* her name *be.*
And I will bless her, and give thee a son also of her: yea, I will
bless her, and she shall be *a mother* of nations; kings of people
shall be of her. Then Abraham fell upon his face, and laughed,
and said in his heart, Shall *a child* be born unto him that is an
hundred years old? and shall Sarah, that is ninety years old,
bear? And Abraham said unto God, O that Ishmael might live
before thee! And God said, Sarah thy wife shall bear thee a
son indeed; and thou shalt call his name Isaac: and I will
establish My covenant with him for an everlasting covenant,
and with his seed after him."
(Genesis 17:15 – 19)

"And the LORD visited Sarah as He had said, and the LORD did unto Sarah as He had spoken. For Sarah conceived, and bare Abraham a son in his old age, at the set time of which God had spoken to him. And Abraham called the name of his son that was born unto him, whom Sarah bare to him, Isaac." (Genesis 21:1 – 3)

Note that I never said God would fulfill His promises when we think they should be. God has His own timetable and He follows that, not ours. It took multiple years for Abraham and Sarah to have a son, but it still came to pass.

God also told Abraham that the children of Israel would be in bondage to Egypt (the nation was not specifically mentioned, but the amount of time was), but they would not stay there. Sure enough, that came to pass:

"And He said unto Abram, Know of a surety that thy seed shall be a stranger in a land *that is* not theirs, and shall serve them; and they shall afflict them four hundred years; And also that nation, whom they shall serve, will I judge: and afterward shall they come out with great substance." (Genesis 15:13 – 14)

"And Pharaoh rose up in the night, he, and all his servants, and all the Egyptians; and there was a great cry in Egypt; for
368

there was not a house where *there was* not one dead. And he called for Moses and Aaron by night, and said, Rise up, *and* get you forth from among my people, both ye and the children of Israel; and go, serve the LORD, as ye have said. Also take your flocks and your herds, as ye have said, and be gone; and bless me also. And the Egyptians were urgent upon the people, that they might send them out of the land in haste; for they said, We *be* all dead *men*."
(Exodus 12:30 – 33)

Those are just three examples of the plethora of promises that God has made and has been faithful with. God is true. God is trustworthy. God keeps His promises. He sticks by His word. Here are some other verses about God's faithfulness:

"Know therefore that the LORD thy God, He *is* God, the faithful God, which keepeth covenant and mercy with them that love Him and keep His commandments to a thousand generations;"
(Deuteronomy 7:9)

"Righteous *art* Thou, O LORD, and upright *are* Thy judgments. Thy testimonies *that* Thou hast commanded *are* righteous and very faithful."
(Psalms 119:137 – 138)

"God *is* faithful, by whom ye were called unto the fellowship of His Son Jesus Christ our Lord."
(1 Corinthians 1:9)

"Faithful *is* He that calleth you, who also will do *it.*"
(1 Thessalonians 5:24)

"But the Lord is faithful, who shall stablish you, and keep *you* from evil."
(2 Thessalonians 3:3)

"*It is* a faithful saying: For if we be dead with *Him,* we shall also live with *Him:* If we suffer, we shall also reign with *Him:* if we deny *Him,* He also will deny us: If we believe not, *yet* He abideth faithful: He cannot deny Himself."
(2 Timothy 2:11 – 13)

"And we know that the Son of God is come, and hath given us an understanding, that we may know Him that is true, and we are in Him that is true, *even* in His Son Jesus Christ. This is the true God, and eternal life."
(1 John 5:20)

__Goodness:__ For this attribute, people either adamantly hold to it or fiercely reject it. One of the largest questions about God revolves around it: "If God is so good, why is there so much evil and suffering in the world?" That question will be expounded on further in "Wrath, Love, and Other Enigmas." However, I'll give a small piece of what is to come with that. Bad things happen as a result of other people, Satan, a sin-cursed world, or God's will. Because humanity has free will, God is not to blame for people's actions. Those are on them specifically. The same could be said of Satan. Disease and other ill-effects of the fall aren't God's fault, either. This sin-cursed world is a result of sin, which we are guilty of, not God.

Now, what about bad things that are allowed by God or that God directly puts into our lives? How can God still be good when He does that? Let's take the life of Joseph for example. Joseph was the favored child of Jacob. So much so that his other brothers hated him for it.[109] They sold him as a slave and Joseph ended up in Egypt. Joseph, after some time, was then falsely accused of sexually assaulting Potiphar's wife. He was thrown in the dungeon. Tell me, what had he done wrong to deserve all of that? Nothing. Did God directly do this to Joseph? No, that was on Joseph's brothers and Potiphar's wife. It was their actions that put Joseph where he was. So, why did God allow it to happen to him? Because of the terrible famine that was coming. God worked out Joseph's terrible situation to where Joseph was able to interpret the dream of Pharaoh and he moved from the prison to the palace.

---

109. This is why, parents, that you ought not have a favorite child among your children. Treat your kids equally. Love your kids equally.

He became the second most powerful man in the world at that time, and it was Joseph that stated this concerning the whole endeavor:

"But as for you, ye thought evil against me; *but* God meant it unto good, to bring to pass, as *it is* this day, to save much people alive."
(Genesis 50:20)

There aren't many I know who had an experience as hard as Joseph's. However, there's another in the Bible who had even more suffering, yet called God good: Job. Like Joseph, Job had done nothing worthy of the tragedy he received. The Bible states that he was "perfect and upright, and one that feared God, and eschewed evil." (Job 1:1) Yet, he lost all of his wealth, his children, and his health. To boot, he was labeled as a sinful man by his three friends. What was his initial response?

"Then Job arose, and rent his mantle, and shaved his head, and fell down upon the ground, and worshipped, And said, Naked came I out of my mother's womb, and naked shall I return thither: the LORD gave, and the LORD hath taken away; blessed be the name of the LORD."
(Job 1:20 – 21)

He responded with worship and praise. Does that mean that Job did not mourn or wonder why this was happening to him? Absolutely not. He struggled with this deeply and most of the rest of the book is about that. Furthermore, Job never found out the reason why this happened in his life, but how much of a benefit has the book of Job been to those who are going through suffering? Job's hardship has helped countless thousands who have lost family members, have come to financial ruin, who are dealing with sickness, etc. It has showed us today that the righteous do not always prosper and that hardships are not always the result of sin. Though Job received calamity, God allowed it for a greater good:[110]

"So the LORD blessed the latter end of Job more than his beginning: for he had fourteen thousand sheep, and six thousand camels, and a thousand yoke of oxen, and a thousand she asses. He had also seven sons and three daughters."

(Job 42:12 – 13)

I want to go to one last passage of a man that was able to say that God was good in the midst of suffering: Jeremiah the weeping prophet. He went through much turmoil as well. He was called to be a prophet when no one would listen. Jeremiah

---

110. That is *not* to say that the new children would be better than the original that died. The part where it says that Job was more blessed in the end is likely referring more to his wealth rather than to his children.

witnessed the destruction of Jerusalem by the Babylonians, as well as his people being taken into captivity. He wrote the book of Lamentations to mourn over all the great losses he had both seen and endured. Yet, in chapter three, there is a change:

"This I recall to my mind, therefore have I hope. *It is of* the LORD'S mercies that we are not consumed, because His compassions fail not. *They are* new every morning: great *is* Thy faithfulness. The LORD *is* my portion, saith my soul; therefore will I hope in Him. The LORD *is* good unto them that wait for Him, to the soul *that* seeketh Him. *It is* good that *a man* should both hope and quietly wait for the salvation of the LORD."
(Lamentations 3:21 – 26)

How could this man say that God is good after such devastation? It was because that Jeremiah recognized that this terrible catastrophe was a result of God's goodness. For God brought judgment to His people because they strayed away from Him. They were worshipping false gods. They were following heathen practices. They were being hypocritical, acting like everything was good between them and God when they really weren't. If God had allowed that to continue, it would only spiral down worse. Because God is good, He must judge sin. And His longsuffering had run out. So even though Jeremiah went through all of this hardship, he knew that God was good.

Each of these men experienced something terrible from a different source. For Joseph, hardship was brought upon him by other people. For Job, Satan. For Jeremiah, God's divine wrath came into play. But all three were allowed by God to take place. Is God still good when He allows bad things to happen? The answer is yes. Just as the refiner makes gold pure by adding heat and pressure to it, God does the same with us. Imagine in your mind the most patient person you know. Do you think they became that patient due to dealing with situations that were very easy and getting good results immediately? No, people become more patient by getting their patience tried. It's why so many stay-at-home mothers are often very patient. They have to deal with screaming, fussy children all the time. So, the key to this whole thing is not looking at the problem to accuse God of not being good, but seeing God's goodness because of the problem. Each of these men had a good ending. I realize some may be scratching their heads about how Jeremiah had a good ending. The truth is, he may not have had one in life, but he has a good ending in heaven now. For Jeremiah was obedient to the end, and he will receive great reward for that.

Innumerable other stories could be expounded upon on how God is good. Instead of going through them, I would challenge you, dear reader, to rather go to the Bible and see if you're able to find a place where God is *not* good. Good luck with that. Even if we may not see it or not agree with it, God is good. Everything that is good comes from Him, and here are some verses about how His believers proclaimed His goodness:

"And Moses told his father in law all that the LORD had done unto Pharaoh and to the Egyptians for Israel's sake, *and* all the travail that had come upon them by the way, and *how* the LORD delivered them. And <u>Jethro rejoiced for all the goodness which the LORD had done to Israel</u>, whom He had delivered out of the hand of the Egyptians."
(Exodus 18:8 – 9)

"And now, O Lord GOD, Thou *art* that God, and Thy words be true, and Thou hast promised this goodness unto Thy servant:"
(2 Samuel 7:28)

"*Oh* how great *is* Thy goodness, which Thou hast laid up for them that fear Thee; *which* Thou hast wrought for them that trust in Thee before the sons of men!"
(Psalms 31:19)

"O taste and see that the LORD *is* good: blessed *is* the man *that* trusteth in Him."
(Psalms 34:8)

"O give thanks unto the LORD, for *He is* good: for His mercy

endureth for ever."

(Psalms 107:1)

"The LORD *is* good, a strong hold in the day of trouble; and

He knoweth them that trust in Him."

(Nahum 1:7)

"Or despisest thou the riches of His goodness and forbearance

and longsuffering; not knowing that the goodness of God

leadeth thee to repentance?"

(Romans 2:4)

"Every good gift and every perfect gift is from above, and

cometh down from the Father of lights, with whom is no

variableness, neither shadow of turning."

(James 1:17)

Immutability: Immutable simply means "unchanging over time or unable to be changed." An example would be $2 + 2 = 4$. Four is the immutable answer to that equation. It will not change. It *cannot* change. No matter what fancy-schmancy math wizardry you try, two and two together ***will always be*** four. Even more so is God. All of the attributes we've talked about will always be. He cannot suddenly get rid of His goodness, or discard His holiness. He will not all of a sudden add deception to His list of attributes. I

377

mean, the fact that He doesn't change is in His name: I AM THAT I AM. Not I AM THAT I WAS or anything like that.[111] No, He is I AM THAT I AM. He is constant and He is unchanging, and that's a very good thing for us.

We know people who change. People who were once quiet and shy turning into people who are outspoken and confident. The same could be said of someone who was kind becoming someone who is cruel. People change a lot, but if God changed, that would be bad news for us. What if what salvation required for the Christian believers of the first century was no longer what God thought was good enough? What if He suddenly wanted us to do works instead of just calling upon the name of Jesus Christ? What if He decided He didn't want humanity saved at all? Can you imagine the kind of chaos we would constantly be going through if God was as fickle as we are? Thank goodness He isn't! But here are also some verses to show how He is immutable:

"God is not a man, that He should lie; neither the son of man, that He should repent: hath He said, and shall He not do it? or hath He spoken, and shall He not make it good?"
(Numbers 23:19)

---

111. I'm not entirely certain if that made technical sense, but I'd like to hope that you understand what I was getting at.

"Of old hast Thou laid the foundation of the earth: and the heavens are the work of Thy hands. They shall perish, but Thou shalt endure: yea, all of them shall wax old like a garment; as a vesture shalt Thou change them, and they shall be changed: But Thou art the same, and Thy years shall have no end."

(Psalms 102:25 – 27)

"For I am the LORD, I change not; therefore ye sons of Jacob are not consumed."

(Malachi 3:6)

"For when God made promise to Abraham, because He could swear by no greater, He sware by Himself, Saying, Surely blessing I will bless thee, and multiplying I will multiply thee. And so, after he had patiently endured, he obtained the promise. For men verily swear by the greater: and an oath for confirmation is to them an end of all strife. Wherein God, willing more abundantly to shew unto the heirs of promise the immutability of His counsel, confirmed it by an oath: That by two immutable things, in which it was impossible for God to lie, we might have a strong consolation, who have fled for refuge to lay hold upon the hope set before us:"

(Hebrews 6:14 – 18)

"Jesus Christ the same yesterday, and to day, and for ever."
(Hebrews 13:8)

"Every good gift and every perfect gift is from above, and
cometh down from the Father of lights, <u>with whom is no</u>
<u>variableness, neither shadow of turning</u>."
(James 1:17)

Now, there is something that a lot of people like to point out:
"In the Old Testament, God required sacrifices and the dietary
law, but He changed that in the New Testament." To clarify, His
nature did not change between the Old and New Testament.
Rather the way He worked with humanity changed due to the fact
that the debt was paid. Jesus fulfilled the law, He did not abolish
it. The sacrifices were a picture of Jesus, the suffering Saviour.
The dietary law was to keep the Jewish people separate and
healthy, as well as show other pictures of holiness. Everything
that is blacklisted in the dietary law is still not good for you today.
Yes, that does include bacon; but again, God did not change. He
just changed the way He deals with us. For those who think that
changing the way He deals with us would be breaking His
immutability, just consider a man dealing with both his wife and
his daughter. He treats them differently, does he not? Does that
mean that he himself has changed? No. The same is true of God.

That is all the attributes of God we are going to go through for now. I've said it numerous times, and I'll say it again: I can't cover everything. I hope these have been a help to the reader. I apologize if a specific attribute of God you may have wanted to go over was not discussed.

Jesus Christ

Jesus Christ is the very core of Christianity. Hence the name, **Christ**ianity. It is only natural that He is a point of tremendous controversy. Unfortunately, however, the controversy that surrounds Him is not only between Christians and lost people, but between Christians and other Christians.

Multitudes of questions have surrounded Jesus Christ of Nazareth: Was He truly God in the flesh? Was He just a prophet? Was He a charlatan? Was He a white guy with long, luscious hair that Loreal would love to advertise? Did He even truly exist?

Depending on who you ask, you'll get drastically different answers to all of these questions. I'll do my best to answer all of these questions, and more, with what the Bible says.

The Eternality of Jesus: Only God has existed for all eternity and never had a beginning. Everything else, whether an angel, a human, an animal, or the vastness of all Creation was brought into existence at some point in time. Even time itself had a beginning, but not God. He is I AM THAT I AM. The self-existing One. The only being that has been since eternity past, but some people fail to realize that the Bible talks about Jesus in the same fashion:

"But thou, Bethlehem Ephratah, *though* thou be little among the thousands of Judah, *yet* out of thee shall He come forth unto me *that is* to be ruler in Israel; <u>whose goings forth *have been* from of old, from everlasting</u>."
(Micah 5:2)

This is the verse that prophesied where Jesus was to be born. There are those who believe that Jesus was a higher being than humanity but not God. Remember, only God has existed from everlasting. Jesus, being God, has always been. Yes, He was born, but He also existed before His birth. It's confusing, but as stated before, we're not going to understand everything. Other Bible translations have tarnished this verse, saying something like "whose origins are from old, from ancient times"[112] or "whose coming forth is from of old, from ancient days."[113] Being from "everlasting" is far different than being from "ancient times." Being from "ancient times" means you're really old, but you had a beginning. Being from everlasting means you had no beginning

---

112. New International Version (NIV) translation.

113. English Standard Version (ESV) translation.

because you were there before the beginning. This word "everlasting" comes from the Hebrew word "עֹלָם עוֹלָם" (pronounced "o-lawm', o-lawm'"), which means "eternal," "always," "without end," or "time out of mind, past or future." That is to say, it is beyond what our mind is able to comprehend, to the past or to the future.

We know this verse refers to Jesus because it's the verse that the chief priests use to tell where the Messiah would be born:

"And when he had gathered all the chief priests and scribes of the people together, he demanded of them where Christ should be born. And they said unto him, In Bethlehem of Judaea: for thus it is written by the prophet, And thou Bethlehem, *in* **the land of Juda, art not the least among the princes of Juda: for out of thee shall come a Governor, that shall rule my people Israel."**
(Matthew 2:4 – 6)

There are also plenty of passages that show Jesus appearing to individuals in the Old Testament before His birth. It is important to note that the Apostle John states that no man has ever physically seen God the Father:

"No man hath seen God at any time; the only begotten Son, which is in the bosom of the Father, He hath declared *Him.*"
(John 1:18)

The glory of God the Father would be too overwhelming for any of us to behold and still live. God Himself tells this to Moses:

"And He said, Thou canst not see My face: for there shall no man see Me, and live."
(Exodus 33:20)

Putting these two statements together leads us to the conclusion that all visible manifestations[114] of the Lord in the Old Testament were God the Son, Jesus:

Abraham:
"And the LORD appeared unto him in the plains of Mamre: and he sat in the tent door in the heat of the day; And he lift up his eyes and looked, and, lo, three men stood by him: and when he saw *them,* he ran to meet them from the tent door, and bowed himself toward the ground, And said, My Lord, if now I have found favour in Thy sight, pass not away, I pray thee, from Thy servant:"
(Genesis 18:1 – 3)

---

114. Note: not all audible. The emphasis is every time someone physically saw God.

<u>Jacob</u>:

"And Jacob was left alone; and there wrestled a man with him until the breaking of the day. And when He saw that he prevailed not against him, He touched the hollow of his thigh; and the hollow of Jacob's thigh was out of joint, as he wrestled with Him. And He said, Let me go, for the day breaketh. And he said, I will not let Thee go, except Thou bless me. And He said unto him, What *is* thy name? And he said, Jacob. And He said, Thy name shall be called no more Jacob, but Israel: for as a prince hast thou power with God and with men, and hast prevailed. And Jacob asked *Him,* and said, Tell *me,* I pray Thee, Thy name. And He said, Wherefore *is* it *that* thou dost ask after My name? And He blessed him there. And Jacob called the name of the place Peniel: for I have seen God face to face, and my life is preserved."

(Genesis 32:24 – 30)

<u>Joshua</u>:

"And it came to pass, when Joshua was by Jericho, that he lifted up his eyes and looked, and, behold, there stood a man over against him with His sword drawn in His hand: and Joshua went unto Him, and said unto Him, *Art* Thou for us, or for our adversaries? And He said, Nay; but *as* captain of the host of the LORD am I now come. And Joshua fell on his face to the earth, and did worship, and said unto Him, What saith my lord unto His servant? And the captain of the LORD'S

385

host said unto Joshua, Loose thy shoe from off thy foot; for the place whereon thou standest *is* holy. And Joshua did so."

(Joshua 5:13 – 15)[115]

Gideon:

"And there came an angel of the LORD, and sat under an oak which *was* in Ophrah, that *pertained* unto Joash the Abiezrite: and his son Gideon threshed wheat by the winepress, to hide *it* from the Midianites. And the angel of the LORD appeared unto him, and said unto him, The LORD *is* with thee, thou mighty man of valour. And Gideon said unto Him, Oh my Lord, if the LORD be with us, why then is all this befallen us? and where *be* all His miracles which our fathers told us of, saying, Did not the LORD bring us up from Egypt? but now the LORD hath forsaken us, and delivered us into the hands of the Midianites. And the LORD looked upon him, and said, Go in this thy might, and thou shalt save Israel from the hand of the Midianites: have not I sent thee? And he said unto Him, Oh my Lord, wherewith shall I save Israel? behold, my family *is* poor in Manasseh, and I *am* the least in my father's house. And the LORD said unto him, Surely I will be with thee, and thou shalt smite the Midianites as one man. And he said unto Him, If now I have found grace in Thy sight, then shew me a sign that Thou talkest with me. Depart not hence, I pray Thee, until I come unto Thee, and bring forth my present, and set *it*

---

115. Only God accepts worship. No angel of God would do so.

before Thee. And He said, I will tarry until thou come again. And Gideon went in, and made ready a kid, and unleavened cakes of an ephah of flour: the flesh he put in a basket, and he put the broth in a pot, and brought *it* out unto Him under the oak, and presented *it*. And the angel of God said unto him, Take the flesh and the unleavened cakes, and lay *them* upon this rock, and pour out the broth. And he did so. Then the angel of the LORD put forth the end of the staff that *was* in His hand, and touched the flesh and the unleavened cakes; and there rose up fire out of the rock, and consumed the flesh and the unleavened cakes. Then the angel of the LORD departed out of his sight. And when Gideon perceived that He *was* an angel of the LORD, Gideon said, Alas, O Lord GOD! for because I have seen an angel of the LORD face to face."
(Judges 6:11 – 22)[116]

<u>Nebuchadnezzar, Shadrach, Meshach, and Abednego</u>:
"And these three men, Shadrach, Meshach, and Abednego, fell down bound into the midst of the burning fiery furnace. Then Nebuchadnezzar the king was astonied, and rose up in haste, *and* spake, and said unto his counsellors, Did not we cast three men bound into the midst of the fire? They answered and said unto the king, True, O king. He answered and said, Lo, I see four men loose, walking in the midst of the

---

116. "Angel of the LORD" can refer to a Christophany. "Angel" simply means "messenger." It doesn't necessarily mean that this wasn't the Lord, though I urge you to study it out for yourself.

fire, and they have no hurt; and the form of the fourth is like
the Son of God."
(Daniel 3:23 – 25)

There are undoubtedly others, but I feel that the point is made. No mere man could exist from the time of Abraham to the time of the Babylonian captivity, and no angel of God would receive worship.

The Virgin Birth of Jesus: It is crucial to note that Jesus was born of a virgin woman. The Bible states it very clearly that Jesus was born of a virgin:

"Therefore the Lord Himself shall give you a sign; Behold, a virgin shall conceive, and bear a Son, and shall call His name Immanuel."
(Isaiah 7:14)

"Behold, a virgin shall be with child, and shall bring forth a Son, and they shall call His name Emmanuel, which being interpreted is, God with us. Then Joseph being raised from sleep did as the angel of the Lord had bidden him, and took unto him his wife: And knew her not till she had brought forth her firstborn Son: and he called His name JESUS."
(Matthew 1:23 – 25)

388

"And the angel said unto her, Fear not, Mary: for thou hast found favour with God. And, behold, thou shalt conceive in thy womb, and bring forth a Son, and shalt call His name JESUS. He shall be great, and shall be called the Son of the Highest: and the Lord God shall give unto Him the throne of His father David: And He shall reign over the house of Jacob for ever; and of His kingdom there shall be no end. Then said Mary unto the angel, <u>How shall this be, seeing I know not a man?</u> And the angel answered and said unto her, The Holy Ghost shall come upon thee, and the power of the Highest shall overshadow thee: therefore also that holy Thing which shall be born of thee shall be called the Son of God."

(Luke 1:30 – 35)

Why was the fact that it had to be a virgin woman that conceived Jesus so important? It is because sin is passed down from parent to child, or, more specifically, *father* to child.[117] Jesus could not have been born of a human father since because the sin nature would have been passed to Him, and He, being God, cannot be sinful. Thus, if Jesus was born of a human father, He would not have been God. Mary had to be a virgin because, if she was not, anyone could have accused her of just conceiving from

---

117. There is probably a very scientific way to go about showing how this is done, but since it deals with the sexual nature, I would rather avoid discussing that where I am able. I would like to keep this book as appropriate as I can while still going through some more mature or taboo subjects. So, I would encourage those who wish to know more to study it out for themselves.

Joseph. If she conceived before Joseph and her came together, it would have been nothing short of a miracle.

The Sinless Life of Jesus: We've talked about it already that Jesus did not sin, could not sin, absolutely would not sin. Whether or not you believe that is up to you, but the Bible shows it as truth:

"For He hath made Him *to be* sin for us, <u>who knew no sin;</u> that we might be made the righteousness of God in Him."
(2 Corinthians 5:21)

"For we have not an high priest which cannot be touched with the feeling of our infirmities; but was in all points tempted like as *we are, <u>yet</u>* <u>without sin</u>."
(Hebrews 4:15)

"For even hereunto were ye called: because Christ also suffered for us, leaving us an example, that ye should follow His steps: <u>who did no sin</u>, neither was guile found in His mouth:"
(1 Peter 2:21 – 22)

"And ye know that He was manifested to take away our sins; and <u>in Him is no sin</u>."
(1 John 3:5)

The temptation of Jesus in Matthew 4 also shows His resolve against sin, but this is another very vital part of Jesus' existence. If Jesus could sin and did sin, He would not be God. If He was not God, He could not provide our salvation on the cross. Our salvation required Him to be sinless because only a sinless man could pay for the salvation of another. A sinner cannot. This is showed in the Old Testament when God required a spotless animal:

"Speak ye unto all the congregation of Israel, saying, In the tenth *day* of this month they shall take to them every man a lamb, according to the house of *their* fathers, a lamb for an house: And if the household be too little for the lamb, let him and his neighbour next unto his house take *it* according to the number of the souls; every man according to his eating shall make your count for the lamb. Your lamb shall be without blemish, a male of the first year: ye shall take *it* out from the sheep, or from the goats: And ye shall keep it up until the fourteenth day of the same month: and the whole assembly of the congregation of Israel shall kill it in the evening. And they shall take of the blood, and strike *it* on the two side posts and on the upper door post of the houses, wherein they shall eat it...For I will pass through the land of Egypt this night, and will smite all the firstborn in the land of Egypt, both man and beast; and against all the gods of Egypt I will execute judgment: I *am* the LORD. And the blood shall be to you for a

391

token upon the houses where ye *are:* and when I see the blood, I will pass over you, and the plague shall not be upon you to destroy *you,* when I smite the land of Egypt."
(Exodus 12:3 – 7, 12 – 13)

"If a soul commit a trespass, and sin through ignorance, in the holy things of the LORD; then he shall bring for his trespass unto the LORD a ram <u>without blemish</u> out of the flocks, with thy estimation by shekels of silver, after the shekel of the sanctuary, for a trespass offering:"
(Leviticus 5:15)

"*Ye shall offer* at your own will a male <u>without blemish</u>, of the beeves, of the sheep, or of the goats. *But* <u>whatsoever hath a blemish, *that* shall ye not offer: for it shall not be acceptable for you</u>."
(Leviticus 22:19 – 20)

There are countless other verses that go over the need for a spotless animal for the different offerings in the book of Leviticus, but animals could not completely redeem mankind to God. Only a being who is all man and all God could: Jesus Christ. If He was all God, there could not have been any sin in Him at all.

<u>Jesus' Submission to the Father</u>: Time to get to another confusing aspect of Jesus. Jesus was fully submitted to God the

392

Father at all times. This was to show us the perfect example of how we are to be. Since we do not have the sinlessness nor miraculous abilities of Jesus, we **must** rely on the Father in our lives. But did Jesus have to? No, He could fully rely upon Himself. For He was all God when He walked this Earth. But Jesus willingly limited Himself to be all man.

Take a moment to consider that. Jesus was just as much human as you and I are, limited just as much as you and I are. This means that Jesus did not know everything. He only knew what God the Father wanted Him to know. This also means that Jesus could not do miracles unless God the Father wanted it to be so. I would dare say that when Satan tempted Jesus to turn the stones into bread that Jesus couldn't. That's up for debate, and it ultimately doesn't matter a whole bunch, but I'm just trying to make the point that Jesus fully submitted to the Father. Bible verses support this as well:

"I can of Mine own self do nothing: as I hear, I judge: and My judgment is just; because I seek not Mine own will, but the will of the Father which hath sent Me."
(John 5:30)

"Then said Jesus unto them, When ye have lifted up the Son of man, then shall ye know that I am *He,* and *that* I do nothing of myself; but as my Father hath taught me, I speak these

things. And He that sent me is with Me: the Father hath not left Me alone; for I do always those things that please Him."
(John 8:28 – 29)

"But I would have you know, that the head of every man is Christ; and the head of the woman *is* the man; <u>and the head of Christ *is* God</u>."
(1 Corinthians 11:3)

"Let this mind be in you, which was also in Christ Jesus: who, being in the form of God, thought it not robbery to be equal with God: But made Himself of no reputation, and took upon Him the form of a servant, and was made in the likeness of men: And being found in fashion as a man, He humbled Himself, and became obedient unto death, even the death of the cross."
(Philippians 2:5 – 8)

"Who, when He was reviled, reviled not again; when He suffered, He threatened not; <u>but committed *Himself* to Him that judgeth righteously</u>:"
(1 Peter 2:23)

<u>The Resurrection of Jesus</u>: One of the most highly talked about, debated, and important subjects in all of the Bible. Jesus

did die on the cross. Many understand and accept that fact. Yes, Jesus really did exist. He was a real person. Here is an account from Josephus, a historian of the first century:

> "Now, there was about this time Jesus, a wise man, if it be lawful to call Him a man, for He was a doer of wonderful works – a teacher of such men as receive the truth with pleasure. He drew over to Him both many of the Jews, and many of the Gentiles. He was [the] Christ; and when Pilate, at the suggestion of the principal men amongst us, had condemned Him to the cross, those that loved Him at the first did not forsake Him, for He appeared to them alive again the third day, as the divine prophets had foretold these and ten thousand other wonderful things concerning Him; and the tribe of Christians, so named from Him, are not extinct at this day."[118]

Believers and non-believers alike agree that Jesus existed. If you go to any competent historian, whether a believer or no, he or she will confirm that there was a man in history named Jesus that was crucified by Romans. Here's the part where people start to divide: He rose again. He took His life back after death as He said He would.

"Now if Christ be preached that He rose from the dead, how say some among you that there is no resurrection of the dead? But if there be no resurrection of the dead, then is Christ not

118. Josephus, Flavius. 1987. "*The Antiquities of the Jews.*" Hendrickson Publishers. Book 18, Chapter 3.

risen: And if Christ be not risen, then *is* our preaching vain, and your faith *is* also vain. Yea, and we are found false witnesses of God; because we have testified of God that He raised up Christ: whom He raised not up, if so be that the dead rise not. For if the dead rise not, then is not Christ raised: And if Christ be not raised, your faith *is* vain; ye are yet in your sins. Then they also which are fallen asleep in Christ are perished. If in this life only we have hope in Christ, we are of all men most miserable. But now is Christ risen from the dead, *and* become the firstfruits of them that slept. For since by man *came* death, by man *came* also the resurrection of the dead. For as in Adam all die, even so in Christ shall all be made alive."
(1 Corinthians 15:12 – 22)

What Paul is saying here is that if Jesus did not rise from the dead, then everyone who follows Christianity is following a false doctrine. That means that everything Jesus said was false. That means that we are not saved and not going to heaven. That is why the resurrection is so crucial because He ***did*** rise from the dead. How do I know that?

Reason #1 – The Tomb was and is Empty

"Now upon the first *day* of the week, very early in the morning, they came unto the sepulchre, bringing the spices which they had prepared, and certain *others* with them. And

396

they found the stone rolled away from the sepulchre. And they entered in, and found not the body of the Lord Jesus."

(Luke 24:1 – 3)

"The first *day* of the week cometh Mary Magdalene early, when it was yet dark, unto the sepulchre, and seeth the stone taken away from the sepulchre. Then she runneth, and cometh to Simon Peter, and to the other disciple, whom Jesus loved, and saith unto them, They have taken away the Lord out of the sepulchre, and we know not where they have laid him. Peter therefore went forth, and that other disciple, and came to the sepulchre. So they ran both together: and the other disciple did outrun Peter, and came first to the sepulchre. And he stooping down, *and looking in,* saw the linen clothes lying; yet went he not in. Then cometh Simon Peter following him, and went into the sepulchre, and seeth the linen clothes lie, And the napkin, that was about his head, not lying with the linen clothes, but wrapped together in a place by itself. Then went in also that other disciple, which came first to the sepulchre, and he saw, and believed. For as yet they knew not the scripture, that He must rise again from the dead."

(John 20:3 – 9)

"In the end of the sabbath, as it began to dawn toward the first *day* of the week, came <u>Mary Magdalene and the other Mary to see the sepulchre.</u> And, behold, there was a great earthquake: for the angel of the Lord descended from heaven, and came and rolled back the stone from the door, and sat upon it. His countenance was like lightning, and his raiment white as snow: <u>And for fear of him the keepers did shake, and became as dead *men.*</u>"
(Matthew 28:1 – 4)

"Now when they were going, behold, <u>some of the watch came into the city, and shewed unto the chief priests all the things that were done</u>. And when they were assembled with the elders, and had taken counsel, they gave large money unto the soldiers, Saying, Say ye, His disciples came by night, and stole Him *away* while we slept. And if this come to the governor's ears, we will persuade him, and secure you. So they took the money, and did as they were taught: and this saying is commonly reported among the Jews until this day."
(Matthew 28:11 – 15)

"And it came to pass, as they were much perplexed thereabout, behold, two men stood by them in shining garments: And as they were afraid, and bowed down *their* faces to the earth, they said unto them, Why seek ye the living among the dead? He is not here, but is risen: remember how He spake unto you when he was yet in Galilee, Saying, The Son of man must be delivered into the hands of sinful men, and be crucified, and the third day rise again. And they remembered his words, And returned from the sepulchre, and told all these things unto the eleven, and to all the rest. It was Mary Magdalene, and Joanna, and Mary *the mother* of James, and other *women that were* with them, which told these things unto the apostles."

(Luke 24:4 – 10)

"The former treatise have I made, O Theophilus, of all that Jesus began both to do and teach, Until the day in which He was taken up, after that He through the Holy Ghost had given commandments unto the apostles whom He had chosen: To whom also He shewed himself alive after His passion by many infallible proofs, being seen of them forty days, and speaking of the things pertaining to the kingdom of God:"

(Acts 1:1 – 3)

"And that He was buried, and that He rose again the third day according to the scriptures: And that He was seen of Cephas, then of the twelve: After that, He was seen of above five hundred brethren at once; of whom the greater part remain unto this present, but some are fallen asleep. After

399

that, <u>He was seen of James</u>; then of all the apostles. And last of all <u>He was seen of me also</u>, as of one born out of due time."

(1 Corinthians 15:4 – 8)

Reason #3 – Jesus said He would Rise Again prior to His Death

"From that time forth began Jesus to shew unto His disciples, how that He must go unto Jerusalem, and suffer many things of the elders and chief priests and scribes, and be killed, and be raised again the third day."

(Matthew 16:21)

"Now the next day, that followed the day of the preparation, the chief priests and Pharisees came together unto Pilate, Saying, Sir, we remember that that deceiver said, while He was yet alive, After three days I will rise again."

(Matthew 27:62 – 63)

"And they were in the way going up to Jerusalem; and Jesus went before them: and they were amazed; and as they followed, they were afraid. And He took again the twelve, and began to tell them what things should happen unto Him, *Saying,* Behold, we go up to Jerusalem; and the Son of man shall be delivered unto the chief priests, and unto the scribes; and they shall condemn Him to death, and shall deliver Him to the Gentiles: And they shall mock Him, and shall scourge

Him, and shall spit upon Him, and shall kill Him: and the

third day He shall rise again."

(Mark 10:32 – 34)

"Jesus answered and said unto them, Destroy this temple, and in three days I will raise it up. Then said the Jews, Forty and six years was this temple in building, and wilt Thou rear it up in three days? But He spake of the temple of His body. When therefore He was risen from the dead, His disciples remembered that He had said this unto them; and they believed the scripture, and the word which Jesus had said."

(John 2:19 – 22)

"Therefore doth My Father love Me, because I lay down My life, that I might take it again. No man taketh it from Me, but I lay it down of Myself. I have power to lay it down, and I have power to take it again. This commandment have I received of My Father."

(John 10:17 – 18)

False Claims Against the Resurrection: There are many claims about how the resurrection of Jesus never happened. I have also compiled how to refute such accusations.

1. The Fraud Theory – "Jesus and the Apostles conned everyone into thinking that He was the Messiah by arranging His

life, cross experience, and supposed resurrection to match the Old Testament prophecies."

<u>Refutations</u>:

- Jesus' family tree was recorded meticulously on both sides, all the way back to Abraham and Adam (Matthew 1:1 – 16, Luke 3:23 – 38). It would be incredibly difficult to forge such family trees without any of the learned scribes and Pharisees finding errors in it. Note that there were numerous individuals in Jesus' day that were well versed in Jewish history and many of them were seeking to find a way to discredit Him.

- The impossibility of Jesus planning the place of His birth (Micah 5:2, Matthew 2:5 – 6), the journey into Egypt when He was less than two years old (Hosea 11:1, Matthew 2:15), the massacre of children at His birthplace (Jeremiah 31:15, Matthew 2:18), the Romans parting His garments while He was on the cross (Psalms 22:18, Matthew 27:35), and countless other things that were completely out of His control, all of which were fulfillments to prophecies.

- Jesus did not fulfill the popular expectations of the first century Hebrews concerning the Messiah. They were expecting a military conqueror. If He wanted their acceptance, He would not have come as a suffering Saviour, fulfilling Old Testament prophecies that weren't even understood, and ultimately disappoint Israel's anticipations.

402

Even the Apostles believed He would liberate them from Rome rather than die as a sacrifice for humanity's sin (Matthew 16:21 – 22, Acts 1:6).

- Jesus resisted being forced into the place of a ruler (John 6:15). This shows that Jesus was not interested in pursuing power and authority.
- Jesus requested people to **not** tell others about His deity or the miracles He performed (Matthew 8:4, 16:20, 17:9, Mark 7:36, Luke 8:56).

2. <u>The Swoon Theory</u> – "Jesus never died, but rather fainted on the cross. Once He was put in the tomb, He was revived by the cool air."

<u>Refutations</u>:

- The nature of crucifixion. Some don't realize that the cause of death for those who are crucified is suffocation. The arms are stretched out while the body hangs, putting tremendous pressure on the lungs. So much pressure that the victim is unable to breathe. The way that the victim combats this is by pulling up on the nails that are in the wrists and pushing up on the nails that are in the ankles. This causes excruciating pain (which was purposeful), but allows the victim to get in a few breaths before slumping back down. This is why crucifixion is so torturous. Taking that information into account, if Jesus had fainted on the cross and wasn't able to pull up on the nails to breathe, He would have most certainly died shortly after.

- The severity of crucifixion. It is said that there are some historical cases where people were removed from the crosses before death, yet still died. This method of execution was extremely effective. The body is unable to handle the enormous trauma that crucifixion brings.

- The Romans' expertise in death. The Roman soldiers were professional executioners. They would have known if Jesus was still alive when He was taken down from the cross. Jesus would have had to still be breathing, and He would have had a heartbeat, both of which are immensely easy to tell.

- The severe scourging Jesus suffered before being placed on the cross. He was beaten with a cat of nine tails, which would have bruised and ripped up His body. This punishment was sometimes used as a means of execution alone. Even excluding the cross, the idea that He would have recovered from such physical trauma and blood-loss in the tomb is very unlikely.

- The spear that pierced His side. The fact that water and blood flowed out is also a definite indicator that Jesus was dead. This can be backed by medical fact, but was not known in the first century and therefore would not have been added to make Jesus' death sound more credible. Also, the fact that He was *stabbed* in the side. Most people can't simply walk away from a spear-wound in their ribs.

- The thousand pound stone that sealed the tomb. If Jesus had somehow survived the scourging, the cross, and fooled the Roman soldiers into thinking He was dead, He still would have been trapped in the tomb. No one man could move the stone, much less a gravely wounded man on the inside. Even if Jesus had somehow moved it, the Roman soldiers were standing guard outside. They would have just killed Him.
- Jesus' condition if He somehow overcame all of those obstacles (surviving being crucified, enduring the scourging and spear puncture, rolling a massive stone away from the tomb, overcoming several Roman soldiers, and then making His way to find His disciples). The disciples would have then called for a physician, not proclaimed Him as a resurrected Lord of life.

3. <u>The Hallucination Theory</u> – "The disciples all had hallucinations of seeing a resurrected Jesus, but Jesus was still dead. The disciples expected and hoped for Jesus' resurrection so much, they saw what they wanted to see instead of the actual truth."

<u>Refutations</u>:
- The empty tomb. If Jesus was still dead, the Roman soldiers or the Pharisees could have easily debunked the claims that

Jesus rose from the dead by showing everyone Jesus' body, but they couldn't because He wasn't there.

- Mass hallucinations don't happen. There were over five hundred witnesses of Jesus in a forty day period. Any medical expert will tell you that people don't share hallucinations. If five hundred people all saw the same thing, that means that it was really there.

- None of the disciples expected Jesus to rise from the dead. When Mary Magdalene saw the empty tomb, her first guess was that someone had stolen Jesus' body (John 20:2). When the Apostles were told by the women that He had risen again, they were all skeptical (Luke 24:11). Even when ten of the Apostles had seen Jesus with their own eyes, Thomas refused to believe them until he could see the nail print in Jesus' wrists and the spear wound in His side (John 20:25).

4. The Spirit Theory – "The spirit of Christ arose, not the physical body of Jesus."

Refutations:
- The empty tomb. Why was the body gone if just the spirit arose?
- Thomas was able to physically feel the nail prints in Jesus' wrists and the spear wound in Jesus' side (John 20:27).
- Jesus was able to eat food after His resurrection (Luke 24:41 – 43).

- Jesus told them He was not a spirit and had the disciples feel Him to prove it (Luke 24:39).

5. The Stolen Body Theory – "The disciples stole Jesus' body while the Roman guards were sleeping." This theory was fabricated by the Pharisees themselves in Matthew 28:12 – 15.

Refutations:
- The laws of legal evidence. How would the Roman soldiers know it was the disciples that stole the body if they were sleeping?
- The idea that *all* of the Roman soldiers were asleep at the same time is very unlikely. They would have rotated sleeping shifts.
- The absurdity of the Roman soldiers *admitting* that they all had fallen asleep, if it were true. The penalty for a guard falling asleep at his post was death. Why not simply lie and say that they were overcome by five hundred zealous disciples? There was no penalty for losing to overwhelming numbers.
- The impossibility of the disciples rolling back the stone without waking any of the Roman soldiers. With their rotating sleeping shifts, Romans often slept with their head touching whatever they were guarding. In this case, it would have been the stone.

- The lack of punishment for the soldiers. If the Roman soldiers had truly fallen asleep while on guard and openly admitted it, why were they not put to death? This was because the Pharisees told their superiors what really happened (Matthew 28:14).

- The unbelieving disciples. The disciples themselves did not believe the resurrection stories at first. If they stole the body to fake a resurrection, why would they be arguing amongst themselves about whether or not it really happened?

- The fact that the disciples gained nothing but suffering and death through their claims. No temporal benefit was bestowed upon them for spreading the Gospel.

- The fact that none of the disciples ever recanted, even while under horrible torture. If they knew that Christianity was a farce, why would they endure such pain and ultimately be put to death?

6. The Wrong Tomb Theory – "The disciples went to the wrong tomb, which was unused, and mistakenly believed that Jesus had risen."

Refutations:

- The absurdity of the idea that everyone went to the wrong tomb. This would have included Mary Magdalene, Mary the mother of James, Salome, Peter, John, and likely countless others.

- The soldiers guarding Jesus' tomb. If everyone went to the wrong tomb, both the Roman soldiers and the Pharisees could have easily pointed out where the correct tomb was. They could have shown the evidence of Jesus' body. If everyone started proclaiming the Jesus was risen after they went to the wrong tomb, why would they not immediately squash that idea with the hard facts?
- The Pharisees' plotting. If everyone went to the wrong tomb, why did the Pharisees make up the lie that the disciples had stolen Jesus' body? Why did they bribe the Roman soldiers to spread that lie if the right tomb was still sealed?

7. <u>The Wrong Victim Theory</u> – "Jesus arranged the entire scenario to achieve status of Messiah and that Judas Iscariot was the one who was crucified, not Jesus."

<u>Refutations</u>
- The empty tomb. If this was all a big lie, where did Judas' body go?
- The imbecility that Judas would agree to and go along with this plan.
- Judas' appearance. How did none of the hundreds of people who were present at the trial and crucifixion not realize that Judas was not Jesus? They knew Jesus' face very well due to His many confrontations with the scribes and Pharisees. They likely knew Judas' face for the same reason.

- The fact that Jesus never appeared to the general public after the resurrection. He only ever appeared to His disciples. If the whole point was to appear as the Messiah after Judas was crucified, Jesus ultimately failed by only showing up to His disciples.

The Second Coming of Jesus: Jesus' first coming has already taken place, though many in that day thought Messiah would come as a military conqueror and not as a suffering Saviour. Jesus' second coming is yet to come to pass. Before it takes place, the Rapture will occur, which will bring all of the living believers to heaven. Immediately after proceeds the Tribulation. Many Bible verses support these instances:

"And as He sat upon the mount of Olives, the disciples came unto Him privately, saying, Tell us, when shall these things be? and what *shall be* the sign of Thy coming, and of the end of the world? And Jesus answered and said unto them, Take heed that no man deceive you...When ye therefore shall see the abomination of desolation, spoken of by Daniel the prophet,[119] stand in the holy place, (whoso readeth, let him

---

119. This is referencing Daniel 12:11, another end times passage. The abomination of desolation means something that is set up in the temple. Daniel prophesied that this would first happen with Antiochus Epiphanes in Daniel 11:31. Antiochus did this by setting up an idol of Jupiter/Zeus in the temple (a false god set up as higher than God) and offered a large pig on the altar (an unclean animal that was forbidden to be offered on the altar). This pictured how the Anti-Christ will do similarly in the Tribulation.

understand:) Then let them which be in Judaea flee into the mountains: Let him which is on the housetop not come down to take any thing out of his house: Neither let him which is in the field return back to take his clothes. And woe unto them that are with child, and to them that give suck in those days! But pray ye that your flight be not in the winter, neither on the sabbath day: For then shall be great tribulation, such as was not since the beginning of the world to this time, no, nor ever shall be. And except those days should be shortened, there should no flesh be saved: but for the elect's sake those days shall be shortened. Then if any man shall say unto you, Lo, here *is* Christ, or there; believe *it* not. For there shall arise false Christs, and false prophets, and shall shew great signs and wonders; insomuch that, if *it were* possible, they shall deceive the very elect. Behold, I have told you before. Wherefore if they shall say unto you, Behold, he is in the desert; go not forth: behold, *he is* in the secret chambers; believe *it* not. For as the lightning cometh out of the east, and shineth even unto the west; so shall also the coming of the Son of man be. For wheresoever the carcase is, there will the eagles be gathered together. Immediately after the tribulation of those days shall the sun be darkened, and the moon shall not give her light, and the stars shall fall from heaven, and the powers of the heavens shall be shaken: And then shall appear the sign of the Son of man in heaven: and then shall all the tribes of the earth mourn, and they shall see the Son of man

411

coming in the clouds of heaven with power and great glory. And He shall send His angels with a great sound of a trumpet, and they shall gather together His elect from the four winds, from one end of heaven to the other."
(Matthew 24:3 – 4, 15 – 31)

However, the next time Jesus Christ comes down to the world, He *will* come as a great conqueror to take the Earth as His own:

"Behold, the day of the LORD cometh, and thy spoil shall be divided in the midst of thee. For I will gather all nations against Jerusalem to battle; and the city shall be taken, and the houses rifled, and the women ravished; and half of the city shall go forth into captivity, and the residue of the people shall not be cut off from the city. Then shall the LORD go forth, and fight against those nations, as when He fought in the day of battle. And His feet shall stand in that day upon the mount of Olives, which *is* before Jerusalem on the east, and the mount of Olives shall cleave in the midst thereof toward the east and toward the west, *and there shall be* a very great valley; and half of the mountain shall remove toward the north, and half of it toward the south. And ye shall flee *to* the valley of the mountains; for the valley of the mountains shall reach unto Azal: yea, ye shall flee, like as ye fled from before

the earthquake in the days of Uzziah king of Judah: and the
LORD my God shall come, *and* all the saints with Thee."
(Zechariah 14:1 – 5)

However, before Jesus comes to Earth after the Tribulation,
He will rapture out all of the Christians before the seven year
Tribulation:

"Behold, I shew you a mystery; We shall not all sleep,[120] but
we shall all be changed, In a moment, in the twinkling of an
eye, at the last trump: for the trumpet shall sound, and the
dead shall be raised incorruptible, and we shall be changed.
For this corruptible must put on incorruption, and this mortal
must put on immortality."
(1 Corinthians 15:51 – 53)

"For the Lord Himself shall descend from heaven with a
shout, with the voice of the archangel, and with the trump of
God: and the dead in Christ shall rise first: Then we which
are alive *and* remain shall be caught up together with them in
the clouds, to meet the Lord in the air: and so shall we ever be
with the Lord."
(1 Thessalonians 4:16 – 17)

---

120. This word "sleep" comes from the Greek word "κοιμάω" (pronounced
"koy-mah'-o"), which not only means "to slumber," but also means "to
decease." Due to the context, it is referring to the latter.

Though, since it is a doctrine that is not heavily discussed in the Scriptures, there is a lot of debate as to when Jesus will rapture out the believers. The three positions would be premillinnialism, postmillinnialism, and amillinnialism. Premillinnialism says that Jesus will rapture us out before the Tribulation. Postmillinnialism says He will do it during or after the Tribulation. Amillinnialism says He won't do it at all and that humanity will just get better and better until it's essentially heaven on Earth (not widely accepted after the two World Wars). The Bible supports Premillinnialism, however this will be more heavily discussed in one of the later volumes of Baptist Apologetics. Other verses about Jesus' second coming:

"In My Father's house are many mansions: if *it were* not *so,* I would have told you. I go to prepare a place for you. And if I go and prepare a place for you, <u>I will come again, and receive you unto Myself</u>; that where I am, *there* ye may be also."
(John 14:2 – 3)

"And while they looked stedfastly toward heaven as He went up, behold, two men stood by them in white apparel; Which also said, Ye men of Galilee, why stand ye gazing up into heaven? this same Jesus, which is taken up from you into heaven, <u>shall so come in like manner as ye have seen him go into heaven</u>."
(Acts 1:10 – 11)

"And Enoch also, the seventh from Adam, prophesied of these, saying, Behold, <u>the Lord cometh with ten thousands of His saints</u>, To execute judgment upon all, and to convince all that are ungodly among them of all their ungodly deeds which they have ungodly committed, and of all their hard *speeches* which ungodly sinners have spoken against Him."
(Jude 1:14 – 15)

The Holy Spirit

Compared to God the Father and Jesus Christ the Son, there won't be as much spoken about the Holy Spirit in this chapter. The simple reason is this:

"Howbeit when He, the Spirit of truth, is come, He will guide you into all truth: for <u>He shall not speak of Himself</u>; but whatsoever He shall hear, *that* shall He speak: and He will shew you things to come. <u>He shall glorify Me</u>: for He shall receive of Mine, and shall shew *it* unto you."
(John 16:13 – 14)

Jesus said this, and if the Holy Spirit refrains from speaking about Himself and rather uplifts Jesus, I feel that we should do the same. There are those out there that exaggerate the Holy Spirit. Most would think of Pentecostal, which is true, but that's hardly the only group that overemphasizes the Holy Spirit. Regardless, we can move into dangerous territory when we start exalting things that Jesus did not. Now, that does **not** mean that we shouldn't exalt the Holy Spirit. We should, He is God, but we can get to a place where it becomes very unhealthy, spiritually speaking – getting wrapped up in just the Spirit, but not emphasizing what Christ did for us, nor the Father's authority.

That being said, de-emphasizing the Holy Spirit is also wrong. The Holy Spirit is not an impersonal force. He is God, just like God the Father and Jesus the Son. He has personality. The Holy Spirit is not some super power. He's not a suit of armor to wear just when going out to battle. He's not a *thing*. He's a *person*. Does He have tremendous power to give to those who ask? Absolutely. But He's not a lucky rabbit's foot or some other good luck charm, nor should He be treated as such. He is not to be overemphasized, but He is also not to be dishonored, either. He deserves reverence and obedience. The balance is crucial. Many things in life are at their best when they are balanced.

Now that we've gotten that out of the way, the Holy Spirit always seems to appear as the quiet laborer. He's working in the background, not trying to bring much attention to Himself, but doing great things all the same:

"And Jesus being full of the Holy Ghost returned from
Jordan, and was led by the Spirit into the wilderness,"
(Luke 4:1)

"And they were all filled with the Holy Ghost, and began to
speak with other tongues, as the Spirit gave them utterance."
(Acts 2:4)

"In whom ye also *trusted,* after that ye heard the word of
truth, the gospel of your salvation: in whom also after that ye
believed, ye were sealed with that holy Spirit of promise,"
(Ephesians 1:13)

Acts definitely looks to be the book that He is most
prominent in, or at the very least, He has His most shining
moments in it. I'll explain why:

The Ministry Change Between the Testaments: Jesus told
His disciples that the Holy Spirit had to come:

"But the Comforter, *which is* the Holy Ghost, whom the
Father will send in My name, He shall teach you all things,
and bring all things to your remembrance, whatsoever I have
said unto you."
(John 14:26)

417

"But when the Comforter is come, whom I will send unto you from the Father, *even* the Spirit of truth, which proceedeth from the Father, He shall testify of Me:"
(John 15:26)

"Nevertheless I tell you the truth; It is expedient for you that I go away: for if I go not away, the Comforter will not come unto you; but if I depart, I will send Him unto you."
(John 16:7)

This begs the question: "Where was the Holy Spirit prior to the Gospels?" We know He existed throughout time because He is God. The Old Testament speaks of the Holy Spirit on several occasions. So, what is Jesus talking about? He is talking about the ministry change of the Holy Spirit. See, because the Holy Spirit worked in the lives of several people in the Old Testament. Saul, to name one:

"And the Spirit of God came upon Saul when he heard those tidings, and his anger was kindled greatly."
(1 Samuel 11:6)

However, we also see the Holy Spirit leave Saul:

"But the Spirit of the LORD departed from Saul, and an evil spirit from the LORD troubled him."
(1 Samuel 16:14)

This was not just a special case with Saul. We see that David was afraid of the Holy Spirit departing from him:

"Cast me not away from thy presence; and take not thy holy Spirit from me."
(Psalms 51:11)

So, in the Old Testament, the Holy Spirit could come upon and depart from individuals. His residence was not permanent on people, it would seem. He could come upon those who were living wickedly, such as Samson (Judges 15:14), or even pagans, such as Balaam (Numbers 24:2). That changed in the book of Acts:

"And, being assembled together with *them,* commanded them that they should not depart from Jerusalem, but wait for the promise of the Father, which, *saith He,* ye have heard of Me. For John truly baptized with water; but ye shall be baptized with the Holy Ghost not many days hence."
(Acts 1:4 – 5)

"And when the day of Pentecost was fully come, they were all with one accord in one place. And suddenly there came a sound from heaven as of a rushing mighty wind, and it filled all the house where they were sitting. And there appeared unto them cloven tongues like as of fire, and it sat upon each of them. And they were all filled with the Holy Ghost, and began to speak with other tongues, as the Spirit gave them utterance."

(Acts 2:1 – 4)

It was this moment where the Holy Spirit changed how He worked. In the Old Testament, He had temporary residence on a select few. In the New Testament, He switched to permanent residence of all believers. This is shown by the fact that we never see anywhere in the New Testament where it says the Spirit departed from someone, as well as the following verses that support it:

"And as I began to speak, the Holy Ghost fell on them, as on us at the beginning. Then remembered I the word of the Lord, how that He said, John indeed baptized with water; but ye shall be baptized with the Holy Ghost. Forasmuch then as God gave them the like gift as *He did* unto us, who believed on the Lord Jesus Christ; what was I, that I could withstand God?"

(Acts 11:15 – 17)

This is part of the passage that deals with Peter leading Cornelius and his family to the Lord. As soon as Cornelius and his family believed on Jesus and were saved, the Holy Spirit came upon them. Unlike in the Old Testament, the Holy Spirit was not choosing to come upon them just for a specific purpose or mission. These were just, if I can say this, ordinary believers. These were not Moseses or Elijahs who did supernatural things through the Spirit's power. They're not even really mentioned again through Scripture. They were just regular people who were saved. This shows us, among other verses, that the Holy Spirit was no longer picking and choosing who to come upon. It was every believer.

"What? know ye not that your body is the temple of the Holy Ghost *which is* in you, which ye have of God, and ye are not your own?"

(1 Corinthians 6:19)

This is the verse that demonstrates permanent residence. In the secular Roman mindset, where did a pagan god dwell? In a temple. That is where it stayed, where it lived. It has a sense of permanence. Paul is using that thought of the day and time to convey that we as believers are the temple of the Holy Spirit. We're not just a hotel room. We're the temple. This conveys other thoughts as well such as the fact that we ought to be holy because temples are holy places, but it also shows that this is the place where the Holy Spirit *lives*, not just vacations. Even getting outside of the secular mindset, think of the Old Testament temple. It was where the Ark of the Covenant stayed. The representation of God's presence; the temple is where it stayed. Similarly, we now hold the Holy Spirit within us as a permanent dwelling. We cannot be separated from Him like David or Saul could.

So, what is so important about the Holy Spirit living within us? First off, God lives within your spirit. That's pretty awesome, but it's not just to be cool. There is a significant purpose:

"But the fruit of the Spirit is love, joy, peace, longsuffering, gentleness, goodness, faith, Meekness, temperance: against such there is no law. And they that are Christ's have crucified the flesh with the affections and lusts. If we live in the Spirit, let us also walk in the Spirit."
(Galatians 5:22 – 25)

Many great people have stated that God loves us as we are, but loves us too much to leave us that way. With the Holy Spirit living within us, He changes us from within. Have you ever wondered why you, as a saved individual, can't have as much enjoyment in sin as you used to before you were saved? It's because the Spirit within you convicts you. God's Spirit cannot mix with sin, so you feel rather sour after getting involved with sin, don't you? You feel wretched and miserable. That's because the Spirit works in us to be like Jesus. To destroy the desires of wickedness and grow the fruit of the Spirit. The fruit of your life shows the root of your heart, after all. If you are saved, you should be showing the fruit of the Spirit. The manifestation that God is working within you. If you don't show any fruit or if you don't feel any guilt for continuing in sin, it might be best to evaluate whether or not you were really saved. This is not to cause true believers to doubt, but you cannot be both a child of God and a child of the devil. Whichever one you are, you will act like your father.

Speaking in Tongues: Speaking in tongues is a big topic today, depending on what crowd you ask. Some may wonder why this topic is under the Holy Spirit. Well, speaking in tongues is always associated with the Holy Spirit first coming upon someone, but when it comes to the importance of speaking in tongues, people usually hold to one of two sides:

1. Super vitally important to your Christian walk.

2. Doesn't matter at all because they don't legitimately happen anymore.

I hold to the latter, and I'll explain why by going over the course of this section. So, what is the reason behind speaking in tongues? Is it for the edification of other believers? Is it a mystical prayer language? Is it to stimulate faith and help us learn how to trust God more fully? The answer to all of those is no. Speaking in tongues has a very specific purpose. Let's dive into the Word to see what that is.

"Charity never faileth: but whether *there be* prophecies, they shall fail; <u>whether *there be* tongues, they shall cease</u>; whether *there be* knowledge, it shall vanish away."
(1 Corinthians 13:8)

First, I would like to point out that Paul states speaking in tongues is not something that will keep on happening. As Pastor John Yates writes the following:

> "Tongues will **permanently cease** in and of themselves...This statement is not debatable. It is simply what the Greek language in this passage actually mean. The specific voice used in the Greek language of this passage indicates that prophecy and knowledge will be brought to an end by the coming of that which is perfect and the middle voice indicates that tongues will cease in and of themselves."[121]

In fact, the time for speaking in tongues is over and I will point out why later. Speaking in tongues was also not prominent in the Old Testament. We don't see people like Abraham, Job,

---

121. Yates, John. Faith Bible Institute Commentary Series, Volume IV (1 Corinthians through Philippians). Monroe, Louisiana. Faith Bible Institute Press. Pages 462 and 463.

David, etc. speaking in tongues, yet they were all very godly individuals. This all shows that speaking in tongues is not essential to someone's Christian walk. Furthermore, the best place to see where speaking in tongues has its place is throughout 1 Corinthians 14:

"Follow after charity, and desire spiritual *gifts,* but rather that ye may prophesy. For he that speaketh in an *unknown* tongue speaketh not unto men, but unto God: for no man understandeth *him;* howbeit in the spirit he speaketh mysteries. But he that prophesieth speaketh unto men *to* edification, and exhortation, and comfort. He that speaketh in an *unknown* tongue edifieth himself; but he that prophesieth edifieth the church. I would that ye all spake with tongues, but rather that ye prophesied: for greater *is* he that prophesieth than he that speaketh with tongues, except he interpret, that the church may receive edifying."
(1 Corinthians 14:1 – 5)

Each time Paul talks about prophesy or prophesying, what he means is the ministering of the revealed Word of God in a known language. So, what Paul is saying here is that the preaching of the Bible in a language people can understand is far better than speaking in a language nobody can understand. These verses aren't commending speaking in tongues, but are actually a rebuke towards the Corinthians' obsession with tongues rather than just analyzing the Scriptures. Proclaiming the Word of God reaches out to the lost and teaches the saved. Speaking in tongues when no one understands does nothing.

Some might argue that speaking in tongues at least "edifieth himself." Some have twisted that to mean that speaking in tongues is good for one's spiritual walk. I disagree. Look closer. It states that "He that speaketh in an *unknown* tongue edifieth himself; but he that prophesieth edifieth the church." That is to show how they contrast and how Paul is still rebuking the Corinthians for this. When someone speaks in tongues, they look oh-so spiritual don't they? It makes them look so filled with the Holy Spirit and they get a bunch of "wow"s and adoration from the Christian commoner masses, so to speak. That buffs up that guy's image, doesn't it? It makes him look good and spiritual. Kinda like the Pharisees that prayed so well and were so pious and such. But what did Jesus call those same Pharisees? Hypocrites. White sepulchers. You see, the person speaking in tongues is trying to edify himself. He's trying to make himself look better, just like the Pharisees. To further drive this point home, Paul has been talking about charity since chapter 13. It is still very much in the context of chapter 14.[122] Those who seek to exalt or edify themselves rather than other believers are not showing the charity

---

122. Note: chapter and verse divisions are not inspired. Sometimes the idea that is in a previous chapter carries over into the next chapter because, originally, it was all just one, undivided body of words.

that Paul exhorts us to show. After all, why else would he mention this at the beginning of chapter 13?

"Though I speak with the tongues of men and of angels, and have not charity, I am become *as* sounding brass, or a tinkling cymbal."
(1 Corinthians 13:1)

If someone is out to just make themselves look good, they do not have an attitude of charity. If they don't have charity, Paul compares their speaking in tongues to just a bunch of noise. Nothing more. Moving on, what is the actual purpose of speaking in tongues, then? Paul goes into that as well:

"In the law it is written, With *men of* other tongues and other lips will I speak unto this people; and yet for all that will they not hear me, saith the Lord. Wherefore <u>tongues are for a sign, not to them that believe, but to them that believe not</u>: but prophesying *serveth* not for them that believe not, but for them which believe."
(1 Corinthians 14:21 – 22)

Speaking in tongues are not a sign to believers. It is actually a sign to those who do ***not*** believe in Jesus Christ. Now, this adds some confusion to the mix, because what is the initial reaction of unbelievers when someone speaks in tongues?

"And they were all amazed, and were in doubt, saying one to another, What meaneth this? Others mocking said, These men are full of new wine."

(Acts 2:12 – 13)

"If therefore the whole church be come together into one place, and all speak with tongues, and there come in *those that are* unlearned, or unbelievers, will they not say that ye are mad?"

(1 Corinthians 14:23)

Unbelievers either think those who speak in tongues are crazy or drunk. That still tracks today. Making Christianity look insane does not bring anyone closer to realizing that Jesus is the Messiah, but it gets even more perplexing. Verse 22 says tongues are for unbelievers, but verse 23 says tongues are not for unbelievers? Is this a contradiction in the Bible? No, the Bible doesn't contradict itself. Rather, look at the key word "unlearned." While thinking on that, look back at 1 Corinthians 14:21. It states "In the law it is written With *men of* other tongues and other lips will I speak unto this people." Who is "this people"? This verse is taken from Isaiah 28:11, where it is indicated that "this people" is referring to Israel.[123]

---

123. Isaiah 28:14 makes it clear when it says "this people which *is* in Jerusalem."

So, we've gotten a step closer to solving the mystery. Speaking in tongues is targeted towards unbelieving Israel. Why? Well, it has always been a sign of judgment for Israel to be spoken to in another language:

"But it shall come to pass, if thou wilt not hearken unto the voice of the LORD thy God, to observe to do all His commandments and His statutes which I command thee this day; that all these curses shall come upon thee, and overtake thee:...The LORD shall bring a nation against thee from far, from the end of the earth, *as swift* as the eagle flieth; a nation whose tongue thou shalt not understand;"
(Deuteronomy 28:15, 49)

In the Old Testament, these verses came to pass with Assyria and Babylon. Destruction and dispersion was brought to Israel. So Israelites who knew the Law, but were not believers in Jesus Christ, would have understood speaking in tongues as a sign from Jehovah God. This would bring about realization that Jesus Christ was sent from Jehovah God. Not only that, but it was a sign of coming judgment that they would need to take heed to. What was Israel's sin in the first century that brought about speaking in tongues? Rejecting the Messiah. Israel, as a whole, never repented or got right with God concerning that. So, what happened? Destruction and dispersion by the Romans in 70 A.D. This dispersion has lasted for centuries and has just now begun to end with Israel becoming a nation again back in 1948. It was after 70 A.D. where the genuine speaking in tongues ended. There is no account in Scripture after 70 A.D. where someone spoke in tongues. There is also no valid instance of speaking in tongues in church history after 70 A.D. The why is all centered around the primary purpose of tongues in the New Testament:

<u>Speaking in tongues was a sign of judgment to unbelieving Israel after they rejected the Messiah. This forewarned judgment came by the Romans in 70 A.D.</u>

Try the spirits: Lastly, we need to be careful of which spirit we listen to. Because the Holy Spirit isn't the only one that speaks to our hearts. Satan sends many spirits our way to get us off the path that God wants for us.

"Beloved, believe not every spirit, but try the spirits whether they are of God: because many false prophets are gone out into the world."
(1 John 4:1)

How do we try these spirits? Simple. Which one matches up with God's Word? Which one adheres to the Bible? The one that matches up with the Bible is going to be the Holy Spirit. The ones that twist Scripture or get away from it are from the enemy, Satan. So, this goes to show that we need to read our Bible because if we don't know it, we won't know which one is of God and which ones are not. Some may think that they will be able to discern which is which by themselves. You won't. First, Satan is very good at making himself look like he's sent from God:

"For such *are* false apostles, deceitful workers, transforming themselves into the apostles of Christ. And no marvel; for Satan himself is transformed into an angel of light."
(2 Corinthians 11:13 – 14)

Secondly, you really can't trust yourself:

"The heart *is* deceitful above all *things,* and desperately wicked: who can know it?"
(Jeremiah 17:9)

Better to trust the book that was written by He who is all-knowing and all-seeing. Better to trust Him than what our measly minds can discern.

Other Points

Jesus' Appearance

I'm sorry, I just can't let it go: contrary to many paintings and countless movies and T.V. shows, Jesus is not Caucasian. Jesus does not have long hair. How can I be so dogmatic? Let me tell you.

When it comes to His skin color, Jesus was a Jewish man. His mother was a Jewish woman. Not only that, but He was a carpenter. Moreover, He eventually left the work of carpentry to start His earthly ministry. Neither of these were luxurious lifestyles. As a carpenter, He worked hard to build things. That means that Jesus was not some effeminate wimp either.[124] He would have been outside a lot, His skin being exposed to the sun. Even more so, when He began His ministry, Jesus was exposed to the elements constantly. Not only with how much He traveled and how much He spoke with multitudes outside, but He had no permanent dwelling:

"And Jesus saith unto him, The foxes have holes, and the birds of the air *have* nests; but the Son of man hath not where to lay *His* head."
(Matthew 8:20)

Jesus' skin was not pale. He would have had very tanned and rough skin. For all of those who think Jesus was white or resembled a white man, that thought is erroneous. I read somewhere that this was started in Medieval times. Evidently, a

---

124. Note: He overthrew tables and chased people out of the temple a couple times. He was no sissy.

painter made some artwork of Jesus to resemble the current European monarch. This was to get into the good graces of said king. I don't know if that's true or not, but it would make sense. Regardless, Jesus did not ever resemble a Caucasian man. He is Jewish and would have an appearance that matched that.

Now, concerning Jesus' hair, it has been shown as shoulder length in almost everything. There are numerous reasons why this would have never been the case with Jesus. The most primary reason would be Jesus' submission to God the Father. Jesus was always ever doing the will of His Father and nothing else. For instance, Satan tempted Jesus in Matthew 4:3 to turn stones to bread. Was there something morally wrong with turning stones into bread? No, but Jesus refused because it was not the will of His Father. Now, that being said, there is something morally wrong with men having long hair:

"Doth not even nature itself teach you, that, if a man have long hair, it is a shame unto him?"
(1 Corinthians 11:14)

Jesus never brought shame upon His Father. Each time God the Father spoke to Jesus, He said He was well pleased with Him (Matthew 3:17, 17:5, Mark 1:11, Luke 3:22, 2 Peter 1:17). This would not be the case if Jesus went contrary to God's Word. Furthermore, Jesus would not have been the Messiah had He not lived in complete harmony with God the Father. Something so simple as having long hair would have done that. Because your hair shows your attitude. Men having long hair and women having very short hair was a sign of rebellion. Jesus was fully submitted to God the Father, never having any rebellion towards Him whatsoever.

One of the things that people bring up in the argument for Jesus' long hair is that He was a Nazarite. This is not true. Jesus was a Nazar*ene*, meaning that He was raised in Nazareth. There is a difference between a Nazarite and a Nazarene. A Nazarite was an individual that took a vow so as to be set apart:

"Speak unto the children of Israel, and say unto them, When either man or woman shall separate *themselves* to vow a vow of a Nazarite, to separate *themselves* unto the LORD: He shall separate *himself* from wine and strong drink, and shall drink no vinegar of wine, or vinegar of strong drink, neither shall he drink any liquor of grapes, nor eat moist grapes, or dried. All the days of his separation shall he eat nothing that is made of the vine tree, from the kernels even to the husk. All the days of the vow of his separation there shall no razor come upon his head: until the days be fulfilled, in the which he separateth *himself* unto the LORD, he shall be holy, *and* shall let the locks of the hair of his head grow. All the days that he separateth *himself* unto the LORD he shall come at no dead body. He

shall not make himself unclean for his father, or for his mother, for his brother, or for his sister, when they die: because the consecration of his God *is* upon his head. All the days of his separation he *is* holy unto the LORD."
(Numbers 6:2 – 8)

If Jesus had been a Nazarite, Scripture records Him blatantly breaking one of these rules:

"While He yet spake, there came from the ruler of the synagogue's *house certain* which said, Thy daughter is dead: why troublest thou the Master any further? As soon as Jesus heard the word that was spoken, He saith unto the ruler of the synagogue, Be not afraid, only believe...And He took the damsel by the hand, and said unto her, Talitha cumi; which is, being interpreted, Damsel, I say unto thee, arise. And straightway the damsel arose, and walked; for she was *of the age* of twelve years. And they were astonished with a great astonishment."
(Mark 5:35 – 6, 41 – 42)

Now, if Jesus was a Nazarite, He would have just broken His Nazarite vow. This was not something to be taken lightly and it would have been sin to break such a vow. For, just look at what someone had to do if he or she had broken the Nazarite vow:

435

"And if any man die very suddenly by him, and he hath defiled the head of his consecration; then he shall shave his head in the day of his cleansing, on the seventh day shall he shave it. And on the eighth day he shall bring two turtles, or two young pigeons, to the priest, to the door of the tabernacle of the congregation: And the priest shall offer the one for a sin offering, and the other for a burnt offering, and make an atonement for him, for that he sinned by the dead, and shall hallow his head that same day. And he shall consecrate unto the LORD the days of his separation, and shall bring a lamb of the first year for a trespass offering: but the days that were before shall be lost, because his separation was defiled."
(Numbers 6:9 – 12)

According to these verses, breaking a Nazarite vow was sin. We know that Jesus never sinned. If Jesus sinned, He was not God. This all proves that Jesus never had a Nazarite vow, therefore disproving the only acceptable reason for Jesus to have long hair. Therefore, <u>Jesus did **_not_** have long hair</u>.

Why make such a big deal about this? Well, as a Christian, I greatly dislike these obvious misrepresentations of my Saviour, especially when they can be used to bring shame upon Him. This would include the idea that Jesus had long hair.

Which One do I Pray to?

The trinity of God is confusing, as stated before. And it can sometimes bring up questions. One that I've heard is which one should be prayed to? The Father, the Son, or the Holy Ghost? Or does it matter? Can you just choose one? Should you just pray to all at once? The more questions you ask, the more your brain begins to hurt (or, at least mine does).

My personal opinion is that it doesn't make too much of a difference. All three are God and God is one. However, we can take examples of what Jesus did while He was on Earth:

"But thou, when thou prayest, enter into thy closet, and when thou hast shut thy door, <u>pray to thy Father</u> which is in secret; and thy Father which seeth in secret shall reward thee openly."
(Matthew 6:6)

"After this manner therefore pray ye: Our <u>Father</u> which art in heaven, Hallowed be Thy name."
(Matthew 6:9)

As well as the example of Paul and Peter, two Apostles in the New Testament:

"Giving thanks always for all things unto God and the Father
in the name of our Lord Jesus Christ;"
(Ephesians 5:20)

"We give thanks to God and the Father of our Lord Jesus
Christ, praying always for you,"
(Colossians 1:3)

"Giving thanks unto the Father, which hath made us meet to
be partakers of the inheritance of the saints in light:"
(Colossians 1:12)

"And if ye call on the Father, who without respect of persons
judgeth according to every man's work, pass the time of your
sojourning *here* in fear:"
(1 Peter 1:17)

So, is it a sin to pray to Jesus or the Holy Spirit? No. Is it as big of a deal as some people make it out to be? Probably not. However, when in doubt, pray to the Father. It does make sense because, of the three, the Father has the most authority.

Summary

- God is three in one. The Father is God, Jesus Christ is God, and the Holy Spirit is God, but they are not three different

Gods. Remember to think of the trinity as time: past is time, present is time, and future is time, but they all fit into one (Matthew 3:16 – 17, John 10:30 – 33).

- God is holy, meaning He cannot be associated with sin at all. It's like trying to mix light and darkness together (1 Peter 1:15 – 16).

- Jesus is eternal (Micah 5:2), was born of a virgin (Isaiah 7:14, Matthew 1:23 – 25), was completely sinless (Hebrews 4:15) died in our place and rose again.

- There are many theories that reject Christ's rising from the dead, but they are all filled with holes.

- The Holy Spirit should be reverenced and obeyed as God, but not exaggeratedly exalted above Jesus and God the Father, for Jesus Himself states that is not of the Holy Spirit (John 16:13 – 14).

- The ministry of the Holy Spirit changed at the day of Pentecost. In the Old Testament, He temporarily resided on specific people for a specific purpose. In the New Testament, He resides in all believers permanently and works in us to mold us to be more like Jesus.

- Speaking in tongues, that was brought on by the Holy Spirit in the New Testament, was a sign of judgment to unbelieving Israel after they rejected the Messiah. This forewarned judgment came by the Romans in 70 A.D. It is no longer something that genuinely happens today (1 Corinthians 14:1 – 5).

CHAPTER FIFTEEN

WRATH, LOVE, AND OTHER ENIGMAS

Introduction

I said I wouldn't cover everything in this book, and I won't. But with this chapter, I will try to answer some of the most common questions people have concerning God. Before diving in, we must realize that if we can't even understand how a bumblebee flies with its fat body and little wings, what hope do we have to understand the complexities of the infinite God who made us? There are some things that we will never be able to comprehend about God and we have to be content with that:

> **"Hast thou not known? hast thou not heard, *that* the everlasting God, the LORD, the Creator of the ends of the earth, fainteth not, neither is weary? *there is* no searching of His understanding."**
> **(Isaiah 40:28)**

Another way to put it: Jesus called us to follow Him, not to understand Him. After all, this is the God that is above time. He *made* time. He is not bound by it. So, God is in the past, the present, and in the future all at the same time. To Him, people who are saved are already with Him in heaven, even though they're still on Earth right now. Does that blow your mind? Finite minds cannot put that which is infinite inside them. So, we are going to explore some of the intricacies of God, but I must put a disclaimer that we may not discern everything about them. So, without further ado, let's get to the complicated questions.

"How can you Justify the 'Inconsistencies' between God's Love and God's Wrath?"

This is a big one I hear often. People don't tend to understand how God's love works perfectly with His justice. How can John say "God is love" (1 John 4:8) when He commands for the extinction of entire people groups, like the Amalekites in 1 Samuel 15:3? It can seem a little contradictory, but there is a reason behind it.

First off, we need to reflect upon sin once more. God hates it, and being a just Judge over all Creation, He must punish it. We can see this in the following verses:

"He that believeth on Him is not condemned: but he that believeth not is condemned already, because he hath not believed in the name of the only begotten Son of God. And this is the condemnation, that light is come into the world, and

men loved darkness rather than light, because their deeds were evil. For every one that doeth evil hateth the light, neither cometh to the light, lest his deeds should be reproved." (John 3:18 – 20)

"So then every one of us shall give account of himself to God." (Romans 14:12)

"For we must all appear before the judgment seat of Christ; that every one may receive the things *done* in *his* body, according to that he hath done, whether *it be* good or bad." (2 Corinthians 5:10)

"And I saw a great white throne, and Him that sat on it, from whose face the earth and the heaven fled away; and there was found no place for them. And I saw the dead, small and great, stand before God; and the books were opened: and another book was opened, which is *the book* of life: and the dead were judged out of those things which were written in the books, according to their works. And the sea gave up the dead which were in it; and death and hell delivered up the dead which were in them: and they were judged every man according to their works. And death and hell were cast into the lake of fire. This is the second death. And whosoever was not found written in the book of life was cast into the lake of fire." (Revelation 20:11 – 15)

Like a judge that must require a price to be paid for someone who broke the law, the Lord must require a price to be paid for someone who committed sin. But here is where God's mercy, love, and patience is shown. Going back to the Amalekites that were sentenced to death in 1 Samuel 15, look at what God says their crime was:

"Thus saith the LORD of hosts, <u>I remember *that* which</u> <u>Amalek did to Israel, how he laid *wait* for him in the way,</u> <u>when he came up from Egypt</u>."
(1 Samuel 15:2)

That happened back in Exodus 17:8 – 13. According to Google,[125] Amalek attacked the Israelites in 1446 B.C. Also according to Google, Saul started his kingly reign around 1020 B.C. If that happens to be remotely correct (I would encourage you to verify this with something more trustworthy than Google), that is around 400 years where God did not judge the Amalekites for attacking an innocent band of people. Not to mention the fact that they were still worshipping heathen gods and committing other atrocities and sins throughout those 400 years. So, what was God doing for those 400 years? Being lazy? Certainly not. Rather, He was giving them time to repent. Time to get things right. He

---

125. I do not recommend putting much faith into Google. I simply did not have anything with which I could find an accurate timeline for this.

was being longsuffering and giving them much more time than they deserved.

Tthe Lord did this with Israel, too, when they got away from Him. Beginning at the time of the judges, Israel had been committing vile acts and then getting right and going back to the sin again eventually. Sure, there were spaces of good times. David and Solomon's reigns are decent examples. But then they had times of great evil. Ahab and Manasseh's reigns are decent examples of that. God didn't immediately bring righteous indignation upon them. No, He gave them all the way until Babylon became an empire. Much longer than they deserved, as well.

That is the connection between God's love and God's wrath. Because of who He is, He must bring judgment to sin, but He loves us so much and is so merciful that He gives us much more time to repent and turn to Him than we could ever deserve. This compounds even more with hell and salvation. Yes, hell is absolutely horrible, and all sinners are destined to go there. That was set in place by God because He is just. He has wrath against sin, but God is also merciful, taking that punishment upon Himself and offering salvation freely to us through Jesus Christ. Once you get the right mindset of how wretched sin is and how patient and merciful God has been with us, the fog of confusion starts to lift and it makes perfect sense.

"If Evolution is False, why do we have DNA that is so close to Chimpanzees?"

It was actually one of my co-workers that believes in the theory of evolution that brought forth this question. I had no idea how to respond to that in the moment. It's a good question, but I thought it was worth the study to find the answer.

There is a good article that explains all of this very well called "A Tale of Two Chromosomes" by Dr. Jean Lightner. It can be found on a website titled "Answers in Genesis."[126] I will summarize the points that Dr. Lightner goes through, but if you want the more sophisticated version, I would encourage you to check out her article.

So, human and ape anatomy is similar. It's one of the reasons evolution can seem somewhat believable at times. One difference is that apes have forty-eight chromosomes while humans have forty-six. If we descended from apes, where did those two chromosomes go? One explanation by evolutionist Dr. Ken Miller[127] is that those two chromosomes fused together and formed a brand new species: humanity. Chromosomal fusion does take place, so this does make sense. However, chromosomal

---

126. The specific URL is the following: answersingenesis.org/genetics/dna-similarities/a-tale-of-two-chromosomes/

127. A biology professor from Brown University, according to the above article.

fusion has been found to happen in the same species without any evolutionary process. Furthermore, the issue is not the number of chromosomes, but the information contained within those chromosomes. If you take a closer look at the molecular level of these chromosomes, you'll find some glaring differences. Dr. Lightner has all the scientific jargon for this piece, so I'll just let her say it:

"Despite the superficial similarities between human and ape chromosomes, there are important differences on the molecular level. There are many protein coding genes in humans that are distinctly human and are not found in chimps. Perhaps more significantly are the differences in genes that don't code for proteins. Genes have been described which code for microRNA (miRNA). The miRNA molecule is not translated, but acts directly to control gene expression. A single miRNA can regulate the expression of dozens or even hundreds of genes. A study of miRNAs expressed in the brain found 51 of 447 new miRNAs were distinctly human and 25 were only found in the chimp. The idea that so many genes were altered so that they are expressed in the proper concentration according to cell type and can effectively control the many different genes they regulate is not what we would expect of chance processes. It is more rational to believe that God created humans distinct from chimps, just as He tells us in the Bible."[128]

Boiled down, she's saying this: Evolutionists say that human and chimpanzee chromosomes are super similar, but they really

128. Lightner, Jean. "A Tale of Two Chromosomes." "Answers in Genesis." November 14, 2007. answersingenesis.org/genetics/dna-similarities/a-tale-of-two-chromosomes/

aren't. I have heard other things as well, such as the amount of chimpanzee DNA is 12% larger than what it is in humans, there's a 2% – 4% difference in the genomes (which means millions and millions of individual components of DNA are different), and so on. I honestly don't know if that is true. I'm not a scientist, a geneticist, a biologist, or anything close to any of those. What I do know is this: God can do whatever He wants in the way that He creates. If He wanted to make human DNA and chimpanzee DNA similar, that's fine. It's His creation, He can do with it what He wants. What that doesn't do is give more weight to evolution.

Again, I urge you to research it for yourself. Remember that the truth makes itself known if you're willing to analyze the evidence honestly and without bias. Sometimes, we may not get the answers we like, but that's the truth. It doesn't shift based on opinion, not even the opinion of billions. Now evolution looks more and more to be something designed so that men could do what they wished and not feel like they have to answer to God. For all of those evolutionists out there, do you really think that the complexities of everything we know could be made by random chance? Can evolution truly make a beautiful sunrise? Or brilliant brains that are able to run math equations? Or build amazing bodies that function according to an intricate system of order? Explosions don't make order, and evolution doesn't create life.

At the end of the day, you will have to choose what you believe. Being fully candid, neither side is likely to win over the other, because we Baptists are pretty stubborn, and evolutionists want to have their way. But I promise you, the facts point towards an intelligent Creator. If you believe this was all made by dirt, pressure, and heat, you will one day have to face that intelligent Creator with that insufficient explanation. Then, it will be too late.

"Why do Bad Things happen in Life if God is Good and in Control over Everything?"[129]

Many a tormented soul has asked this question. Because very evil and tragic things take place in this world. They happen to those who seem to deserve them, but they also happen to those who seem to not be worthy of such harshness. How can God be good if such horrible circumstances take place? The way I see it, bad things that happen to us come from one of four sources:

1. People: God created mankind with free will and the ability to make choices. Because of that, God will not force anyone to do anything. In retrospect, God will not force anyone to stop doing what they have chosen to do. If a person has chosen to murder another human, God will not overtake their mind and order that person to stop. So, we, as sinful creatures, often choose to do wrong things that will bring harm onto other people. People

---

129. Also see the "Goodness" section under "Attributes of God" in "Chapter Fourteen: The Triune God." They touch on this as well.

murder. People rape. People steal. Consequently, the victims of those crimes are subject to loss. Sometimes great loss. Sometimes little loss. But loss nonetheless. And that is not to be attributed to the fault of God since He did not commit it. It was done by a person.

2. Satan: Satan works to destroy mankind. He wishes to destroy us physically, mentally, and emotionally, but he especially wants to destroy us spiritually. Ultimately, Satan wants to drag every person he can down to hell with him, but once a man or a woman cries out to Jesus for salvation, Satan can never cause that person to experience hell. He can never change that person's eternal fate. So, he tries everything he can to keep people from trusting in God. Sometimes that is with luxury and success, but Satan also uses hardship. He wants people to think that God is so good that nothing bad could ever happen.[130] That way, when tragedy hits, people's view of God is shattered and instead of realizing that God allows bad things to happen in life, people make the assumption that God can't exist because their idea of God wasn't validated. That is a lie from Satan after working his own evil schemes.

---

130. As stated before, God is completely good, but sometimes allowing bad things to come in our lives is actually a part of His goodness. Just like a parent allowing his or her children to reap the consequences of their wrong actions. It may seem like a bad thing to the children, but it helps them to learn from their mistakes and grow from it.

3. A Cursed World: Because of the introduction of sin into this world via Adam and Eve's fall, the world has been cursed by sin. This world is imperfect. Chaotic storms occur. Animals can be violent and savage. Disease spreads. Bad things happen because sin has devastated this world. Sometimes, bad things do not happen because of other people, Satan, or God. Sometimes, they can happen just because of our surroundings. Take Mephibosheth in 2 Samuel 4:4 for instance. His nurse dropped him by accident as a toddler and it caused him to be lame on both of his legs. This was, as far as I can tell, unintended by all beings. We cannot blame God for accidents or consequences of a fallen world. He originally created the world in absolute perfection. It was man that tainted it. God is guiltless.

4. God: Now, this is the trickiest one to talk about. First, know that God is good in every way possible. He is righteous and beyond perfection. That being said, God does allow everything that happens to happen. He is in complete control of everything that exists. God does not *cause* everything to happen, but God does *allow* everything to happen. A good example of this is the beginning of the book of Job. Now, Satan caused the hardships that Job faced, but God allowed them. In that particular instance, God allowed it to prove Job's faithfulness to Him. There are times when God allows bad things in our lives to grow us. There are times when God allows bad things in our lives to enable us to help others who are going through similar situations. God also

450

sometimes allows unfortunate circumstances to come into our lives in order to prevent something far, far worse from taking place.[131] Of course, there are times God does bring judgment upon humanity for sin. The Lord does not allow those terrible tragedies to happen so that He can laugh at us or because He enjoys inflicting pain. He has a grand purpose to everything, and should we all submit to His will, I know that everything would be better in the end.

God is still good despite all of these. God is not responsible for the actions of people, Satan, or a sin-cursed world, for God is good to give us free will instead of just making us do whatever He wants. However, because of that we are free to do evil things. When it comes to the sin-cursed world, that is a consequence of humanity's sin, not God's fault. As for God's allowance of evil in our lives or His judgment, both of those are results of His goodness. Contrary to popular belief, God is good to let evil come our way to grow us. Imagine a parent that shielded his or her child from **everything** potentially harmful or uncomfortable. That itself would ultimately be harmful for the child. Because chores are uncomfortable, and if a child goes through his or her entire

---

131. I realize that can be a little vague, so here's an example: Imagine a toddler is playing with a ball next to a busy street. He accidentally knocks the ball into the road and chases after it right as a semi comes barreling down the road. The child's father sees what is about to happen, sprints to his child, snatches him by the arm and pulls him off the road before the semi hits him. Because of how tight the father's grip was and how fast he pulled the child back, he actually hurt the child, but he also saved the child from the far worse fate of being crushed by a semi. God does the same at times.

adolescence not gaining a work ethic through daily chores, he or she is bound to be lazy, or that same child won't be prepared for the wave of work that is bound to come after moving out. With God, our all-wise Father, He knows what is best for us. That means that whatever hardship may come our way is going to be ultimately for good if we trust Him through it. Concerning God's divine wrath, God would not be good if He did not meet out judgment for sin. Just as a judge would not be a good judge after overlooking someone breaking the law. At the end of the day, God is still good even if bad things may come in our lives.

"How can we have Free Will if God is Sovereign over Everything?"

This one is a bit of a head-scratcher at some points, but here it is in a nutshell: God gave us free will and the ability to make our own decisions, but He is so wise that He can take our decisions and still work His ultimate will with them. How? Well, take the idea of time-travel. It's a well-liked subject in a lot of movies, books, and even video games. A good example of this is *Legend of Zelda: Majora's Mask*. In a quick summary, the goal of the video game is this: you have three days to stop an evil imp with magical powers from destroying the world. In order to stop him, though, you need to go to defeat four different bosses in four different locations, each of which basically takes the three full days, but here's the kicker – you can time travel. You can go back to the first day whenever you want.[132] I bring all that up to say that you, as the player, become very aware of what someone is going to do before they do it. Because you've already seen it happen before. So, you can start using people's actions for your own benefit. You know when Sakon is going to try and steal the bomb merchant's wares, so you can stop him and get a gift from the bomb merchant. Did Sakon and the bomb merchant still both make their own decisions? Absolutely. You didn't make it for them; but because you knew it was going to happen, you could use it for your own will.

That's one way we can start to wrap our mind around how God can use our free will actions to accomplish His will. He has already seen the end of time and everything until then. He knows what we're going to do. He sees all of history as one big picture. To Him, it's like a road-map while we are walking through it. We can't see the beginning or the end because we're in the midst of it. He sees everything. He even sees what path we're going to take. Could He not ensure that a certain road is blocked so we take the right path? He very easily could. A more biblical example would be most of the book of Esther. It was not God's will for Haman to murder Mordecai. Haman made the decision to hang Mordecai on a gallows, not the Lord, yet the Lord used that very gallows to be

---

132. For those of you who know the game, I am simplifying it so that those who don't know it can understand it without going too in depth with the details.

Haman's demise. Haman's free will decision used by the Lord to accomplish His sovereign will.

Furthermore, God's knowledge is infinite. He understands everything about us more than we ever can. This shows that we can still make our own decisions that God can use to see that His will is accomplished.

"Why doesn't God just Weigh our Good and our Bad in order to let us into Heaven?"

If we did it that way, we would all go to hell. If there is any sin on our account, no matter how small or how large our good works may be, we cannot be in God's presence. God doesn't weigh our good and our bad to see which is heavier because that would automatically doom us all to hell.

"But we are all as an unclean *thing*, and all our righteousnesses *are* as filthy rags; and we all do fade as a leaf; and our iniquities, like the wind, have taken us away."
(Isaiah 64:6)

"For the wages of sin is death; but the gift of God is eternal life through Jesus Christ our Lord."
(Romans 6:23)

"For by grace are ye saved through faith; and that not of yourselves: *it is* the gift of God: <u>Not of works, lest any man should boast.</u>"
(Ephesians 2:8 – 9)

"For whosoever shall keep the whole law, and yet offend in one *point,* he is guilty of all."
(James 2:10)

<u>"Why didn't God make the World without Evil?"</u>

This is an easy one. He *did*.

"And God saw every thing that he had made, and, behold, *it was* very good. And the evening and the morning were the sixth day."
(Genesis 1:31)

God fashioned everything in perfection. It was Lucifer who brought sin into existence, and it was mankind that brought sin to Earth. Adam and Eve chose to disobey God, and the corruption of sin poisoned everything on this planet. In short, we messed it up, not God.

From this statement usually stems another question: why didn't God just make it so Adam and Eve couldn't sin? I will illustrate this with a movie that came out in late 2021 called *Ron's Gone Wrong*. In this movie, a company by the name of Bubble makes a line of robot companions called "B-bots" that are designed to help people make friends. B-bots are basically walking social-medias that agree to everything you say and like everything you like. A young boy named Barney wants one as well, but his father gets him a broken one called Ron. Due to his malfunctions, Ron doesn't do everything a regular B-bot is supposed to do. He doesn't always agree with Barney and has different interests. Ron and Barney even argue and fight from time to time. Throughout the movie, Barney comes to realize that he likes Ron as he is because Ron acts more like a real person rather than a yes-man robot. Near the end of the movie, Ron actually gets fixed and becomes just like all the other B-bots. Barney is devastated because Ron lost his unique personality and just agrees to everything Barney says. When Ron lost his individuality, Barney and Ron's relationship transitioned from a friendship to a master-servant relationship.[133]

Now, take that analogy and apply it to God when He formed mankind. If the Lord wanted mindless robots that would perform His will without any choice, He certainly could have made us that way, but God wanted more than a master-servant relationship with

___

133. For those of you who are wondering, the movie doesn't end there but I don't want to spoil any more than I already have. It was a decent movie, in my opinion and worth watching.

us.[134] He wanted a Father-child relationship. He wanted us to choose Him, not be forced to obey Him without any free will. He wanted His love to be reciprocated, which is impossible for a creature that cannot choose.

So, when asking, "Why didn't God just make it so Adam and Eve couldn't sin," people need to be aware that there would be no choice if Adam and Eve couldn't sin. If there was no choice, there would be no way to actually love God. You wouldn't be able to do anything else, and that's not love. God does not want anyone to be forced to choose Him. It is against His nature.

"Can God Make a Rock so Big that He couldn't Lift it?"

In truth, this is just a dumb question. Why would God *want* to make a rock so big that He couldn't lift it? What would be the point? However, I have found that this question does open the door to answers of some other questions. See, because God cannot contradict Himself. Therefore, He actually *can't* make a rock so big that He couldn't lift it.

---

134. Please don't misunderstand. We are to have a Master-servant relationship with God, but what I'm trying to convey is that God did not want it to end there. He endeavors to be closer to us than that.

Other Points

Followers, Not Understanders

It is a good thing to want to understand things. I'll state that again for emphasis: it is good to want to study and learn and understand things. That's a *good* thing, But, at the end of the day, there will be so many questions concerning God. We won't understand everything. For some, that might be a stumbling block. How can we not have the answers to the questions?! But that's just the way it is. So, there are countless questions, and there will be more countless questions in the future; but we need to make our peace with that because, as created finite beings, we will not have the ability to comprehend the self-existing infinite being that is God.

So, what to do about this? Well, we need to have a heart of the follower. There's a reason Jesus told us to be like little children:

"And Jesus called a little child unto Him, and set him in the midst of them, And said, Verily I say unto you, Except ye be converted, and become as little children, ye shall not enter into the kingdom of heaven."
(Matthew 18:2 – 3)

Why did Jesus say this? Well, think of how children are. One attribute is their immense trust. A child knows that his or her parents can be trusted. They don't always understand things that adults do, so they trust that their parents are seeking for the best for them and follow. I understand this analogy falls apart if you add too many factors, but I ask for you to humor me. Think of it like this: a mother and father tell their six-year-old son that they are going to Disney World. The six-year-old then proclaims to them, "Unless you prove to me how that is possible, I will not believe it!" Do kids do that? Not typically. Some may have a little disbelief, but if you look up videos of when parents told their kids they were going to Disney World, those kids instantly start screaming happily and jumping up and down. They do that because they trust their parents. Do they understand all of what goes into getting a family trip to Disney World? No, but they don't have to. They just need to follow as their parents take care of everything.

That is the heart that we need to have towards our Father. Again, it's good to understand the things that we can understand, but the things we can't? Just trust that your Father has it taken care of. So, some questions are going to go unanswered in this life. You need to be okay with that, as do I, because He's got it covered. Just follow Him.

EPILOGUE

SPEAK THE TRUTH IN LOVE

By themselves, truth and love are unbalanced. Take a conversation with someone who is four-hundred pounds and is dangerously unhealthy in the way he eats. Truth by itself is cold and harsh. Telling this man pure truth, like "You're fat. You need to stop eating so much. If you don't, you'll die prematurely." may be what he needs to hear, but it's also hurtful. The hurt that comes with it may either discourage him from doing anything about it or make him angry enough to disregard your words.

Love, on the other hand, seeks to make everyone feel good when it is not grounded in truth.[135] Pure love will tell him "Oh, you're not overweight. You're just a different body type." It may make the man happier in the moment, but it's a lie and it isn't addressing the problem. Rather, it encourages him to continue his unhealthy habit. Pure truth and pure love are unbalanced in the same way when we talk to people about the Lord.

---

135. To clarify, if you genuinely love someone, you will tell them the truth because you care about their well-being. But this "love" that I'm using here has more the idea of "I just want everyone to be happy." Just to make sure everyone understands that.

One who holds to truth alone becomes cruel and unfeeling, pushing people away from God because he or she appears to portray God as a merciless master. You may be doctrinally correct, but nobody will care about your doctrine if you don't first show that you care about them. Those who hold only to love make God seem like He cares little for righteousness and will applaud anyone's and everyone's life choices, no matter how right or wrong they are. Love alone may get a big following, but people are wrongly indoctrinated about who God is and what He expects of His children. But when someone speaks truth with love, something miraculous happens. The truth is not vicious because it is balanced out with compassion and sympathy. The love is not unprincipled because it is rooted in verity. And that is when God is correctly portrayed, for He is both truth and love:

"Jesus saith unto him, I am the way, the truth, and the life: no man cometh unto the Father, but by me."
(John 14:6)

"He that loveth not knoweth not God; for God is love."
(1 John 4:8)

So, what am I getting at with this? Well, we've been going over the defense of the faith throughout this book. We have been studying out the truth of the Bible. We've discussed many evils of this world. We've looked at various godly principles. It is my hope that I have endowed my readers with the truth that they need to correctly live out the teachings of Christ. ***But!*** If you read this book and intend to go and just fling out truth at people in a Pharisaical fashion, it is ***ALL FOR NOTHING!*** Paul put it this way:

"Though I speak with the tongues of men and of angels, and have not charity, I am become *as* sounding brass, or a tinkling cymbal. And though I have *the gift of* prophecy, and understand all mysteries, and all knowledge; and though I have all faith, so that I could remove mountains, and have not charity, I am nothing. And though I bestow all my goods to feed *the poor,* and though I give my body to be burned, and have not charity, it profiteth me nothing."
(1 Corinthians 13:1 – 3)

Paul here is saying that just having truth is not good enough. Charity must be shown to the world. Because truth alone will kill the desire for God like a winter storm kills a fair rose. The truth that people are sinners and are going to hell is definitely enough to terrify them, but without the knowledge of God's love, what good is it? The fear of the cold truth will either cause them to try to work their way to be good enough for heaven, or they may give up and say, "If this is the best it will ever get, I might as well enjoy it." Is this not shown to us in the realms of every works-based faith? There are both zealots who keep every single law that is given them, and those who simply give in, knowing they could never keep all of the laws. Legalism and hopelessness. That is what truth alone can lead to. And what of those who have become angry at God for His strict stance against sin? There are plenty of atheists and agnostics that are endeavoring to prove God doesn't exist simply because they hate everything about His truth, but once people realize that God *loves* them with a passion that is so deep, they can never truly understand it, everything changes.

Allow me to put forth an example. Say there are two boys growing up in public school. One is named Lee, and the other is named Quentin. With Lee, his father cares about how he does in school and sports, and little else. Lee's father is very success-oriented when it comes to his son, and his son doesn't disappoint. Lee is a good student. Smart, polite, likeable. If Lee gets A's, behaves well, and does well on the football field, his father is pleased, but Lee's father does not display love to his son often. He is cold, and when Lee has difficulty in school, he rails on his son. Lee is being shown that, in order to receive praise and acceptance from his father, he needs to do everything right. If he doesn't, he's scorned. This eventually leads to Lee resenting his father. He realizes that he can never be the perfect son that his father desires and gives up trying. Lee becomes deeply bitter against his father and will likely have a hard time reconciling with him in the future.

On the opposite end, there is Quentin. He is not an ideal student, especially in math. Quentin has a tendency to day-dream during class periods and is slow with some of the curriculum. He does not have the best self-esteem when it comes to his grades or his performances, but there is another drastic difference between Quentin and Lee: Quentin knows his father loves him, regardless of how he does in school. Quentin's dad always lets him know that he loves him. He wants Quentin to do good in school, but it isn't a requirement to his dad's affection. Because of his dad's love, Quentin tries his very best because he knows it will make his dad happy, but even when he doesn't, his dad always tells him "As long as you did your best, I'm proud of you." He has a fantastic relationship with his father to this day.

You see the difference? Without love, a relationship with God doesn't really work, does it? And so we need to be the same when we establish relationships with lost people. Showing no love and all truth will be nothing beneficial to them. So, if you're going to use the information in this book, use it with compassion and a heart for people, not just to prove people wrong and demonstrate how smart you are.

ABOUT THE AUTHOR

Nicholas M. Krohn has always had a love for both writing and the Lord. Nicholas received Jesus Christ as his Lord and Saviour at the age of nine, thanks to his faith-filled mother and a godly church. After his salvation, Nicholas spent most of his childhood free time jotting down fantastical stories. When he was a teenager, Nicholas discovered that writing was his calling from God. When attending Heartland Baptist Bible College, Nicholas began seriously writing and self-publishing novels with the desire that they would both wholesomely entertain readers yet bring glory to God's name. It was here that he met his wife, Marissa, whom he married in 2017 (and who is an invaluable part of Nicholas' writing process by means of cover art, editing, inspiration, and simply saying "That doesn't make sense" when certain ideas are thrown at her). Halfway through college, Nicholas also realized that he could do more than just write Christian Fiction. After deep study in the Bible and graduating from Heartland Baptist Bible College in 2020, Nicholas made it his mission to not only point to the Lord with his fiction novels but to expound on the Word of God itself through commentaries, in-depth studies, and other such works of literature. Nicholas continues to pursue this work while living in Iowa with his wife and children.

OTHER KROHN'STORIES BOOKS

(All of which are available on Amazon)

MARISSA KROHN

The Silent Princess (*Children's book*)

NICHOLAS M. KROHN

BAPTIST APOLOGETICS SERIES

Baptist Apologetics: Volume One

BIBLE COMMENTARY SERIES

Krohn's Commentary of the Book of Ruth

Krohn's Commentary of the First Book of Samuel

Krohn's Commentary of the Second Book of Samuel

THE SCOEFIELD SERIES (*HISTORICAL FICTION*)

Scoefield

Engel

Blume

THE ZALIAN CHRONICLES (*CHRISTIAN FANTASY*)

Heroes & Thieves I: The Noble Bandit

Heroes & Thieves II: A Bundle of Fools

Heroes & Thieves III: Clapia's Rebirth

Heroes & Thieves IV: Two Wastelands

PROTECTOR EDITIONS

Heroes & Thieves: Protector Edition I

KROHN'STORIES POETRY

Trains, Bridges, Cups, & Cheese

The Rambling of a Cart Pusher

STANDALONE NOVELS

The Polish Ghost

CONTACT US

Website: krohnstories.storiad.com

Facebook Group: Krohn'Stories Books

Instagram: krohnstoriesbooks

Email: krohnstories@gmail.com

Fan mail, inquiries, suggestions, and critiques are all welcome. We will do our best to reply to all messages/emails but cannot promise due to a busy schedule. Please be appropriate. Any swearing, vulgarity, threatening, or otherwise inappropriate messages/emails will be deleted without any response.